M000250480

INTERURBANS SPECIAL 99

The Short Line
DOODLEBUG

Galloping Geese and Other Railcritters
by Edmund Keilty

INTERURBAN PRESS
GLENDALE, CALIFORNIA

(Front Endsheet) THIS WAS AMER-
ICA in 1921. The motorman is all
business as he helps passengers
with toddlers off the Muscatine,
Burlington & Southern's railbus,
just arrived in the teeming rail
center of Burlington, Iowa. News-
boys in knickers look on; it's hot,
but 1921 decorum demands that the
solid citizen keep coats, ties and
hats on. In the background sits one
of the MB&S's Bettendorf-Savant
steam cars.
Ray Buhrmaster Collection

(Rear Endsheet) AN OPEN-AIR
delight was this Fairbanks-Morse
Sheffield gas car of the Cornwall &
Lebanon, a 22-mile Pennsylvania
short line which later merged into
the Pennsylvania Railroad. This
photo was taken at the Mt. Gretna
station about 1922 or 1923.
Author's Collection

THE AUTHOR would like to thank
the following persons for help in as-
sembling the data that went into the
making of this book. Many others—too
numerous to mention—helped, too. With-
out these people, a book like this would be
impossible.
  Russell Tedder, Crossett, Ark.
  Tom King, Kingsport, Tenn.
  Mal Connery, Durham, N.C.
  Louis Saillard, Hammond, La.
  Richard Wallin, Springfield, Ill.
  Bill Pollard, Conway, Ark.
  Jim Mottram, Poplar Bluff, Ark.
  John Taubeneck, Seattle, Wash.

The Short Line Doodlebug

© 1988 by Edmund Keilty

All rights reserved. No part of this book may be used or
reproduced without written permission from the publisher,
except in the case of brief quotations used in reviews.

Manufactured in the United States of America
First Printing: Fall 1988

Published by:
INTERURBAN PRESS
P. O. Box 6444
Glendale, California 91205

Library of Congress Cataloging-in-Publication Data

Keilty, Edmund.
    The short line doodlebug.

    (Interurbans special ; 99)
    Includes index.
    1. Railroad motor-cars—United States. I. Title. II. Series.
TF494.K46   1988   625'.6   88-22991
ISBN 0-916374-77-7

Table of Contents

7 INTRODUCTION

11 ALABAMA

14 ALASKA

16 ARIZONA

18 ARKANSAS

21 CALIFORNIA

30 COLORADO

35 CONNECTICUT

35 DELAWARE

36 FLORIDA

39 GEORGIA

44 HAWAII

46 IDAHO

48 ILLINOIS

52 INDIANA

54 IOWA

56 KANSAS

58 KENTUCKY

61 LOUISIANA

64 MAINE

66 MARYLAND

69 MASSACHUSETTS

72 MICHIGAN

73 MINNESOTA

78 MISSISSIPPI

80 MISSOURI

83 MONTANA

84 NEBRASKA

85 NEVADA

89 NEW HAMPSHIRE

90 NEW JERSEY

93 NEW MEXICO

94 NEW YORK

98 NORTH CAROLINA

103 NORTH DAKOTA— SOUTH DAKOTA

105 OHIO

107 OKLAHOMA

109 OREGON

114 PENNSYLVANIA

120 RHODE ISLAND

121 SOUTH CAROLINA

122 TENNESSEE

124 TEXAS

131 UTAH

133 VERMONT

135 VIRGINIA

137 WASHINGTON

142 WEST VIRGINIA

144 WISCONSIN

147 WYOMING

148 INDEX

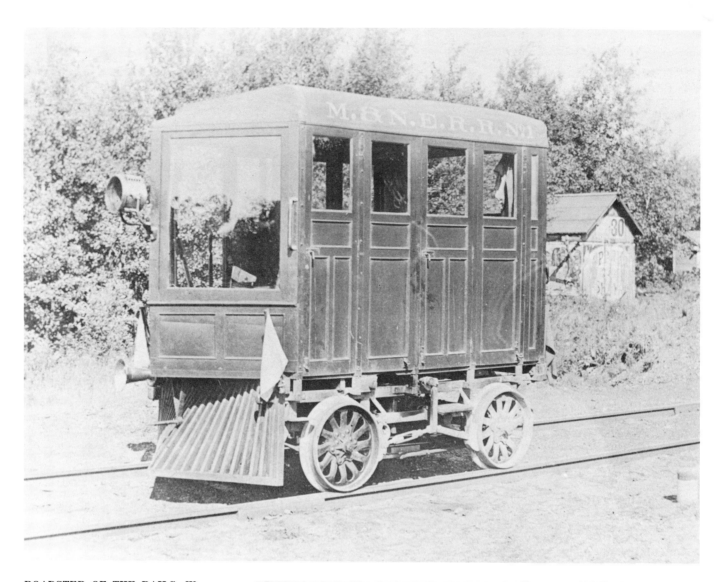

ROADSTER OF THE RAILS: We show you this view of a dandy little railcar, higher than it is long. Perhaps a speeder with an elegant cabin atop, complete with pointy nose. It ran on the Manistee & Northeastern.
Author's Collection

A SMALL CROWD awaits boarding time for Nevada Central 103, a four-wheel dinky of a railcar with a racy wedge-front, shown at Battle Mountain, Nev., circa 1916. Soon it will head across the desert for Austin, the southern end of the line.
Felix Reifschneider Collection

Introduction

WHEN WE FIRST contemplated this series of books on the subject of self-propelled railcars, the thought was that one volume would suffice to cover the whole subject. Our estimate soon proved to be overly optimistic, and this is the third book of the series.

This book has been by far the most difficult to research and write for a number of reasons.

Since the second book of the series, *Doodlebug Country,* subtitled "The Rail Motorcar on the Class I Railroads of the United States," it seemed logical to devote this book to Class II railroads of the United States.

During the era we are largely concerned with—the 1920s and 1930s—the dividing line between classes was clearly and simply defined by the Interstate Commerce Commission: any railroad with gross receipts over a million dollars was a Class I line, any with less than that was a Class II.

The parameters of our subject in the other books had also been simple: the car, of course, must be self-propelled and be used in revenue service. This left a large group of cars that qualified on this criteria but were owned by lines not operating in interstate commerce, thus not reporting to the ICC.

Many of these lines were purely local in nature and were often streetcar lines that were for one reason or another never electrified. Some of these operations were tiny—one or two cars and a couple of miles of track—others such as the operations on Manhattan Island, had hundreds of cars. Such large operations are out of our area of coverage, because they have already been written about to some extent.

The small lines, however, have been almost entirely neglected, so it seems logical to include them.

Another problem area was railroads that became parts of larger systems so long ago that very little is known about the cars involved. This problem was resolved by deciding to use everything that wasn't included in *Doodlebug Country,* so long as we were able to obtain enough information to confirm that the car operated in regular service and not an experimental unit that got very little, if any, revenue service.

By far the greatest problem has been the fact that a high percentage of the small railroads that makes the bulk of these short lines, ceased to exist 30, 40 or 50 years ago, and in many cases operated for only 10 or 20 years. The only evidence that they operated rail motorcars was brief mentions in the *Official Railway Equipment Register* or the *Official Guide* or periodicals of the period.

In a surprising number of cases, more evidence as to the type of, builder and other vital statistics eventually came to light, but there are still a number of these mystery cars, cars we are sure that existed, but on which we lack information. In general we have included these cars.

Another category is cars which lack convincing evidence that they existed. Usually the source is some type of periodical with no further proof. In these cases we have decided that unless photographic documentation exists, we should ignore these reports. The other side of this problem is more frustrating: sometimes we have come across a photo of a car with no sign of the railroad it ran on, or any other evidence to help in identification.

Heretofore, our arrangement of material has been purely alphabetical, but the great number of railroads involved and their often obscure locations, made us decide on the state-by-state approach. For the locations of most of these obscure railroads, we can refer the reader to the Rand-McNally Railroad Atlas of the year 1928, which has been reprinted by the Kalmbach Publishing Co.

There is no doubt that much of this information is incomplete. In any project of this nature, there is a natural tendency to delay publication until that last bit of information can be confirmed, or that last photo obtained. But your author is becoming, as the British say, a bit long of tooth. And, having seen some worthwhile endeavors die with their authors, it behooves me to get this opus into print with the hope that it will inspire others to fill in the blanks and correct the errors.

ENORMOUS SNOWPLOW on the front of Meister car 24 ought to get its plucky passengers to the outside world no matter what. California's Hetch-Hetchy Railway operated five of these cars in connection with its main job of serving the City of San Francisco's big mountain water project.
Railway Negative Exchange, Author's Collection

Standard Cars Commonly Used by Short Line Railroads

BUILDER	MODEL NO.	LENGTH	WEIGHT (LBS.)	DRIVE
Brill	55	43'	30,000	68hp gas-mech.
Brill	75	55'	50,000	175hp gas-mech.
Edwards	10	32'	20,000	80hp gas-mech.
Edwards	20	43'	34,000	108hp gas-mech.
Gen. El.		70'	100,000	175hp gas-elect.
Fair-Morse	19	20'	9,000	25hp gas-mech.
Fair-Morse	24	30'	26,000	50hp gas-mech.
McKeen		55'	60,000	200hp gas-mech.
McKeen		70'	75,000	200hp gas-mech.
Mack	AB	27'	11,000	45hp gas-mech.
Mack	AC	35'	20,000	64hp gas-mech.

TYPICAL CARS operated by America's short line railroads are illustrated in these photos and drawings from vintage publications. Shown are: the General Electric motor car which was "streamlined" as early as 1909 and was an early success; two Brill models; the Mack AC railbus with its "Bulldog" snout; the No. 24 Fairbanks-Morse gasoline car; and, on page 10, the Edwards Model 20, a great favorite with lines in the Southeast. *All: Author's Collection*

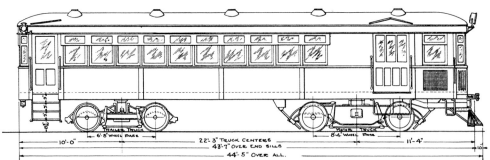

Fig. 545—Brill Model 65 Gasoline Motor Car with Six-Cylinder Engine. Length of Baggage Compartment, 12 ft. 4 in.; Total Seating Capacity, 41; Weight, 31,000 lb.

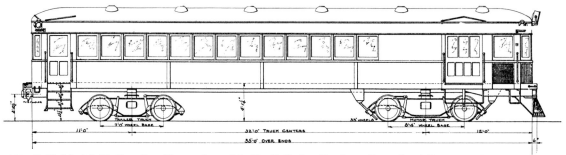

Fig. 546—Brill Model 75 Gasoline Motor Car with Six-Cylinder Engine. Length of Baggage Compartment 16 ft. 3 in.; Total Seating Capacity, 59; Weight, 50,000 lb.

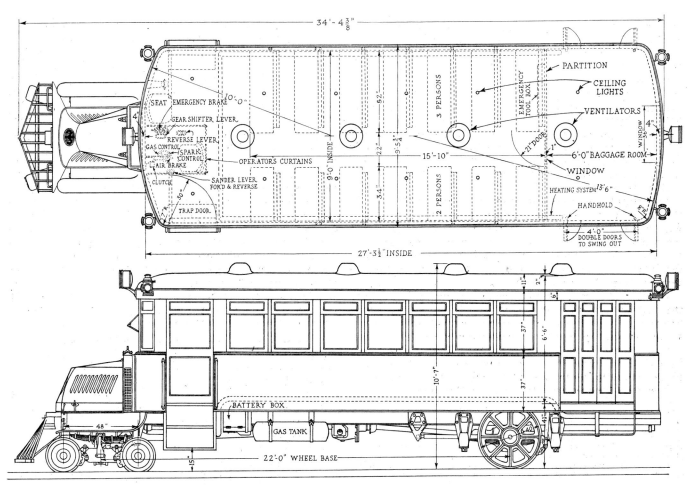

Plan and side views of Mack AC rail car with baggage compartment and seats for 36 passengers

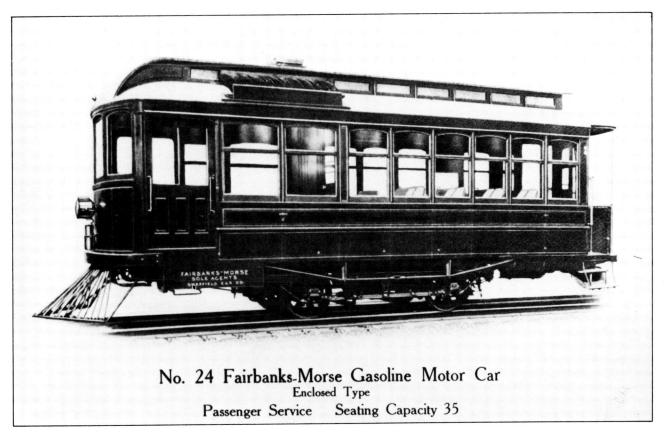

No. 24 Fairbanks-Morse Gasoline Motor Car
Enclosed Type
Passenger Service   Seating Capacity 35

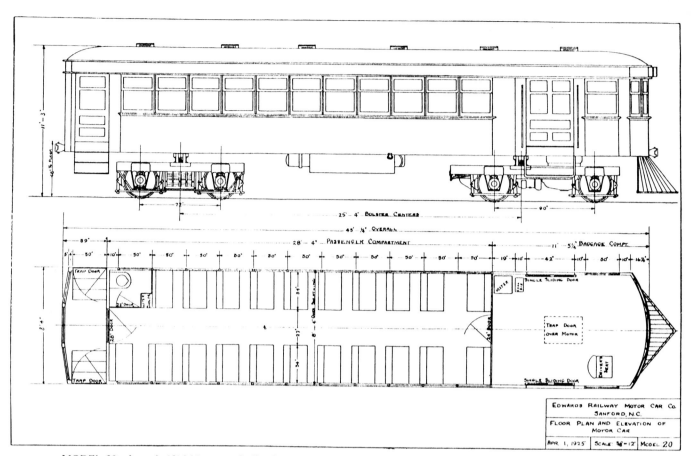

MODEL 20—Length 43' ¼" over end sills; Seats 42 passengers, has one toilet and baggage compartment 11'5¼"
long. Weight 30,000 lbs. Motor is located in truck below floor, giving entire floor space for revenue purposes.

Alabama

AREA: 51,609 sq. miles
CAPITAL: Montgomery
POPULATION (1927): 2,549,000

IN CONTRAST to the rest of the Deep South, the state of Alabama had relatively few short lines.

Two of them, the Alabama, Tennessee & Northern and the Tennessee, Alabama & Georgia, were fairly large by short-line standards and still exist (although cut down in size) as branches of the Burlington Northern and the Southern, respectively.

The Birmingham and Southeastern was of fair size and had the distinction of operating a modest fleet of Edwards cars as late as 1964. The Chattahoochee Valley still exists as a very truncated switching line in the Lanett area.

(Top Photo) CROOKED BELL adorns the front of Tennessee, Alabama & Georgia Brill 500, shown at Chattanooga, Tenn., in 1951.
Author's Collection

COMBINE CARS 51 and 52 of the Alabama, Tennessee & Northern show off their EMC heritage in these two views dating to 1938.
(Middle Photo) Author's Collection; (Bottom Photo) George E. Votava Collection

ROAD NOS.	BUILDER	DATE	BLDR. NO.	ENGINE & DRIVE	BODY TYPE	LGTH.	WT.	DISPOSITION	NOTES & COMMENTS
ALABAMA & FLORIDA RR (Orig. Ala. Florida & Gulf) Cotsworth, Ala. to Gramwood, Fla., 28.8 mi. (Abandoned)									
500	Edwards			Buda 50hp gas- mech.	4 win. OP bag. 16 pass.	31'9"	10T		Model 10, may have been secondhand
(1 car)	Evans	1939		Internation. Diesel-mech.	2 win. bag. 4 pass.				"Autorailer"
ASHLAND RY. (Orig. Alabama Northern) Pyriton to Ashland, Ala. 7.1 mi. (Abandoned)									
									Two motor cars listed in 1928 "Equipment Register"
ALABAMA, TENNESSEE & NORTHERN RR CORP. Mobile to Reform, Ala. 220 mi. Merged into SL-SF RR									
(1 car)	Indiana	1922		Indiana gas- mech.	29 pass. motor bus	30'		scrapped 1929	
(1 car)	Indiana	1923		Indiana gas- mech.	29 pass. motor bus	30'		scrapped 1929	
51	EMC St. Louis	5/27	209 1425	Winton 120 275hp GE	8 win. RPO bag. 37 pass.	75'	58T	scrapped	Ex-CB&Q 9835, acquired 10/36
52	EMC St. Louis	5/27	210 1425	Winton 120 275hp GE	8 win. RPO bag. 37 pass.	75'	58T	scrapped	Ex-CB&Q 9836, acquired 10/36
CHATTAHOOCHEE VALLEY RY. CO. Standing Rock to Bleeker, Ala. 41.5 mi. (9 mi. still in operation)									
316	Brill Ry. Storage Battery	1915	19833	battery-electric	4 wheel, 8 win. st. car	34'			
317	Brill Ry. Storage Battery	1915		battery-electric	4 wheel, 8 win. st. car	34'			
BIRMINGHAM & SOUTHEASTERN RR CO. Union Springs to Eclectic, Ala. (Abandoned)									
500	Edwards	1923		Buda GL66 60hp gas.	6 win. OP, bag. 25 pass.	31'9"	10T		Model 10, ex-Washington & Lincolnton RR (Ga.) acquired 1929
501	Edwards	1925		Buda gas-mech.	9 win. bag. 36 pass.	45'	17T		
502	Edwards	1926		2 Buda gas- mech.	9 win. bag. 36 pass.	45'	17T	wrecked 11/63	Ex-Cen. of Ga. No. 10, ex-ex-Marion & Rye Valley (Va.) acquired 1938
MOBILE & PENSACOLA RY. & NAV. CO. Volanta, Ala. 2 mi. (Abandoned)									
(1 car)									One gas-elect. car listed in 1918 (McGraw Elect. Ry. List, 8/18)
PEOPLES RR CO. Fairhope, Ala. 1.5 mi. (Abandoned)									
(1 car)									One gas car and trailer listed in McGraw Elect. Ry. List 8/18
SUMPTER & CHOCTAW RY. CO. Lilita to Choctaw City, Ala., 22.6 mi. (Abandoned)									
500	Edwards	1923		Buda 100hp gas-mech.	5 win. OP bag. 20 pass.	30'	9T	demotorized, used as trailer	
TENNESSEE, ALABAMA & GEORGIA RY. Gadsden, Ala. to Chattanooga, Tenn. 91.7 mi. (Merged into Southern System)									
500	Brill	1922	21588	Midwest 68hp, gas-mech.	10 win. bag. 43 pass.	43'	14½T	scrapped	
501	Brill	1923	21836	Midwest 68hp, gas-mech.	10 win. bag. 43 pass.	43'	14½T	scrapped	A third car was ordered (Brill 22185) but canceled (1925)

STRANGE COINCIDENCE: On these pages we present three cars 500 working for three different railroads. Photo at right is of Alabama & Florida 500, snapped at Cowarts, Ala., on September 5, 1937.
H.H. Pollitt

EDWARDS MODEL 10 was a smaller version. Birmingham & Southeastern 500 is pictured at right at Tallassee, Ala., in 1937.
Author's Collection

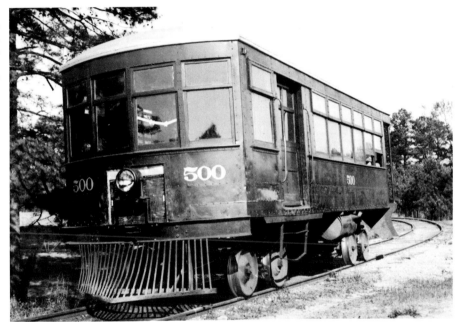

DEMOTORIZED Edwards No. 500 served the Sumpter & Choctaw. It is shown at Bellamy, Ala., in 1959 with most of its paint gone.
Harold K. Vollrath Collection

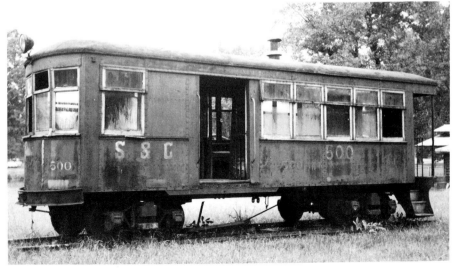

Alaska

AREA: 590,884 sq. miles
CAPITAL: Juneau
POPULATION (1927): 54,899

I SUPPOSE it is rather stretching the point to include the Chitina Auto Railer and the Yakutat & Southern Railroad as bona-fide railroads.

The Chitina line, which used the north end of the Copper River & Northwestern Railway after it was abandoned in 1938, was maintained—at least during the war years—as a public road by the Alaska Road Commission. During World War II the road was surveyed by the Army, but apparently was never used by the military.

The Yakutat & Southern Railroad served the city of Yakutat, a small fishing port on Alaska's south coast about halfway between Seward and Juneau, and its airport, which was about four miles away. The only equipment was an ex-Army Chevrolet 4X4 and a small four-wheel gondola car. Its chief function seems to have been to transport fish to the airport.

I suspect these rather fragile lines survived only until their motive power wore out.

The Seward Peninsula Railroad was built around the turn of the century to serve the gold fields in the Nome area. Eventually, when the gold petered out, it too was taken over by the Alaska Road Commission and was designated a public highway.

After something of a revival during the war, when the Army used it, it reverted to public status. During this time private individuals operated small home-built railcars as a tourist attraction during the summer months, pretty much in the manner of a small bus line on a highway. In this case, the highway had tracks on it!

Eventually, the Road Commission converted the rail line into a regular highway, but we do know that it operated in the rail mode until at least the late 1950s.

The other two railroads in Alaska that had railcars—the Alaska Northern and the Tanana Valley—were both incorporated into the Alaska Railroad.

Alaska's other major railroad, the White Pass & Yukon, actually operated mostly in Canada. It had a Paige sedan that was fitted out to run on the WP&Y's narrow-gauge rails. I think this car existed, but no mention was made of it in any of several books on this line, so it may not have been in service very long.

BUS AND TRUCK on flanged wheels both served the Chitina Auto Railer. The photo dates to the World War II year of 1942, when the railroad was used as a "public road" by the Alaska Road Commission.
Author's Collection

TANANA VALLEY used this Edison-Beach battery car, shown probably in a builder's photo.
Author's Collection

TINY TURNTABLE served the Seward Peninsula and its three-foot-gauge car 97. Below, right, is the former Army truck serving the Yakutat & Southern. *Both: Melvin Beaton*

ROAD NOS.	BUILDER	DATE	BLDR. NO.	ENGINE & DRIVE	BODY TYPE	LGTH.	WT.	DISPOSITION	NOTES & COMMENTS
ALASKA NORTHERN RR (orig. Alaska Central) Seward to Kern Creek, Ala. 72 mi. (Incorporated into Alaska RR)									
1	Fair-Morse	1911		F-M 50hp gas-mech.	8 win. wood clere. roof, 4 wheel bag. 35 pass.	34′ 2″	13T	to Alaska RR	Type 24
2	Fair-Morse	1911		F-M 50hp gas-mech.	8 win. wood clere. roof, 4 wheel bag. 35 pass.	34′ 2″	13T	to Alaska RR	Type 24
	Fair-Morse			Sheffield 25hp gas-mech.	4 wheel open	15′ 6″	2½ T	to Alaska RR	Type 22
CHITINA AUTO RAILER Chitina to McCarthy, Ala. 70 mi. (used north end of the ex-Copper River & Northwestern)									
(1 car)	Ford Evans			Ford V-8 gas-mech.	3 win. hood type bus				"Auto Railer"
(1 car)	Ford			Ford 4 cyl. gas-mech.	Model T open pick-up				
SEWARD PENINSULA RR (3 foot gauge) Nome to Bunker Hill, Ala. 70 mi.									Small gas rail bus used around 1912
97	Home Built	ca. 1950		Ford "A" gas-mech.	3 win. 2 drs. 4 wheel wooden				For tourist, summer only

ROAD NOS.	BUILDER	DATE	BLDR. NO.	ENGINE & DRIVE	BODY TYPE	LGTH.	WT.	DISPOSITION	NOTES & COMMENTS
TANANA VALLEY RR (3 ft. gauge) Chena to Chatanika and Fairbanks, Ala. 39 mi. (Incorporated into Alaska RR)									
(1 car)	Edison-Beach	1912		Edison battery electric	5 win. 4 wh. bag. 20 pass.	28'		to Alaska RR	
80				Pierce gas-mech.	4 wheel, open "toast rack" style, abt. 15 pass.			to Alaska RR	
YAKUTAT & Southern RR. Yakutat to Yakutat Airport, 4 miles									
(1 car)	Chevrolet	1949		Chev. 6 gas	Army 4x4				Ex-U.S. Army
WHITE PASS & YUKON RY., Skagway, Alaska to White Horse, Yukon, 3 ft. gauge, 110.7 mi. (Service suspended 1985)									
1	Paige Co. shops	1933		Paige gas	4 door sedan, 4 wh. ld. tk.	18'4"	3T		

Arizona

AREA: 113,909 sq. miles
CAPITAL: Phoenix
POPULATION (1927): 459,000

MOST OF ARIZONA'S short lines were dependent on the mining industry, and as this industry declined, its short lines did, too. The number of short lines in the state was small. The last to run railcars, the Tucson, Cornelia & Gila Bend, is now in somewhat a state of suspended animation because of labor problems and the depressed price of copper.

Except for the Verde Tunnel & Smelter, which seems to have accumulated a fair number of cars, one or two cars was the norm.

One somewhat unusual operation was the Yuma Valley Railroad, which was owned by the United States Department of the Interior and was used in the building of some of the dams on the Colorado River. To serve passengers in this hot and arid area of the country, a McKeen car from the San Diego, Cuyamaca & Eastern was acquired in the middle teens.

After the completion of the dam work, about 1925, the car was transferred to the Alaska Railroad, another government agency, thus going from the hottest operational area to one of the coldest in the United States.

In Alaska, the car was soon demotorized and used as a trailer. During one period in World War II it was used as a mobile PX when the Army operated the Alaska Railroad.

ENORMOUS HEADLIGHT assures plenty of illumination for Tucson, Cornelia & Gila Bend Edward unit No. 401. The line served the large copper mines at Ajo, Ariz., and passenger service was strictly secondary. *Randolph Brandt Collection*

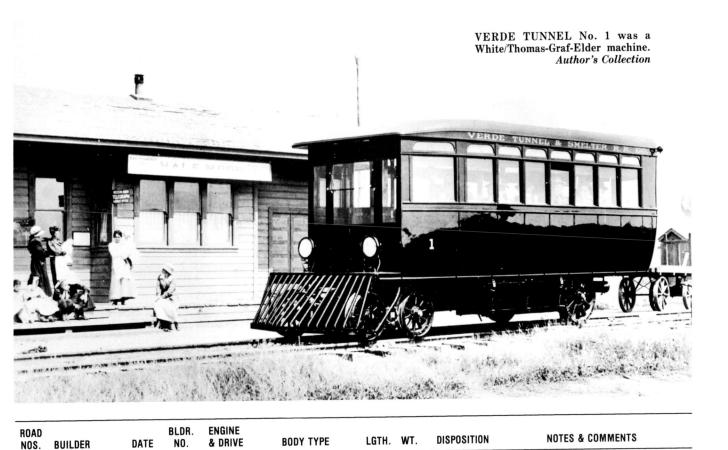

VERDE TUNNEL No. 1 was a
White/Thomas-Graf-Elder machine.
Author's Collection

ROAD NOS.	BUILDER	DATE	BLDR. NO.	ENGINE & DRIVE	BODY TYPE	LGTH.	WT.	DISPOSITION	NOTES & COMMENTS
ARIZONA SOUTHERN, Red Rock to Silver Bell, Arizona, 20 miles (Abandoned)									
none	Pierce-Arrow			Pierce-Arrow	open truck				
MAGMA ARIZONA RR, Magma to Superior, Ariz. 28 miles (In operation)									
1	White			White gas	11 win. CE bag-pass.			retired 1935	Ex-Arizona & New Mexico No. 301. Doors on right side only.
2	North West	1936		Ford V-8	baggage-pass.			retired 1939	Doors each side and back
TUCSON, CORNELIA & GILA BEND, Gila to Ajo, Ariz. 43 miles (In operation)									
6	White-Bender	11/20		White 4 cyl. gas-mech.	open bus, 4 doors, 4 wheel				
7	White-Bender	1921		White 4 cyl. gas-mech.	open bus, 5 doors, 4 wheel				
401	Edwards	1927		Buda 80hp gas-mech.	8 win. OP, bag. pass.	32'	10T	presented to "Travel Town" (L.A.)	"Travel Town" traded this car for some old streetcars. Now at a museum.
VERDE TUNNEL & SMELTER RR. Clarksdale to Jerome, Ariz. (11 miles) (Abandoned)									
1	White Thomas-Graf Edler			White 4 cyl. 40hp gas	8 win. hood type bus				4 wheel lead truck
30	?								
110	?			gas-mech.					
111	?			gas-mech.					
112A				trailer	baggage				
YUMA VALLEY RR (U.S. DEPT. OF INTERIOR, BUREAU OF RECLAMATION) Yuma to Mexican border, Ariz. 25 miles (Abandoned)									
1	McKeen	1910		McKeen 200hp gas-mech.	12 win. CE bag-pass.	55'	34T	to Alaska RR 1925 (M108)	Ex-San Diego, Cuyamaca & Eastern "Cuyamaca." Baggage section installed by Yuma Valley, 1916.
MASCOT & WESTERN RR, Mascot to Wilcox, Ariz. 15 miles (Abandoned)									
Black Cat					open truck, 4 wheel lead truck				

Arkansas

AREA: 53,104 sq. miles
CAPITAL: Little Rock
POPULATION (1927): 1,752,204

M OST OF THE SHORT LINES of Arkansas have been involved in the lumbering industry, and as a result there are still a fair number in operation, especially in the southwestern area of the state.

The geography of the state can be divided into two areas: the northwestern part which is mountainous, and the southeastern section of Delta country flatlands. The two trunk lines of the area, the Missouri Pacific and the Cotton Belt, lie in the flatlands. One road, the Missouri and Northern Arkansas, built its line at a right angle to the MOP/SSW.

Having the north end of the line in mountainous country and the south end on the billiard table delta region led to operational problems that were among the reasons that this line never achieved trunk-line status. For a period it did achieve the status of a Class I railroad, but its operations were much more akin to those of your classic short line.

In any event, the M&NA probably had the worst luck of any railcar operator. In 1912 two new General Electric gas-electric cars were purchased in an attempt to revitalize and cut expenses of the passenger service.

For a couple of years all went well, but on August 5, 1914, while operating under trackage rights on the Kansas City Southern, gas-electric car No. 103 ran head-on into a KCS passenger train at Tipton Ford, Missouri. In the tragic fire that resulted, 43 people died.

Despite this calamity, the M&NA bought another car which was used until the mid-1920s when the prosperity of the era prompted the company to resume conventional steam-hauled passenger trains. The cars were traded off to the Midland Valley Railroad of Oklahoma.

This prosperity did not last, and in 1938 a pair of American Car and Foundry-built gas railcars was purchased, again with the idea of improving service while cutting expenses. Again all went well until August 23, 1946, when car 705 ran into a milk truck at a grade crossing near Harrison, Arkansas. Both the operator of the railcar and the truck driver were killed. There were no other injuries, but both vehicles were demolished.

On the following September 2, the other ACF car hit an auto near Green Forest, so unnerving the operator he was unable to continue his run.

The M&NA has one other notable car, a Brill type 55 car, the last motor car that Brill was to build. It was built in 1937, long after any previous order for the type 55 was filled. This car was used on the flat portion of the road between Helena and Kensett. It faithfully carried out its duties until it was retired in 1949.

EL DORADO & WESSON GE car (right) was used as a trailer. Missouri & North Arkansas GE car 102 is shown in a builder's photo.
(Top Photo) Paul Dunn;
(Bottom Photo) George E. Votava
Collection

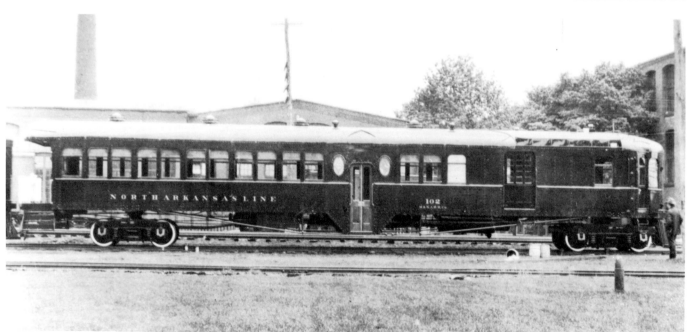

GRIMY EXTERIOR hides the charm of Missouri & Arkansas ACF streamlined car 726 at Harrison, Ark., in 1947. See page 105, *Doodlebug Country*, for a roster of this line which actually belongs in the short-line column.
Harold K. Vollrath Collection

ELBERTA ZEPHYR was a home-made low-tech streamlining effort by the Prescott and Northwestern. Sign on shed reads: No Admittance, No Loafing, No Smoking, Keep Out!
Author's Collection

ROAD NOS.	BUILDER	DATE	BLDR. NO.	ENGINE & DRIVE	BODY TYPE	LGTH.	WT.	DISPOSITION	NOTES & COMMENTS
ARKANSAS RR CO., Isom to Star City, Ark., 17.8 miles. (Abandoned)									
(1 car)	Four wheel drive	1921		Wisconsin A 4 cyl. gas	8 win. CE 4 whl. wooden	25'	6T	gone by 1929	
ARKANSAS NORTHWESTERN RR, Bentonville to Rogers, Ark. 6 miles. (Merged into Frisco System)									
100	McKeen	1911	121	200hp McKeen gas-mech.	15 win. CE bag. 60 pass.	70'	40T	to Saratoga & Encamp. Valley	Car was built for Peoples Elect. Ry., Muskogee, Okla., was repossessed by McKeen
BLYTHEVILLE, LEACHVILLE & ARKANSAS SOUTHERN RR Co., Leachville to Amorel, Ark. 21.5 miles. (Merged into Cotton Belt, 1928)									
		1911		gas-mech.	15 pass. bus			retired 1917	
DE QUEEN & EASTERN RR. CO.-TEXAS, OKLAHOMA & EASTERN RR CO., Dierks, Ark. to Valient, Okla., 75.85 miles. (In operation)									
5				gas-mech.	12 pass. bus			scrapped 1935	
7	International	1935		International gas-mech.	4 win. hood type bus, 4 whl. lead truck, bag. 20 pass.				Pulled small four-wheeled baggage trailer
DONIPHAN, KENSETT & SEARCY RY., Doniphan to Searcy, Ark., 6 miles. (In operation)									
(1 car)				gas-mech.	motor bus				

19

ROAD NOS.	BUILDER	DATE	BLDR. NO.	ENGINE & DRIVE	BODY TYPE	LGTH.	WT.	DISPOSITION	NOTES & COMMENTS
EL DORADO & WESSON RY., El Dorado to Wesson, Ark., 10 miles. (6 miles now in operation)									
5	Gen. Elect. Wason	10/12	3750 12920	GE GM16C1 175hp gas-el.	14 win. CE bag. 79 pass.	70'	51T	demotorized, used as trailer	Ex-CRI&P 9041, acquired 1933, not known if ever used as a motor
FT. SMITH, SUBIACO & ROCK ISLAND RR CO., Paris to Dardenelle, Ark., 39 miles. (Abandoned)									
A-1	Brill Service	1923	21705	Midwest 68hp gas-mech.	10 win. bag. 43 pass.	43'	15T	burned	
GRAYSONIA, NASHVILLE & ASHDOWN RR., Nashville to Ashdown, Ark., 32 miles. (In operation)									
46	Chevrolet	1946		Chevrolet 6 cyl gas-mech.	1 ton pickup truck			to maint. of way service 1953	
100	Brill White	6/23	21808	White 40hp gas-mech.	8 win. CE 30 pass. bag. 4 whl. lead truck	31' 6"	10½T	retired 1929	Brill Model 43
500	Brill White	1925	22192	White 50hp gas-mech.	8 win. CE 30 pass. bag. 4 whl. lead truck	31' 6"	10½T	burned 1925	Brill Model 43
600	Edwards	1925	141	(2) Cont. 144 103hp gas-mech.	9 win. bag. 39 pass.	43'	22T	retired 6/32	Ex-Col. & Sou. 500, ex-ex-CB&Q 504. Acq. 6/29. Body now a store in Hope, Ark.
JONESBORO, LAKE CITY & EASTERN RR CO. Jonesboro to Barfield, Ark. and branches; 84.9 mi. (Merged into SL-SF, 1925)									
(1 car)	McKeen	1906		McKeen 200hp gas-mech.					Very little known about this car, probably kept for very short time
33		1/20			10 pass. motorbus	17'		made into insp. car '22	
101	White Southland	9/22		White 4045, 60hp gas	7 win. 6 pass. motor bus	22' 4"	6T	to SL-SF No. 2900 (1925)	
110	Gen. Elect. Wason	5/11	3710 10270	GE GM16A1 275hp GE	12 win. CE bag. 47 pass.	58'	40½T	to SL-SF '25. Sec. 2117	Acq. 1924, ex-Okla. Nor. 110, ex-ex-Dan Patch 5
111	Gen. Elect. Wason	5/13	3744 12226	GE GM16C1 275hp gas el.	17 win. OP bag. 90 pass.	71'	49T	to SL-SF '25. Sec. 2111	Acq. 1924, ex-Okla. Nor. 111, ex-ex-Chicago, Peoria & St. Louis No. 104
HOXIE-WALNUT RIDGE RY. Hoxie to Walnut Ridge, Ark. 2 mi. (Abandoned)									
(1 car)	Fairbanks-Morse	1907		Sheffield 12½hp gas	4 wheel, open, 12 pass.	15' 6"	2¼T		Replaced horse car
PRESCOTT & NORTHWESTERN RR CO. Prescott to Highland, Ark. 33 mi. (Abandoned)									
22	co. shops				4 wheel bag.				"Elberta Zephyr"
KANSAS CITY & MEMPHIS RY. CO. Rogers to Siloam Springs and Fayetteville, Ark. 57 mi. (Abandoned)									
200	Federal			Battery-el.	8 win. OP bag. 30 pass.	38' 11"		returned	Sold to Cassville & Exeter Ry. Used as a trailer.
ST. LOUIS, KENNETT & SOUTHEASTERN RR. Kennett to Piggott, Ark. 16.8 mi. (Merged into SL-SF 1927)									
80	Edwards	1923		Buda 100hp gas-mech.	8 win. bag. 25 pass.	26' 4"	9T	to SL-SF No. 80	
81	Edwards	1923		Trailer	9 win. 32 pass.	26' 4"	8½T	to SL-SF No. 81	
SEARCY & KENSETT RY. Searcy to Kensett, Ark. 4 mi. Used Missouri & Northern Arkansas RR tracks. (Abandoned)									
(1 car)	Stover	1909		Stover 60hp gas-mech.	6 win. OP 4 wheel, 20 pass.	abt. 20'	6T		Orig. CRI&P 2553, first 9005. Acquired 1911.
WARREN & OUACHITA VALLEY RY. Warren to Banks, Ark. 16 mi. (Abandoned)									
1	Gen. Elect. Wason	3/12	3720	GE GM16B 175hp gas-el.	15 win. OP bag. 88 pass.	67'	45T	rebuilt to trailer	Ex-SP&S 1102, ex-ex-Dan Patch No. 8, acquired 9/24
6	Gen. Elect. Wason	2/11	3704	GE GM10B2 125hp gas-el.	10 win. RE bag. 88 pass.	57'	39T	rebuilt to trailer	Ex-Dan Patch No. 6, ex-ex-Gen. Elect. demo No. 4, acquired 1916

California

AREA: 158,693 sq. miles
CAPITAL: Sacramento
POPULATION (1927): 3,426,861

IN A REFRESHING contrast to most of the other states of the Union, California still has a goodly number of short lines in operation.

Such familiar names as the Santa Maria Valley, California Western, Modesto and Empire Traction Co., Trona Railway, Sierra Railway, to mention a few, are still in operation. Gone are such stalwart lines as the Nevada County Narrow Gauge, Pacific Coast Railway, Ocean Shore, and the San Joaquin & Eastern.

Perhaps more of these lines were associated with the lumbering industry than any other, but other industries, such as mining, agriculture, and construction, were also represented.

Equally as diverse were the types of equipment used. The California Western had cars built by Mack, Edwards, Skagit, and American Car & Foundry, all of them secondhand. The Tonopah & Tidewater (which never got very close to either Tonopah or Tidewater) had a brand-new St. Louis-Electro Motive gas-electric car that for a time pulled a through Pullman to and from Los Angeles, making connections with the Union Pacific at Crucero.

Not to be outdone, the T&T connection at Death Valley Junction, the Death Valley Railroad, acquired a 3' gauge Brill type 55 gas-mechanical car. Strangely enough, the EMD car went to the Sonora-Baja California Railroad in Mexico, and the Brill to the American Potash Co. in New Mexico, and the last I

heard both bodies are still around.

The Visalia Electric Railroad acquired one of the Dan Patch Lines' huge General Electric gas-electrics. This car went from the VER to the Northwestern Pacific, and finally ended up as an emergency work car on the San Francisco Bay Bridge.

Besides the cars built in the east, a number of cars were built by local firms, and the most famous of these—Hall-Scott—not only built cars for the local market, but even for international use. Meister Car Co. and Thomson-Graf-Edler both built lightweight equipment that was widely used in the west.

Besides all this, there were plenty of those special home-built cars so prevalent on short lines all over the country.

The Holton Interurban Railway had a predecessor of the auto railer back in 1917, but most of these units tended to

be modifications of trucks and automobiles, with the Model T Ford as the vehicle of choice, as it was all over the country.

While we have not included the Yosemite Valley or the McCloud River in our rosters, they both dabbled a bit with railcars. The Yosemite Valley had a modified sedan, which was probably an inspection car, and in 1924 rented one of the Western Pacific's under-utilized Brill type 55 gas cars. It apparently didn't work out and was returned.

The McCloud River Line briefly tried out a station wagon-type vehicle with a four-wheel lead truck and a special rubber tire with a metal flange developed by Goodrich around 1933. The parent organization had a couple of home-built railcars built, which were used to transport logging crews and were not in regular revenue service.

THROUGH THE DESERT ran Tonopah & Tidewater EMC car 99 (above right). Ventura County No. 3 is a 1913 Hall-Scott motor.
Both: Al Barker Collection

NEAT BUILDING and arch at Chowchilla had to be shown along with Chowchilla Pacific Hall-Scott motor 101.

Randolph Brandt Collection

NEVADA COUNTY narrow-gauge Ford truck sports a huge bell, baggage truck.

W.C. Whittaker Collection

ORIGIN of this open Holton Interurban bus is not known.

Roger Ciapponi

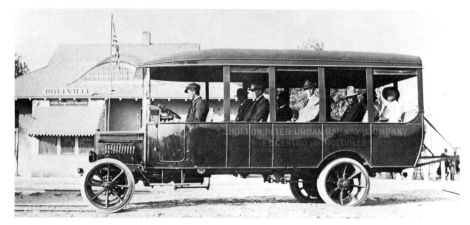

RESTORED Santa Maria Valley 9, a Fairmont Ford, is shown at the Pacific Southwest Railway Museum at Campo, Calif., in 1984. Brill Model 55 No. 5 of the Death Valley RR awaits movement at Death Valley Jct. about 1929.
(Above) W.C. Whittaker Collection;
(Above, right) Randolph Brandt Collection

FORD MODEL T truck serves as Pacific Coast Ry. baggage truck with high number of 4000.
W.C. Whittaker Collection

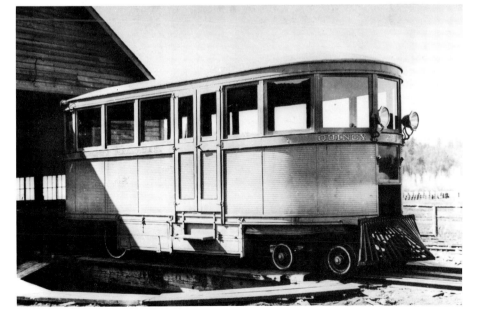

QUINCY RAILROAD 49 has the distinctive look of a Meister car.
Bert Ward Collection

ROAD NOS.	BUILDER	DATE	BLDR. NO.	ENGINE & DRIVE	BODY TYPE	LGTH.	WT.	DISPOSITION	NOTES & COMMENTS
BURLINGAME RY. Burlingame, Calif. 1½ mi. (Abandoned 1917)									
1	Federal	1912		battery, 4-10hp motors	4 wheel wood st.car 26 pass.	27' 6"			
CALIFORNIA WESTERN RAILWAY & NAVIGATION CO. Ft. Bragg to Willits, Calif. 39.6 mi. (In operation)									
M-80	Mack Cummings	10/23	60014	Mack AC 80hp gas-mech.	7 win. bag. 22 pass.	37' 10"	14½T	Wrecked in 1964	Ex-Mack demo, baggage door at rear
M-100	Edwards	1926		2 Buda 108hp gas-mech.	9 win. bag. 36 pass.	43'	17T	in service	Rebuilt with diesel engines. Rebuilt with new body.
M-200	Skagit	1927		Buda JH 6 150hp gas	10 win. CE bag. 50 pass. short hood	44'	20½T	to Pt. Richmond Castro Pt. Ry. Pac. Loco. Assoc.	Ex-Trona Ry. No. 22, acquired 1941. Ex-ex-Longview, Portland & Nor.
M-300	Amer. Car & Foundry	1935	1432	Hall-Scott 168hp GM	17 win. CE bag. 57 pass.	64' 1"	26T	in service	Acquired 1963, ex-Salt Lake, Garfield & Western, MC-3, ex-ex-Aberdeen & Rockfish 106, ex-ex-ex-Seaboard Air Line 2026.
CHOWCHILLA PACIFIC RY. Chowchilla to Dairyland, Calif. 10 mi. (Merged into Southern Pacific)									
100	Meister?			gas-mech.	4 wheel, 5 win. CE	abt. 20'			
101	Hall-Scott	1915	22	Hall-Scott 150hp GM	8 win. bag. 26 pass.	54'		to Visalia Elect. 1924	Visalia Elect. No. 301
DEATH VALLEY RR CO. (3 ft. gauge) Death Valley Junction to Ryan, Calif. 20.34 mi. (Abandoned)									
5	Brill	1928	22499	Brill 55, 58hp GM	10 win. bag. 40 pass.	42'	15½T	to Amer. Potash, 12/31	Now at Laws (Calif.) Railroad Museum
DIAMOND & CALDOR RY. CO. (3 ft. gauge) Diamond Springs to Caldor, Calif. 33 miles (Abandoned)									
(1 car)	Thomas	1909		Thomas gas.	5 pass. open sedan, 4 wh. lead truck				
(1 car)	Ford	ca. 1920		Ford 4 cyl. gas-mech.	Model T, 4 wheel, open				
(1 car)	Ford	ca. 1925		Ford 4 cyl. gas-mech.	5 pass. 4 wh. lead truck, open car				
10	Co. Shops			Studebaker gas-mech.	open with closed cab abt. 12 pass.	23'		to Camino, Cable & Nor. (Scenic) RR	
FRESNO INTERURBAN RY. CO. Hammond to Belmont Ave., Calif. 16.88 mi. (Merged into Santa Fe)									
1	Hall-Scott	1914	21	Hall-Scott 150hp GM	12 win. bag. abt. 50 pass.	70'		to AT&SF 1926	Apparently was demotorized and used in maint. of way service on the AT&SF.
HETCH HETCHY RR, Hetch Hetchy Jct. to Mather, Calif. 68 mi. (Abandoned 1949)									
19	White Meister	1920		White 4 cyl. gas-mech.	open bus, 3 door, 12 pass.		7½T	on display at El Portal (Yosemite)	4 wheel lead truck. Had self-contained ''turntable'' built into car.
20	White Bender			White 4 cyl. gas-mech.	open bus, 5 drs. per side, 23 pass.		3T	scrapped 1949	4 wheel lead truck, ex-highway bus
21	White Meister	1922		White 4 cyl. gas-mech.	open bus, 5 drs. per side, 23 pass.			scrapped 1949	4 wheel lead truck, ex-highway bus
22	White Meister	1922		White 4 cyl. gas-mech.	open mail-express trk.			wrecked 1922	4 wheel lead truck, ex-highway bus. Chassis went to build No. 24.
23	White Meister			White 4 cyl. gas-mech.			6½T		4 wheel lead truck
24	Meister	1925			5 win. CE 30 pass.		5T	Demot. 1927. Scrapped '49	4 wheel lead truck. Parts from No. 22 used in construction, engine housed at rear.

ROAD NOS.	BUILDER	DATE	BLDR. NO.	ENGINE & DRIVE	BODY TYPE	LGTH.	WT.	DISPOSITION	NOTES & COMMENTS
HOLTON INTERURBAN RY. CO. Holtville to El Centro, Calif. 11 miles. In operation. (Owned and operated by the SP)									
3	Hall-Scott Holman	1909	2	Hall-Scott 100hp GM	Clere. roof, wooden bag. pass.				
4	Fair.-Morse Sheffield			30hp gas-mech.	open 4 wh. st.car 20	22'	4½ T		
5	Hall-Scott	1911	7	Hall-Scott 150hp GM	11 win. bag. 44 pass.			sold to Valley and Siletz (Ore.)	Valley & Siletz No. 9
(1 car)	Moreland	1917		Moreland gas-mech.	open flatbed truck	15'6"	3½ T		Early form of ''auto-railer'', could run on either track or road.
(1 car)					open bus abt. 10 pass.				
HUENEME, MALIBU & PORT LOS ANGELES RY.									
(1 car)	Co. Shops	1912		gas motor					

HIGHWAY BUS was given flanged wheels and resumed life as Hetch-Hetchy 20, a White with a Bender body. Those side curtains sometimes came in handy in unpredictable Sierra weather.
W.C. Whittaker Collection

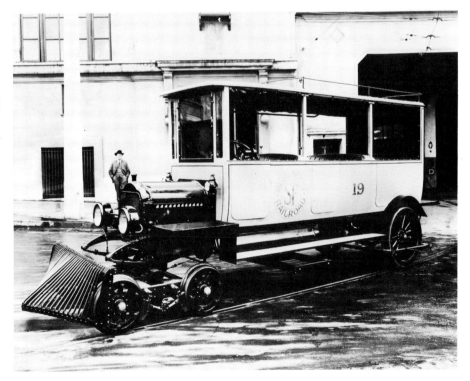

A WHITE-MEISTER UNIT on the Hetch-Hetchy was No. 19, posed in front of San Francisco Municipal Railway's Geary St. barns. Both the Muni and the H-H were owned by the City.
Charles Smallwood Collection

SKUNK & SUPER SKUNK gather in one photo on the California Western. The M-300 is an ACF motor purchased in 1963 from the Salt Lake, Garfield & Western. The steam train with Stillwell coaches is sometimes called the Super Skunk.

Edward Freitas

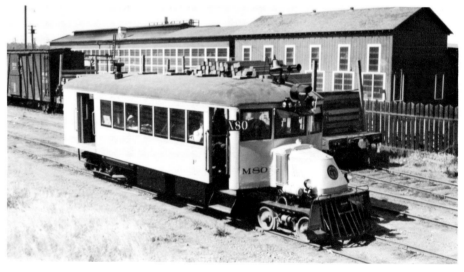

TWO MORE SKUNKS: The M-80, a Bulldog Mack, and the M-200, of Skagit parentage, are shown serving on the California Western in 1947 and 1941 respectively.

(Middle Photo) Jim Buckley Collection; (Bottom Photo) Stephen D. Maguire Collection

ROAD NOS.	BUILDER	DATE	BLDR. NO.	ENGINE & DRIVE	BODY TYPE	LGTH.	WT.	DISPOSITION	NOTES & COMMENTS
LOS ANGELES & SAN DIEGO BEACH RY. San Diego to La Jolla, Calif. 15.75 mi. (Abandoned 1919)									
1	McKeen	1907		McKeen 200hp gas-mech.	12 win., CE 75 pass.	55'	30½T		
2	McKeen	1908		McKeen 200hp gas-mech.					
14	Federal	1912		trailer (ex. bty.-elect.)	7 win. 4 wh., wood st.car	26' 6"			Ex-San Diego & Imperial Beach Ry. (Mexico & San Diego Ry.) battery car No. 1.
15	Federal	1912		trailer (ex. bty.-elect.)	7 win. 4 wh., wood st.car	26' 6"			Ex-SD&IB (M&SD) battery car No. 2.
51	Ort Iron Works	1917		Mack 4 cyl. gas-mech.	6 win. CE abt 20 pass.			sold	4 wheel lead truck
MINERETS & WESTERN RR. Pinedale to Wishon, Calif. 52.69 mi. (9.24 on trackage rights) (Abandoned)									
1	Meister			Midwest 4 cyl. gas-mech.	9 win. CE 45 pass.	33'			Had "trailing truck" at rear to support rear hung engine.
MOUNT TAMALPAIS & MUIR WOODS RY., Mill Valley to Summit Mt. Tamalpais, Calif. 8.19 mi. (Abandoned)									
1		1905		gas-mech.	open 6 pass. sedan			retired 1914	
2	Co. Shops	1909		Stoddard-Dayton gas.	4 wheel CE 4 win. wood 25 pass.				
3	Kissel	1916		Kissel gas-mech.	4 win. CE 20 pass. hood type bus				Had two very small four wheel trucks
4	Fair.-Morse			Fair.-Morse gas-mech.					
Booster				upright boiler steam	open, 4 rows of seats, 4 wheel				
MODESTO & EMPIRE TRACTION CO. Modesto to Empire, Calif. 5.2 mi. (In operation)									
11	Ry. Store. Btty. Beach	1913		Battery Electric	4 wheel st. car	27' 6"			
NEVADA COUNTY NARROW GAUGE RR (3 ft. gauge) Colfax to Nevada City, Calif. 20.65 mi. (Abandoned)									
1	Ford Co. Shops			Ford A 4 cyl. gas-mech.	3 win. hood type truck, 4 wh. lead truck				Pulls 4 wheel closed van.
PACIFIC COAST RY. CO. (3 ft. gauge), Port San Luis to Los Olivos, Calif. and branches, 104.14 miles. (Abandoned)									
4000	Ford Co. Shops			Ford T 4 cyl. gas-mech.	closed chassis with van body				
OCEAN SHORE RY. San Francisco to Tunitas, Calif. 38 miles. (Abandoned)									
61	Meister	1917		Buda SSU 60hp gas-mech.	6 win. CE bag. 31 pass, open rear obs.	40' 4"	11T	sold to Long Bell Lbr. Co.	
62	Meister	1917		Buda SSU 60hp gas-mech.	10 win. CE bag. 31 pass.	40' 4"	11T	sold to La Crosse & Sou. Eastern 1920	
QUINCY RR., Quincy Jct. to Quincy, Calif. 5.29 mi. (In operation)									
49	Meister	1918		Buda SSU 60hp gas-mech.	7 win. CE 25 pass.	abt. 25'	7T		
M-1				trailer					
SAN DIEGO CUYAMACA & EASTERN RR, San Diego to Cuyamaca, Calif. (Abandoned)									
Cuya-maca	McKeen	1908		McKeen 200hp gas-mech.	14 win. CE bag. 75 pass.	55'	34T	sold to Yuma Valley Ry.	Eventually went to Alaska RR
SAN JOAQUIN & EASTERN RR CO. El Prado to Cascada, Calif. 55.91 miles. (Abandoned)									
501	White Thomas Graf Edler	1923		White 4 cyl. gas-mech.	8 win. CE 24 pass.			scrapped '33	4 wheel lead truck

ROAD NOS.	BUILDER	DATE	BLDR. NO.	ENGINE & DRIVE	BODY TYPE	LGTH.	WT.	DISPOSITION	NOTES & COMMENTS
SACRAMENTO VALLEY & EASTERN RY. Pitt River to Bully Hill, Calif. 15.93 mi. (Abandoned)									
(1 car)				gas-mech.	4 wh. open "speeder," 3 rows of seats, curtain sides	abt 12'			
(1 car)				gas-mech.	4 wh. open "speeder," 3 rows of seats, curtain sides				
SANTA ANA & ORANGE MOTOR CO. Santa Ana to Orange, Calif. 4 mi. bought by Pacific Electric 1901, narrow gauge									
5	Baker Iron Works	1898		upright steam dbl. oscillating	open 4 wh. wood st. cars 30 pass.	19'9"	9T	scrapped 10/20	Ex-132, prob. ex-cable trailer
6	Baker Iron Works	1898		upright steam dbl. oscillating rebuilt with 2 cyl 24hp Olds gas engine	open 4 wh. wood st. cars 30 pass.	19'9"	9T	scrapped 10/20	Ex-133, prob. ex-cable trailer
10	Barney & Smith	1897		Mitchell 30hp gas eng.	open 4 wheel, 4 bench st. car	28'	9T	reconverted to elect. '14	Ex-elect. car, ex-LAIU No. (2)757, ex-ex-R&A No. 20.
SANTA MARIA VALLEY RR CO., Bettaravia to Roadamite, Calif. 17.77 mi. (In operation)									
9	Fairmont Ford	1932		Ford A 4 cyl. gas-mech.	2 win. 4 whl. hood front				Now at Pacific Southwest Ry. Museum, Campo, Calif.
SIERRA RY. OF CALIFORNIA, Oakdale to Toulumne, Calif. 56.65 mi. (In operation)									
2	Ford Co. Shops			Ford T 4 cyl. gas-mech.	pickup truck body, 4 wh lead truck				
STOCKTON TERMINAL & EASTERN RR, Stockton to Belluta, Calif. 18.5 mi. (In operation)									
100	Hall-Scott Holman	1912	6	Hall-Scott 100hp GM	7 win. wooden bag. 25 pass.	31'		retired 1933, scrap. 1939	
(1 car)	Mitchell	1909		Mitchell gas-mech.	7 pass. open sedan				
(1 car)	Garford	1913		Studebaker gas-mech.	7 pass. open sedan				
MEXICO & SAN DIEGO RY. (ex-Sou. San Diego 7 Imperial Beach Ry.) Sou. San Diego to Imperial Beach, Calif. 1.1 mi. (Abandoned)									
(1 car)	Fair.-Morse	1910		Sheffield 30hp gas	open 4 wh. st. car, wooden	22'	4½T	sold, perhaps to Holton I-U	
1	Federal	1912		Edison 200 cell, bty. elect.	7 win. 4 wh. st. car, 20 pass.	26'6"		sold to Los Angeles & San Diego Beach	Demotorized, arched windows
2	Federal	1912		Edison 200 cell, bty. elect.	7 win. 4 wh. st. car, 20 pass.	26'6"		sold to Los Angeles & San Diego Beach	Demotorized, square windows
TONOPAH & TIDEWATER RR CO., Ludlow, Calif. to Beatty, Nev. 169 mi. (Abandoned)									
99	EMC St. Louis	1928	349 1484	Winton 120 275hp gas-elec.	10 win. bag. 45 pass.		54T	sold to Sonora-Baja Calif. RR 1943	Used as pay car on S-BC
VENTURA COUNTY RY., Oxnard to Port Hueneme, 5 mi. (In operation)									
001	Fair.-Morse	1905		Sheffield gas-mech.	open "speeder" 4 wheel car				
002	Fair.-Morse			Sheffield gas-mech.	4 wheel, open st. car body				
003	Hall-Scott	1913		Hall-Scott 150hp GM	10 win. bag. 46 pass.	50'		sold for scrap	Was put on display for a time but was so badly vandalized it was scrapped
TRONA RY., Searles to Trona, Calif. 30.8 mi. (In operation)									
22	Skagit	1928		Buda JH 6 150hp GM	10 win. CE, 50 pass. bag.	44'	20½T	sold to Cal. West. Ry. '41 (M-200)	Purchased from Long View, Portland & Northern Ry.

ROAD NOS.	BUILDER	DATE	BLDR. NO.	ENGINE & DRIVE	BODY TYPE	LGTH.	WT.	DISPOSITION	NOTES & COMMENTS
VISALIA ELECTRIC RY., Exeter to Elderwood, Calif. 23.1 mi. Subsidiary of SP (In operation)									
301	Hall-Scott	1915	22	Hall-Scott 150hp GM	8 win. bag. 26 pass.	54'			Ex-Chowchilla Pacific 101, acquired 1924
450	Gen. Elect. Wason	1912	3735 12050	GE 16A5 175hp gas-elec.	17 win. bag. 73 pass.	72'	55T	to NWP	Ex-Dan Patch No. 9
YREKA WESTERN RR, Yreka to Montague, Calif. 6 mi. (In operation)									
5	Hall-Scott Holman	1908	1	Hall-Scott 100hp GM	8 win. OP, bag. 30 pass. clere. roof, wooden		18T	scrapped '35	
(1 car)	Fair.-Morse Sheffield			Sheffield gas-mech.	open 4 wheel "speeder"				

CONDUCTOR and engineer of San Joaquin & Eastern 501 wait patiently for the photographer to finish his business. *H. Johnson Collection*

Colorado

AREA: 104,207 sq. miles
CAPITAL: Denver
POPULATION (1927): 1,074,000

THE FIRST THING that comes to mind when one thinks about rail motor cars in Colorado is that gaggle of quaint but somewhat bedraggled "Galloping Geese" of the Rio Grande Southern Railway.

Born of necessity to radically cut operating costs, with no thought of esthetics, they soon became perhaps the most beloved railcars in the United States, and without doubt the most written about. This tends to obscure the fact that the most successful rail motor car operation in the United States is going on right now in Colorado.

I refer to the Manitou & Pikes Peak Railroad. I know there will be those that say this isn't a "real railroad" since it caters almost exclusively to tourists, does not connect with any other railroad, and uses a rack system. But it was long listed in the *Official Guide,* is incorporated and is listed in such financial guides as *Moody's Railroads.*

The bottom line is that its fleet of diesel-electric and diesel-hydraulic railcars has been carrying increasing loads of happy tourists, and (wonder of wonders in railroading) at a profit!

The only short line in Colorado that operated conventional factory-built cars was the Denver Laramie & Northwestern, which later became part of the Great Western Ry. Early in the century this line purchased two McKeen cars, and a Fairbanks-Morse type 24 car.

The other lines in the state, the Midland Terminal, the narrow-gauge Uintah, the Silverton & Northern, and the San Cristobal made do with home-built or modified cars.

FAR-FLUNG FAME was achieved by the Rio Grande Southern's squadron of Galloping Geese, including No. 3, shown here in two eras. The original Pierce-Arrow configuration is below in Ridgeway, Colo., in 1940. Unit was later rebuilt, above, with a Wayne bus body.

Jack Avery, Louis A. Marre/
Gordon Mott Collection;
Author's Collection

WINDING, rugged, narrow-gauge RGS roadway is clearly evident in the Goose view above.
Author's Collection

HOME-BUILT is this Manitou & Pikes Peak cog train. The popular tourist railroad certainly is one of the few that keeps on ordering new "doodlebugs" in the modern era.
Author's Collection

DIMINUTIVE Silverton Northern railbus *Casey Jones* rests long after the battle, on display in Silverton, Colo., northern terminus of the narrow-gauge Rio Grande branch (now the Durango & Silverton).
Bob Hanft;
W.C. Whittaker Collection

ROAD NOS.	BUILDER	DATE	BLDR. NO.	ENGINE & DRIVE	BODY TYPE	LGTH.	WT.	DISPOSITION	NOTES & COMMENTS
BEAVER-PENROSE & NORTHERN RY. Beaver to Penrose, Colo. 6.21 mi. (Abandoned 1918)									
(1 car)	Stevens-Duryea			Stevens gas-mech.	sedan with Brougham body				Formerly personal sedan of Spencer Penrose (owner of Broadmoor Hotel, Colorado Springs, Colo.)
COLORADO RR. Delagua to Barnes, Colo. (Abandoned)									
1	McGuire-Cummings			gas-elect.	baggage, ex-elect.				Ex-Fox & Illinois Union (Ill.) No. 7. Acquired 1940.
DENVER, LARAMIE & NORTHWESTERN RY., Elm to Wattenberg, Colo. 27.3 mi. (Purchased by Great Western Ry. 1917)									
GREAT WESTERN RY. CO., Longmont to Eaton, Colo. and branches 86.74 mi. (In operation)									
M-1 Greely	McKeen	1/11	107	McKeen 200hp gas-mech.	14 win. CE bag. 75 pass.	70'	37T	sold to UP 1928 (Sec. M-4)	Ex-DL&NW same number
M-2 Denver	McKeen	12/10	89	McKeen 200hp gas-mech.	14 win. CE bag. 75 pass.	70'	37T	sold to UP 1928 (M-5)	Ex-DL&NW same number
M-3	Fair.-Morse Brill	2/16		Fair-Morse 50hp gas	8 win. 4 wheel wooden, clere. roof, bag. 35 pass.	34' 3"	13T	scrapped 7/30	Ex-DL&NW same number. Type 24 F-M car.
EL DORADO SPRINGS RY. CO., Marshall to El Dorado Springs, Colo. Became part of the Denver Interurban Ry.									
1	Fair.-Morse ?	1910		gas-mech.	open "speeder" facing inside seats, 8 pass.				
GEORGETOWN & GRAY'S PEAK, Silver Plume to McClellan, Colo. 16.4 mi. (Abandoned 1918)									
				gas-mech.	9 win. 4 wheel 3 doors, wood			sold	
MANITOU & PIKES PEAK RY. CO., Manitou to Summit Pikes Peak, Colo. 8.9 mi. Cog rail system. (In operation)									
7	Co. Shops	1938		Gen. Mot. gas-mech.	24 pass.			stored	
14	Swiss Loco. & Machine	1963	4441	Diesel-electric	9 win. 80 pass.			in operation	
15	Swiss Loco. & Machine	1963	4442	Diesel-electric	9 win. 80 pass.			in operation	
16	Swiss Loco. & Machine	1968	4778	Diesel-electric	9 win. 80 pass.			in operation	
17	Swiss Loco. & Machine	1968	4779	Diesel-electric	9 win. 80 pass.			in operation	
18	Swiss Loco. & Machine	1976		(4) 300hp Cummins, Dies. Hydr.	22 win. articulated units			in operation	
19	Swiss Loco. & Machine	1976		(4) 300hp Cummins, Dies. Hydr.	22 win. articulated units			in operation	
MIDLAND TERMINAL RY., Colorado Springs to Cripple Creek, Colo. 39.43 mi. (Abandoned 1948)									
101	Co. Shops	1934			10 win. ex-st. car, bag. 8 pass. hood front			scrapped	Ex-Colorado Springs streetcar
102	Co. Shops	1937		(2) Buda 118hp Dies. mech.	2 win. ex-st. car, bag. 8 pass.	42'	18T	scrapped abt. 1943	Ex-Colorado Springs streetcar
RIO GRANDE SOUTHERN RR CO., Durango to Ridgeway, Colo. 162.6 mi. (3 ft. gauge) (Abandoned 1952)									
1	Co. Shops Buick	6/31		Buick 6 gas-mech.	Buick sedan front, stake body rear 4 wh. lead trk. sing rear wheel	20'	2½T	scrapped 1933	
2	Co. Shops Buick	8/31		Buick 6 gas-mech.	Buick sedan front, box rear 2 truck	29' 11"	5T	at Colo. Ry. Museum	Rebuilt with Pierce-Arrow body

EX-FOX & ILLINOIS UNION No. 7
served the Colorado Railroad as a
box motor. Its Illinois traction heritage is quite evident.
Randolph Brandt Collection

MIDLAND TERMINAL operated a
pair of ex-Colorado Springs streetcars. Number 101 kept its deck roof.
Author's Collection

ROAD NOS.	BUILDER	DATE	BLDR. NO.	ENGINE & DRIVE	BODY TYPE	LGTH.	WT.	DISPOSITION	NOTES & COMMENTS
3	Co. Shops Pierce-Arrow	12/31		Pierce-Arrow 33 gas-mech.	3 truck Pierce-Arrow front, box rear	43′3″	7½T	at Knotts Berry Farm, Buena Park, Ca.	Rebuilt with Wayne body
4	Co. Shops Pierce-Arrow	5/32		Pierce-Arrow 33 gas-mech.	3 truck Pierce-Arrow front, box rear	43′3″	7½T	at Telluride, Colo.	Rebuilt with GMC engine, Wayne body
5	Co. Shops Pierce-Arrow	6/33		Pierce-Arrow 36 gas-mech.	3 truck Pierce-Arrow front, box rear	43′3″	7½T	at Dolores, Colo.	Rebuilt with GMC engine, Wayne body
6	Co. Shops Buick	1/34		Buick 6 gas-mech.	2 truck, Buick cab, flatbed	25′6″	4½T	at Colo. Ry. Mus. Golden, Colo.	Rebuilt with Pierce-Arrow cab and engine
7	Co. Shops Pierce-Arrow	10/36		Ford 36 V-8 gas-mech.	3 truck, Pierce-Arrow, sedan, box body	46′	8T	at Colo. Ry. Mus. Golden, Colo.	Used in dismantling Crested Butte branch 1954.

SAN CRISTOBAL RY., Lake City to Saparino, Colo. 35 mi. (Abandoned 1935)

1	Pierce-Arrow McFarland-Eggers	1928 1933		Pierce-Arrow 6 80hp gas-mech.	7 pass. Pierce-Arrow sedan & box frt. sect.	21′	7T		Originally had four wheel front truck single drive wheel, rebuilt with two four wheel trucks with a longer freight section, new length 43′9″

ROAD NOS.	BUILDER	DATE	BLDR. NO.	ENGINE & DRIVE	BODY TYPE	LGTH.	WT.	DISPOSITION	NOTES & COMMENTS

SAN LUIS VALLEY SOUTHERN RY. CO., Blanco to Jarasco, Colo. 31.5 mi. 1 mile (In operation)

ROAD NOS.	BUILDER	DATE	BLDR. NO.	ENGINE & DRIVE	BODY TYPE	LGTH.	WT.	DISPOSITION	NOTES & COMMENTS
M-1 ?		6/17		Waukesha 12hp gas-mech.	4 win. wood, 12 pass.	14'		wrecked 1918	
M-3		1924							
M-4					trailer				

SILVERTON NORTHERN RR CO. (3 ft. gauge) Silverton to Animas Forks, 14.1, Silverton to Gladstone, Colo. 7.3 miles (Abandoned 1941)

ROAD NOS.	BUILDER	DATE	BLDR. NO.	ENGINE & DRIVE	BODY TYPE	LGTH.	WT.	DISPOSITION	NOTES & COMMENTS
Mary M	Mack	1905		Mack gas-mech.	23 pass.				
1	Stover	1908	114	Stover 30hp gas-mech.	4 win. 2 dr. 4 wh. wood, 12 pass.			parts used to build "Casey Jones"	
Casey Jones	Sunnyside Mining Co.	1914		Cadillac V-8 gas-mech.	5 win. 4 wheel wooden bus	18' 11"		on display at Silverton	

UINTAH RY. CO. (3 ft. gauge), Mack, Colo. to Watson, Utah, 63.1 mi. (Abandoned 1939)

ROAD NOS.	BUILDER	DATE	BLDR. NO.	ENGINE & DRIVE	BODY TYPE	LGTH.	WT.	DISPOSITION	NOTES & COMMENTS
31				Steam, conv. to unknown drive	10 win. 6 drs. 4 wheel, hood front			rebuilt to caboose	Rebuilt without hood front
50	Mack	1905		Mack gas	open bus, 3 rows of seats				Had 4 wheel lead and drive truck

McKEEN CARS, it seems, were everywhere and the Denver, Laramie & Northwestern owned two including the one pictured here.
Author's Collection

SAN LUIS VALLEY SOUTHERN motor M-300 eluded the author's search for roster data, but here it is anyway, big as life.
Author's Collection

Connecticut

AREA: 5,009 sq. miles
CAPITAL: Hartford
POPULATION (1927): 1,074,000

PROBABLY DUE to the fact that the New York, New Haven & Hartford Railroad had an almost complete monopoly on public transit in Connecticut, there almost weren't any short lines in the state. The only exception was the Norfolk Branch Railway, which took over an abandoned branch of the New Haven and tried unsuccessfully to run it with a much-rebuilt Sykes car originally owned by the Boston & Maine.

James Ashley originally obtained this car to try to revive the West River Railroad of Vermont. After struggling vainly to get the operation on a paying basis, Ashley took his car to Connecticut, where the results were no better.

The only other operation, and a very marginal one, was conducted on some de-electrified tracks of the Connecticut Co., the New Haven's statewide streetcar operation. Two cars served some factories in Hartford that depended on the line for freight service.

ROAD NOS.	BUILDER	DATE	BLDR. NO.	ENGINE & DRIVE	BODY TYPE	LGTH.	WT.	DISPOSITION	NOTES & COMMENTS
CONNECTICUT CO. (former streetcar line in Hartford)									
2022	Wason Co. Shops	1912 1930		gas-electric	Cen. door, wooden bag.			to Conn. Ry. Museum	Former elect. car
2023	Wason Co. Shops	1910 1930		gas-electric	Cen. door, wooden bag.				Former elect. car
NORFOLK BRANCH RY., East Canaan to Norfolk, Conn., 6½ mi. (Abandoned) (ex-branch of the NYNH&H)									
(1 car)	Sykes St. Louis Brill	1925	1329A 22367	Brill gas-elect.	8 win. bag. 30 pass. front hood	52′8″	33½T		Ex-Bost. & Maine, 1120, built as gas-mech. with Sterling engine. Also operated on West River RR in 1934.

Delaware

AREA: 2,057 sq. miles
CAPITAL: Dover
POPULATION (1927): 540,000

DELAWARE HAD only one short line headquartered in the state that operated rail motor cars. The Wilmington, New Castle & Delaware City Traction Co. was conceived (as its name suggests) as a streetcar line, but was never electrified and used battery cars during its short period of operation.

The Maryland & Delaware Coast Railway, a Maryland-based line, operated railcars in Delaware over a line that extended completely across the state.

ROAD NOS.	BUILDER	DATE	BLDR. NO.	ENGINE & DRIVE	BODY TYPE	LGTH.	WT.	DISPOSITION	NOTES & COMMENTS
WILMINGTON, NEW CASTLE & DELAWARE CITY TRACTION CO., Dobbinsville to Delaware City, Del., 10 mi. (Abandoned)									
1	Federal	1911		(4) 12½hp el. 205 cell battery-elec.	8 win. 4 whl. 30 pass.	32′			Used on the Ephrata & Lebanon St. Ry. for a time
2	Federal	1912		(4) 12½hp, el. mot. 225 cell	9 win. bag. 34 pass.				
3	Federal	1913		(4) 12½hp, el. mot. 225 cell	9 win. bag. 34 pass.				

Florida

AREA: 58,560 sq. miles
CAPITAL: Tallahassee
POPULATION (1927): 1,363,000

PASSENGER TRAIN SCHEDULES

RIDE
"THE BAY LINE"
Gasoline Passenger Cars

NO DETOURS

Takes You Direct to Your
Destination

These all-steel passenger cars
are operated on a Double Daily Schedule
between Dothan Ala., Cottondale, Fla.
and Panama City, Fla.

No Smoke, Cinders or Dust
clean and comfortable

Ride these cars and avoid the dust,
dirt, the danger, crowded seats,
and close contact with
diseased and undesirable
persons encountered in
traveling by buses
over the highway

October 1928

NO DETOURS, promises this 1928
doodlebug timetable on the Atlanta
& San Andrews Bay line.
Author's Collection

THIS IS THE ONE AND ONLY
Smalley railcar (see *Interurbans
Without Wires*, page 189) built in the
early 1920s for the Susquehanna and
New York Railroad. It was a failure,
and was demotorized, winding up on
the Live Oak Perry and Gulf which
used it as a trailer until after World
War II when it was repowered with
a surplus White engine.
Author's Collection

THROUGH THE Florida celery belt
ran the Sanford Traction. This postcard view features Fairbanks-Morse
gas-mechanical car 2.
Author's Collection

TWO OF FLORIDA'S "major" short
lines are still in existence and are
quite prosperous, thank you. They are
the Apalachicola Northern Railroad, and
the Atlanta & St. Andrews Bay Railway
Co. These lines serve, on an exclusive
basis, the ports of Panama City
(A&SAB), and Apalachicola-Port St. Joe
(AN) in the Florida "panhandle" area.

Another pair of lines in this same area,
which in fact was under common management for a period and was officially
merged under Southern Railway ownership, was the South Georgia and the
Live Oak, Perry and Gulf railways.

With the help of Russell Tedder, now
president of the Ashley, Drew and
Northern Railway, operating out of
Crossett, Ark., we were able to put
together rosters of these two lines,
which turned out to be much more of a
job than we expected it would be.

In the lower portions of the state,
short-line operations were few and are all
long gone. One operation is worthy of
note. It had the rather grandiose title of
the Trans-Florida Central Railroad.
Logically enough it started on the East
Coast at Sebastian, but only managed to
get 10 miles to Fellsmere, well short of
the Gulf Coast.

The T-FCR'S motive power consisted
of some of the most ingenious rebuilding
of old Model T Fords and other trucks
one could imagine. They were used to
haul laborers to the sugar cane fields in
the area. The trucks also hauled a couple
of odd-looking side-door coaches, apparently built on old flat carbodies.

36

ROAD NOS.	BUILDER	DATE	BLDR. NO.	ENGINE & DRIVE	BODY TYPE	LGTH.	WT.	DISPOSITION	NOTES & COMMENTS
APALACHICOLA NORTHERN RR CO., Chattahoochee to Port St. Joe, Florida 96 mi. (In operation)									
24	Osgood Bradley El. Mot. Corp.	1/27	8973 194	(2) Winton 106 220hp GE	12 win. bag. 54 pass.	72' 10"	63T	scrapped	Ex-Lehigh Valley No. 24, acquired 1/38
75	Gen. Elect. Wason	12/11	3721	Sterling 250hp gas-elect.	13 win. CE bag. 91 pass.	68'	46T	scrapped 12/48	Ex-Clinchfield No. 75, who replaced orig. engine with the Sterling, ex-ex-Delaware & Hudson No. 2000
T-76	Osgood Bradley	1/27	8974	Trailer	RPO-baggage		27T	scrapped	Ex-Lehigh Valley T-76, acquired 1/38
ATLANTA & ST. ANDREWS BAY RY. CO., Dotham, Ala. to Panama City, Florida, 88 mi. (In operation)									
500	Edwards	1928		Buda GL-6 108hp gas-M	7 win. bag. 28 pass.	31' 6"	11½T		
501	Edwards	1928		Buda GL-6 108hp gas-M	7 win. bag. 28 pass.	31' 6"	11½T		
503	Edwards	1928		(2) Buda GL-6 108hp gas-M	7 win. RPO bag. 28 pass.	43'	30½T	sold to Tallulah Falls Ry. (Ga.)	
510	Edwards	1928		Buda GL-6 108hp gas-M	9 win. 36 pass.	31' 6"	11½T		May have been fitted out as a business car
CENTRAL OF FLORIDA RY. CO., Daytona to Sea Breeze, Fla. 5 mi. (Abandoned)									
1	Amer. Car & Foun	1914		Battery elect.	7 win. 4 wheel streetcar				
2	Amer. Car & Foun	1914		Battery elect.	7 win. 4 wheel streetcar				
3	Amer. Car & Foun	1915		Battery elect.	7 win. 4 wheel streetcar				
5	St. Louis	1914	1047	Battery elect.	7 win. 4 wheel streetcar				
11	St. Louis	1914	1048	Battery-elect.	7 win. 4 wheel streetcar				
CHARLOTTE HARBOR & NORTHERN RY. CO., South Boca Grande to South Mulberry, Fla. 94.5 mi. (Merged into Seaboard Air Line RR)									
A	Federal	1912 ?		Battery elect.	7 win. 4 wheel, 28 pass. st.car				
LIVE OAK, PERRY & GULF RR CO., Live Oak to Springdale, Fla., 87.69 mi. (Merged into Southern System)									
MC-1	Janney, Steinmetz & Co.			Everett 6 cyl. gas-mech.	wood, OP bag. 20 pass.	16'			Ex-Tampa & Jacksonville, acquired 1913

EDWARDS got all of Atlanta & San Andrews Bay's railcar business. Here's the 510. *Ray W. Buhrmaster*

HOME-BUILT from Ford and I-H chassis, these ungainly trucks plied the rails of the Trans-Florida Central, even hauling trains of harvest workers. *Melvin Beaton*

ROAD NOS.	BUILDER	DATE	BLDR. NO.	ENGINE & DRIVE	BODY TYPE	LGTH.	WT.	DISPOSITION	NOTES & COMMENTS
Jitney (MC-?) ?	Co. Shops	1925		Buick gas-mech.				retired circa 1937	
MC-6 Marie	Brill			Brill 75, 175hp gas-mech.	13 win. 59 pass. baggage	55'	25T	sold 1941 to Cuban line	Acquired secondhand, 1937 (ex-PRR 4728?), prob. used as private car
206	Smalley Co. Shops	1925 1947		White diesel-mech.	14 win., bag. 40 pass.	about 60'	about 30T	scrapped 1955	Built for Susquehanna & New York RR (PA.), demotorized by them, sold to LOP&G in 1943, remotorized by company shops 1947. Used mostly as standby car on South Georgia RR (both lines were owned by Brooks-Scanlon Lbr. Co.).

MIAMI TRACTION CO., Miami, Fla. (Abandoned)

ROAD NOS.	BUILDER	DATE	BLDR. NO.	ENGINE & DRIVE	BODY TYPE	LGTH.	WT.	DISPOSITION	NOTES & COMMENTS
1100-01	Brill	1914	19680	Battery elect. car	4 wheel 7 win. streetcar	26'1"			
1102-03	Brill	1914	19682	Battery elect. car	4 wheel 7 win. streetcar	26"1"			
1104-05	Brill	1914	19920	Battery elect. car	4 wheel 7 win. streetcar	26'1"			

SANFORD TRACTION CO., Sanford, Fla. (Abandoned)

ROAD NOS.	BUILDER	DATE	BLDR. NO.	ENGINE & DRIVE	BODY TYPE	LGTH.	WT.	DISPOSITION	NOTES & COMMENTS
1 & 2	Fair.-Morse Brill	1909		Fair.-Morse 50hp gas-mech.	8 win. 4 whl. 35 pass. bag. wood, clere. roof	34'2"	13T		Model 24

TAMPA & JACKSONVILLE RY., Emathia to Sampson City, Fla. (Merged into Seaboard Air Line RR)

ROAD NOS.	BUILDER	DATE	BLDR. NO.	ENGINE & DRIVE	BODY TYPE	LGTH.	WT.	DISPOSITION	NOTES & COMMENTS
MC-1	Janney, Steinmetz & Co.			6 cyl Everett gas-mech.	wood, OP, 20 pass. baggage	16'		sold 1913 to Live Oak, Perry & Gulf RR	1916 "Official Guide" lists trains 9 & 10 (Gainesville to Sampson City) as being motors, so there may have been other cars.

TRANS-FLORIDA CENTRAL RR CO., Fellsmere to Sebastian, Fla. 10 mi. (Abandoned 1952)

ROAD NOS.	BUILDER	DATE	BLDR. NO.	ENGINE & DRIVE	BODY TYPE	LGTH.	WT.	DISPOSITION	NOTES & COMMENTS
59	International Co. Shops			Intl. gas-mech.	closed truck				
"Beast"				(2) Model T gas-mech.	"speeder" chassis hood front				
3 cars	Ford			Ford gas-mech.	pickup truck chassis				Various home-built bodies, may have been more than three

Georgia

AREA: 58,876 sq. miles
CAPITAL: Atlanta
POPULATION (1927): 3,171,000

IF I WERE TO AWARD the title, "Short Line Capital of the United States," it would go to Georgia. Texas had more lines, but they were spread over an area five times greater. In his book, *Mixed Train Daily* (E.P. Dutton & Co., 1947), author Lucius Beebe wrote that Georgia was "... the Big Rock Candy Mountain of railroad historians, the mecca of the faithful among aficiona-

dos of the high iron in its homelier ways and more simplified devisings."

Not only were there over 30 of this type of line, there also were two miniature "empires," the Pidcocks in the south part of the state, and Forrest Greene's (love that name) in the north.

Greene was also the owner of the Georgia Car and Locomotive Co., a dealer in used railroad equipment that seems to have specialized in rail motor cars, obtaining them from all over the country and reselling them mostly in the south and in Cuba. Most of this equipment consisted of lightweight cars from Edwards and Brill, but several lines had

heavyweight cars built by General Electric and other builders.

Probably the most unusual cars were owned by the Collins & Glenville, who purchased a pair of Savannah single-truck Birney cars, equipped them with Buick engines and a pair of arch-bar freight trucks. They apparently managed to get along without the usual Birney-type folding passenger doors.

Most of the short lines of Georgia that managed to survive past World War II have been merged into the mega-railroads now in that area, particularly the Southern (Norfolk Southern) System.

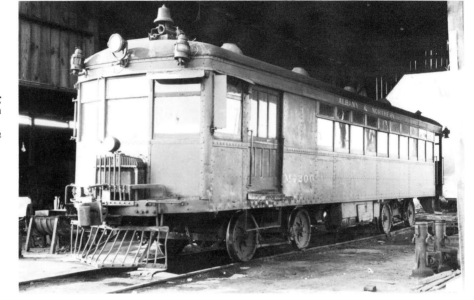

BRILL M-1200 was originally a Big Four Railroad car, but wound up on the Albany & Northern.
Author's Collection

YELLOW BUS (manufacturer, not color) was a mainstay of the Georgia Northern. This photo was taken in Moultrie, Ga., on June 7, 1938.
William Monypeny,
Louis Saillard Collection

YES, IT'S a Birney body on double arch-bar trucks. No. 7 was a Savannah streetcar in electric days. The Collins & Glenville owned two such cars. *Author's Collection*

ROAD NOS.	BUILDER	DATE	BLDR. NO.	ENGINE & DRIVE	BODY TYPE	LGTH.	WT.	DISPOSITION	NOTES & COMMENTS
ALBANY & NORTHERN RY., Albany to Cordele, Ga. 35.3 mi. (Abandoned)									
M-1200	Brill	1925	22182	Brill 55 68hp gas	10 win. bag. 43 pass.	42' 7"	15T		Ex-East Jordan & Sou. (Mich.) M-1200, ex-ex-CCC&SL (Big 4) M-1200
BOWDEN RY., Bowden to Bowden Jct., Ga. 12 mi. (Abandoned)									
102	Mack Brill	3/21	70002 21265	Mack AB 35hp gas-mech.	8 win. bus 25 pass.	27'	6½T		Ex-U.S. Army, Camp Humphrey
(1 car)	International			International gas-mech.	motor truck, 4 wheel lead truck				
CHATTAHOOCHIE VALLEY RY. CO., West Point, Ga. to Bleeker, Ala. 41.46 mi. (9 miles still in operation in Alabama)									
316	Ry. Stor. Btty. Brill	1915	15833	Battery elec.	8 win. 4 wheel, 24 pass. st. car				
(1 car)	Ry. Stor. Btty. Brill	1917		Battery elec.	8 win. 4 wheel, 24 pass. st. car				2 motor cars listed in '30s "Equip. Register."
CLARKESVILLE RR CO., Clarkesville, Ga. 1.25 mi. (Abandoned)									
Two gas cars listed in "McGraw Electric Railway List," August 1918.									
COLLINS & GLENVILLE RR, Collins to Glenville, Ga., 23 mi. (Abandoned)									
6	Co. Shops St. Louis Car	1922	1271	Buick 6 gas	8 win. Birney body, 28 pass. 2 arch bar trucks	28'			Ex-Savannah, Ga., single truck Birney streetcar
7	Co. Shops St. Louis Car	1922		Buick 6 gas	8 win. Birney body, 28 pass. 2 arch bar trucks				Ex-Savannah, Ga., single truck Birney streetcar
(1 car)	Co. Shops	1926		International gas	5 win. OP wood bag. pass.				
FAIRBURN & ATLANTA RY. & ELECTRIC CO., Fairburn to College Park, Ga. 10.6 mi. (Abandoned)									
3 units	Fair.-Morse	1911		Fair.-Morse gas-mech.	4 wheel wood				
2 units	Ry. Stor. Btty.	1916		Battery elec.	4 wheel wood				
(1 car)	Co. Shops	1916		Mitchell gas	7 win. 4 wh. 28 pass.	26'			

EARLY railcar was 52-ton General Electric No. 10 of the Macon & Birmingham, photographed in 1916.
John B. Allen Collection

BOBTAIL BUS belonged to the Milledgeville Railway. No. 1641 was photographed in 1946 at Hardwick, Ga.
W.F. Beckum,
John B. Allen Collection

ROAD NOS.	BUILDER	DATE	BLDR. NO.	ENGINE & DRIVE	BODY TYPE	LGTH.	WT.	DISPOSITION	NOTES & COMMENTS
GAINESVILLE MIDLAND RY. CO., Gainesville to Athens, Ga. and branches 74 mi. (In operation)									
500	Yellow Truck & Coach			Yellow gas	4 win. bus, 4 wheel lead truck				
501	Yellow Truck & Coach				4 win. bus, 4 wheel lead truck				
GAINESVILLE & NORTHWESTERN RR, Gainesville to North Helen, Ga. 35.1 mi. (Abandoned)									
(1 car)	Edwards			Buda gas 108hp	10 win. bag. 40 pass.	43′	17T		May have been sold to the Chesapeake and Western (Va.)
GEORGIA NORTHERN RY. CO., Boston to Albany, Ga., 66.78 mi. (Merged into the Southern System)									
2	St. Louis Fair.-Morse	1939	1598	F.M. 800hp dies. elect.	bag. RPO, round front	81′	114T		Ex-Southern Ry. No. 2
MT-2	St. Louis	1939	1599	Trailer	21 win. 76 pass.	72′9″	57T		Ex-Southern Ry. No. MT-2

STREAMLINED cars were not often seen on short lines, but here's ex-Southern Ry. No. 2, built by St. Louis Car and Fairbanks-Morse, on the Georgia Northern.
Author's Collection

ROAD NOS.	BUILDER	DATE	BLDR. NO.	ENGINE & DRIVE	BODY TYPE	LGTH.	WT.	DISPOSITION	NOTES & COMMENTS
MC12	Edwards	1932		Buda 75hp gas-mech.	7 win. bag. 25 pass.	32'	10T		
14	Yellow			Yellow gas-mech.	6 win. bus, 20 pass.				
M-55	Brill	1923	21566	Midwest 68hp gas-mech.	10 win. bag. 43 pass.	43'	15T		Ex-Western Pacific
M-56	Brill			Midwest 68hp gas-mech.	10 win. bag. 43 pass.	43'	15T		
527	Brill	1924	21983	Midwest 68hp gas-mech.	10 win. bag. 43 pass.	43'	15T		Ex-Missouri Pacific 527, ex-ex-San Antonio, Uvalde & Gulf 200. Acq. 5/40.
528	Brill			Midwest 68hp gas-mech.	10 win. bag. 43 pass.	43'	15T		

GREENE COUNTY RR CO., Apalachee to Monroe, Ga. 20 mi. (Abandoned)

100				gas-mech.	bag. pass.				

HAWKINSVILLE & FLORIDA SOUTHERN RY. CO., Hawkinsville to Camilla, Fla. 90 mi. (Northern section abandoned; southern section, Ga. Ash. & Camilla)

25	Gen. Elect. Wason	10/12	3751	GE FM16-C1 175hp GE	8 win. OP bag. 42 pass.	42'	39T	sold to Midland Vy. No. 5 12/22	Ex-Pitt. Lake Erie 500, acquired 10/15
26	Gen. Elect. Wason	7/12	3728	GE GM16C 175hp GE	14 win. CE bag. 91 pass.	70'	52T	sold to Midland Vy. No. 4, 12/22	Ex-SL-SF (Louisiana Sou.), acquired 1916
100	Wason	1912	12630	Trailer	15 win. OP 74 pass.	44' 10"		to Mid. Vy. T-3 12/22	Ex-Pitt. & Lake Erie 700, acquired 10/15

MACON & BIRMINGHAM RY. CO., Solkee (Macon) to La Grange, Ga. (Abandoned 1926)

10	Gen. Elect. Wason	9/12	3729	GE GM16C1 175hp GE	15 win. CE bag. 91 pass.	70'	52T	sold 1919	Ex-SL-SF (first) 2111
12	Gen. Elect. Wason	8/12	3734	GE GM16C1 175hp GE	15 win. CE bag. 91 pass.	70'	52T	sold 11/18	Ex-SL-SF 2116

MILLEDGEVILLE RY., Milledgeville to State Sanitarium, Ga. 3.5 mi. (Became part of Georgia RR)

1	Brill	1913	18331	Battery elec.	7 win. 4 wheel, deck roof st. car 26 pass.	26'	8T		
2	Brill	1913	18942	Battery elec.	7 win. 4 wheel, deck roof st. car 26 pass.	26'	8T		
1641				gas-mech.	3 win. 4 wh.				

ST. MARYS RR CO., Kingsland to St. Marys, Ga. 10.75 mi. (In operation)

100	Brill	1924	22121	Midwest 68hp gas	10 win. bag. 43 pass.	43'	14½T		Ex-Missouri Pacific 536, ex-ex-Asherton & Gulf 103

ROAD NOS.	BUILDER	DATE	BLDR. NO.	ENGINE & DRIVE	BODY TYPE	LGTH.	WT.	DISPOSITION	NOTES & COMMENTS
1180	Electro-Mot. Osgood Bradly	8/26	163 8795	Winton 120, 275hp GE	10 win. bag. 54 pass.	64'	47T	to Nat. Mus. of Trans.	Ex-Boston & Maine 1180, acq. 1946

ST. SIMONS RY. CO. St. Simons Island, Ga. 1.7 mi. (Abandoned)
McGraw Electric Railway List, Auf. 1918 lists ''two gas cars.''

SOUTH GEORGIA RY. CO., Adel, Ga. to Perry, Fla. 76 mi. (Merged into the Southern System)

ROAD NOS.	BUILDER	DATE	BLDR. NO.	ENGINE & DRIVE	BODY TYPE	LGTH.	WT.	DISPOSITION	NOTES & COMMENTS
16	Hall-Scott	9/14	18	Hall-Scott 150hp gas-mech.	9 win. bag. 35 pass.	54'		demotorized	Ex-St. Joseph Valley 204, acquired circa 1924. May not have been used as motor car.
100	Kalamazoo	6/40		Chevrolet gas-mech.	7 win. CE, 26 pass. bag. door at rear			retired 1952	
M-200	Brill	7/25	22128	Brill 75, 175hp gas-mech.	RPO baggage	55'	31T	sold, 1938 to Cummins Diesel	Ex-NYC M-200, orig. NYC M-101, re-engined with 150hp Cummins Diesel 1937. Acquired 11/36.,
MT-1	Brill	7/25	22129	Trailer	10 win. 40 pass.	50' 10"	41½T	sold, 1938 to Cummins Diesel	Ex-NYC MT-1, orig. NYC 01, acquired 11/36

TALLULAH FALLS RY. CO., Cornelia, Ga. to Franklin, NC, 57.1 mi. (Abandoned)

ROAD NOS.	BUILDER	DATE	BLDR. NO.	ENGINE & DRIVE	BODY TYPE	LGTH.	WT.	DISPOSITION	NOTES & COMMENTS
201	Edwards	1928		(2) Buda 108hp gas-mech.	RPO bag. 2 bag. doors	43'	30½T	demotorized	Ex-Atlanta & St. Andrews Bay 503. Originally had a 7 window passenger section

WASHINGTON & LINCOLNTON RR CO., Washington to Lincolnton, Ga. 5.11 mi. (Abandoned)

ROAD NOS.	BUILDER	DATE	BLDR. NO.	ENGINE & DRIVE	BODY TYPE	LGTH.	WT.	DISPOSITION	NOTES & COMMENTS
(1 car)	Edwards	1923		Buda GL66 60hp gas-mech.	6 win. OP bag. 25 pass.	31'9"	10T	sold to Birm. & Sou. East. 1929	Model 10

LOOKS LIKE the whole class is taking a ride on St. Mary's Railroad Brill No. 100 in 1949. This car started out on the Missouri Pacific.
Author's Collection

(Top Photos) MOTORMAN Charlie Holden poses at the controls of South Georgia No. 100, shown in second photo crossing the Seaboard Air Line at Greenville, Fla.
Both: Tom King Collection

Hawaii

AREA: 6,424 sq. miles
CAPITAL: Honolulu
POPULATION (1960): 632,772

HAWAII HAS the distinction of being the only state that had nothing *but* short-line railroads.

Of course most of these lines were miniscule, built to serve sugar plantations, but there were two that were fairly large, even by "mainland" short-line standards.

The largest and most famous was, of course, the Oahu Railway, which devel-oped a fairly large passenger service, mostly carrying tourists before World War II. It also was noted for building all of its own rail motor cars.

The other line, on the "Big Island," was the Hawaii Consolidated Railway. This railroad relied mostly on rail buses and trucks that used White and Mack chassis.

WHITE and Thomson-Graf-Elder teamed up to fashion this motor-trailer combo for the Hawaii Consol-idated, operating on the Big Island out of Hilo.   *White*

ARCH WINDOWS and wooden sides give Oahu Railway M-1 a classic Midwest Interurban look. The 3-foot gauge OR operated west and around the island from Honolulu.
                    Author's Collection

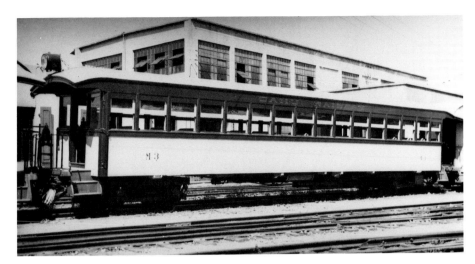

OAHU RAILWAY M-3 is shown in use as a trailer in later days; like the M-1, it was built in company shops.
Author's Collection

ROAD NOS.	BUILDER	DATE	BLDR. NO.	ENGINE & DRIVE	BODY TYPE	LGTH.	WT.	DISPOSITION	NOTES & COMMENTS
HAWAII CONSOLIDATED RY. Hilo area of Hawaii Island, 103.8 mi. (Abandoned)									
Motor 1	White Thomas-Graf-Edler	1927		White 50A gas-mech.					
Motor 2	Hall-Scott	1913	3	Hall-Scott 100hp gas.	13 win. OP wood, cler. roof			retired 1925	Body ex-Hilo Ry. passenger car.
Motor 3	White Thom, Graf, Edler	1925		White 50A 50hp gas	6 win. bus, 4 wheel lead trk.				
Motor 6	Mack	4/28	70021	Mack AB 30hp gas-mech.	truck body, 4 wheel lead trk.				
Trailer 1	Thom. Graf-Edler	1925		Trailer	6 win. CE 4 wheel				
Trailer 2	Thom. Graf-Edler	1925		Trailer	6 win. CE 4 wheel				
OAHU RY., Honolulu to Kahuka, Hawaii, 117.45 mi. (including branches) 3 ft. gauge (Abandoned)									
M1	Ry. Motors Co. Shops	1927		(2) Cont. 15H 103hp GM	17 win. open rear plat. wood, 62 pass.	54'	27T	scrapped 1951	Paired arch windows
M2	Ry. Motors Co. Shops	1927		(2) Cont. 15H 103hp GM	17 win. open rear plat. wood, 62 pass.			scrapped 1951	Paired arch windows
M3	Ry. Motors Co. Shops			(1) Cont. 15H 103hp gas	16 win. OP wooden	50'		conv. to trail., scrapped 1951	
M4	Ry. Motors Co. Shops			(1) Cont. 15H 103hp gas	16 win. OP wooden	50'		used for a period as a model RR clubhouse, then scrapped in '50s	
M5	Ford Co. Shops	1929		Ford A 4 cyl gas-mech.	motor truck with bus body				

Idaho

AREA: 83,557 sq. miles
CAPITAL: Boise
POPULATION (1927): 534,000

DESPITE ITS rather isolated location, Idaho had seven lines that operated rail motor cars. They ranged from the streetcar type of operation in Lewiston, with only a couple of miles of track, to the Gilmour & Pittsburgh with 120 miles. These were very modest operations with only two cars at the most.

The Camas Prairie Railroad, which ran from Riparia, Wash., to Grangeville and Stites, Idaho, and was owned jointly by the Northern Pacific and the Union Pacific, used gas-electric cars for a number of years, but they were always owned by the Northern Pacific.

(Top Photo) ROUND-END McKeen car M-60 of the Pacific & Idaho Northern was actually borrowed from the Oregon Short Line and returned in 1936.
Author's Collection

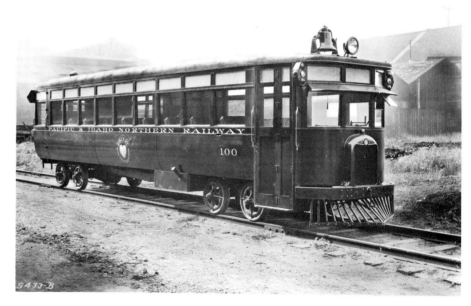

BARELY LONG ENOUGH for the company's name on the side is No. 100 of the Pacific & Idaho Northern. The car was built by California Body Building (not a gymnasium).
Railway Negative Exchange

STORAGE BATTERY cars were built in 1913 for the Twin Falls Railway. Original sales literature said they could be used singly for passenger service or in tandem as a freight locomotive. *Author's Collection*

POTLATCHER was the name given to Washington Idaho & Montana No. 11, a semi-streamlined Fairmont gas-mechanical car. It is shown at Potlatch, Idaho, in 1946.

George E. Votava

ROAD NOS.	BUILDER	DATE	BLDR. NO.	ENGINE & DRIVE	BODY TYPE	LGTH.	WT.	DISPOSITION	NOTES & COMMENTS
CALDWELL TRACTION CO., Caldwell to Lake Lowell, Idaho, 7 mi. (Abandoned)									
1 & 2 (?)	Fair.-Morse Sheffield			F-M 30hp gas	4 whl. open 20 pass. st. car			sold to Lewistown Term. 1913	
GILMOUR & PITTSBURGH RR CO., Armstead, Mont. to Salmon, Idaho, 120 mi. (Abandoned)									
650	Mack Brill	10/21	70011 21363	Mack AB 30hp gas-mech.	5 win. bus, bag. 17 pass. bag. sect. in rear	28'8"	6T	scrapped 7/40	
B-7	St. Louis Elect. Mot.	1926	1348B 107	Winton 106 175hp GE	12 win. RPO bag. 47 pass.	59½'	39T		Ex-NP B-7
LEWISTOWN TERMINAL RR, Lewistown, Idaho (Abandoned)									
(1 car)	Fair.-Morse Sheffield			FM 30hp GM	4 wheel open streetcar 20 pass.			sold to Mitchell, ND, 1915	Ex-Caldwell, Idaho, acq. 12/13
NEZPERCE RR, Craigmont to Nezperce, Idaho (13.4 mi. in operation)									
(1 car)	GMC	1915		GMC gas	5 win. 4 wh. hood type bus body				
(1 car)	Ford			Ford gas					
PACIFIC & IDAHO NORTHERN RY. CO., Weiser to New Meadows, Idaho, 89.9 mi. (Acquired by the Union Pacific)									
T-50	McKeen	1909		Trailer	RPO baggage	31'	12½T	probably ex-OSL	
M-60	McKeen	1909	51	McKeen 200hp gas-mech.	8 win. CE bag. 12 pass. bag. door also in rear	55'	30T	returned to OSL 8/36	Borrowed from Ore. Short Line
100	Calif. Body Bldg. Co.	1924		Dorris 6 cyl 80hp gas	9 win. 33 pass. bag. door rear	33'	8½T	retired	
TWIN FALLS RY. CO., Twin Falls to Shoshone Falls, 12 mi. (Abandoned)									
100	Ry. Stor. Btty.	1913		Edison btty. (4) 10hp Mot. 190 cells	8 win. 4 whl. wood, bag. 32 pass.	38'	19T		"Continental" wheel suspension 19' wheel base
101	Ry. Stor. Btty.	1913		Edison btty. (4) 10hp Mot. 190 cells	8 win. 4 whl. wood, bag. 32 pass.	38'	19T		"Continental" wheel suspension 19' wheel base
WASHINGTON, IDAHO & MONTANA RY. CO., Palouse to Purdue, Idaho, 50 mi. (Acquired by the Milwaukee Road)									
11 Pot-lacher	Fairmont	1937		Fairmont gas-mech.	3 win. CE, 6 whl. bag. 12 pass. bag. sect. at rear	33'8"		retired '55	

Illinois

AREA: 56,400 sq. miles
CAPITAL: Springfield
POPULATION (1927): 7,296,000

WITH ALL THE trunk-line railroads crossing the state at every angle to converge on the Chicago and St. Louis area, you might think that there would be little room for short lines in Illinois.

It may therefore come as a surprise to discover there were indeed many short lines, in contrast with the other states adjoining it.

Some of these lines were built with the hope of being electrified, some of them were, many fell by the wayside early on.

Other lines were built on the wreckage of larger railroads that went bankrupt. When the Chicago, Peoria and St. Louis was dissolved, no less than four new lines were created.

And when the Cincinnati, Indianapolis & Western was taken over by the Baltimore & Ohio, the Slidell to Olney branch was not included, but was broken up into three different lines, all of which struggled on for a few more years with

no more success than the CI&W

In general it can be said that most of the older short lines of Illinois were financially weak, and about the only ones that have survived were "captive" lines of the large electric utilities.

Now, all the recent mergers and bankruptcies have led to a new generation of short lines taking over parts of the old trunk lines. Some have been fairly successful, while others lasted but a short time. It is not without reason that these lines were let go by their previous owners.

NOT FOR PASSENGERS is the Fox & Illinois Union No. 7, a McGuire-Cummings product with interurban box motor lines. *Author's Collection*

LORDLY Chicago Springfield & St. Louis No. 101 would look at home on any big midwest interurban if only it had trolley poles. This builder's photo was taken by Brill.
Author's Collection

LONG HOOD lends a regal look to this Hall-Scott powered railbus. The Illinois Terminal operated her from Alton to Grafton on non-electrified trackage.   *Author's Collection*

ROAD NOS.	BUILDER	DATE	BLDR. NO.	ENGINE & DRIVE	BODY TYPE	LGTH.	WT.	DISPOSITION	NOTES & COMMENTS
AURORA, DE KALB & ROCKFORD TRACTION CO., Aurora to De Kalb, Ill. 30 mi. Electrified in 1910.									
2		1907		Whiting 4 6x6 gas					
4		1907		Whiting 4 6x6 gas					
6	Kuhlman	1907		Batten 4 cyl 6x8 gas	8 win. st. car, 35 pass.	36'	10T		
8	Kuhlman	1907		Batten 4 cyl 7x7 gas	8 win. st. car, 35 pass.	36'	10T		
(1 car)	Fair.-Morse Sheffield			Sheffield gas	open 4 whl.				
BLOOMINGTON, PONTIAC & JOLIET ELECT. RY. (Abandoned)									
(1 car)	White	1924		White 4 cyl. gas	motor bus				
CHICAGO & ILLINOIS MIDLAND RY. CO., Pekin to Taylorsville, Ill. (121 mi. in operation)									
105	Brill Service	1923	22566	Midwest 68hp gas	10 win. 43 pass.	43'	14½T	sold	Ex-Western Pacific, rebuilt (without bag. section) for use as a business car
CHICAGO, PEORIA & ST. LOUIS RR CO. Peoria, Ill. to St. Louis, Mo. 242 mi. (Abandoned)									
47	Co. Shops	1914		Trailer	ex-steam coach				Coach rebuilt for use as trailer
50	Co. Shops	1914		Trailer	ex-steam coach				Coach rebuilt for use as trailer
100				gas-mech.					Other data unknown
101	Gen. Elect. Wason	2/13	3747 12225	GE GM16C1 175hp GE	17 win. OP bag. 91 pass.	70'	49T	to Okla., Kan. & Mo. 3/16	Ex-GE demo. No. 14, RPO sect. installed 1914. OK&M No. 108.
102	Gen. Elect. Wason	4/13	3746 12225	GE GM16C1 175hp GE	17 win. OP bag. 91 pass.	70'	49T	to Okla., Kan. & Mo. 3/16	OK&M No. 107
103	Gen. Elect. Wason	5/13	3743	GE GM16C1 175hp GE	17 win. OP bag. 91 pass.	70'	49T	to OK&M 12/15	OK&M No. 106
104	Gen. Elect.	5/13	3744	GE GM16C1	17 win. OP bag.	70'	49T	to Okmulgee Nor. 3/16	ON No. 111, to Jonesboro Lake City & Eastern, No. 14, to Frisco, second No. 2111
CHICAGO, SPRINGFIELD & ST. LOUIS RY. CO., Springfield to Alton, Ill. 78.78 mi. (Abandoned) (Formed from part of the Chi. Peoria & St. Louis)									
101	Brill	1927	22556	Brill 75, 190hp GM	13 win. bag. 50 pass.	50'	27½T	burned 2/29	
151	Brill	1927	22557	Brill 55 68hp GM	3 win. RPO bag. 10 pass.	43'	14½T		
301	Brill	1927	22558	Trailer	RPO-baggage	50'	23T		

ROAD NOS.	BUILDER	DATE	BLDR. NO.	ENGINE & DRIVE	BODY TYPE	LGTH.	WT.	DISPOSITION	NOTES & COMMENTS
FOX & ILLINOIS UNION RY., Yorkville to Morris, Ill. (Abandoned)									
7	McGuire-Cummings			gas-elect.	1 door bag. ex-elect.			sold to Colo. Ry. 1941	
GALESBURG GREAT EASTERN RR CO., Victoria to Wataga, Ill., 10 mi. (Abandoned 1961)									
Zephyr Jr.	Chevrolet			Chevrolet 6 gas-mech.	2 door station wagon			sold for scrap 1961	
HANOVER RY., Hanover to Hanover Jct., Ill. 2.5 mi. (Abandoned)									
(1 car)	Stover			Stover 30hp gas-mech.	6 win. 2 door bus, long hood			sold	
THE ILLINOIS CENTRAL ELECTRIC, Lewiston to Farmington, Ill., 33 mi. (Abandoned 1928)									
1	Fair.-Morse	1906		gas-mech.	open				Very little known about these cars
2	Fair.-Morse	1906		gas-mech.	open				
3				gas-mech.	7 win. OP 4 wheel, st.car	abt. 25'			
4				gas-mech.					
ILLINOIS TERMINAL RAILROAD SYSTEM, Alton to Grafton Div. (ex-Chicago, Peoria & St. Louis-Alton & Eastern) 15 mi. (Abandoned)									
204	American Car & Foundry			Hall-Scott gas-mech.	6 win. hood type bus, 4 wheel lead truck				
206	White				6 win. hood type school bus body, 4 wheel lead truck			to Nat. Mus. of Transport	
JACKSONVILLE & HAVANA RR CO., Jacksonville to Havana, Ill., 41.75 mi. (Abandoned 1937) (Formed from part of CP&SL)									
251	Brill	1926	22400	Brill 75 175hp GM	13 win. bag. 50 pass.	55'	25T	returned to Brill 11/30	
M-14	Co. Shops	1930		General Mot. gas	GMC panel truck			scrapped 10/37	
M-16	Co. Shops	1934		General Mot. gas	truck with cab from an auto & home-built bag. section			scrapped 10/37	
(1 car)	Co. Shops			trailer	truck chass.				
JEFFERSON SOUTHWESTERN RR, Mt. Vernon, Ill. (Abandoned 1927)									
100	Brill	1923	21897	Midwest 68hp gas-mech.	10 win. bag. 46 pass.	43'	14½T		A Bowen car operated on this line ca. 1920, probably as a demonstrator
MACOMB & WESTERN ILLINOIS RR, Macomb to Littleton, Ill. (Abandoned)									
2	St. Louis Car Co.	1903	427	gas-mech.				burned 1907	
LEE COUNTY CENTRAL ELECTRIC RY., Amboy to Middlebury, Ill. 12.11 mi.									
3 ?	St. Louis	1892		Hart Parr 30hp gas	wood, OP 4 wheel, ex-horse car			scrapped 1915	Ex-Charles City Western No. 3
MIDLOTHIAN & BLUE ISLAND RR, Midlothian to Blue Island, Ill. (electric streetcar line) (Abandoned 1928)									
(1 car)	Autocar	1916 ?		gas				retired '28	
OIL BELT RY.									
(1 car)	McGuire-Cummings Drake	1913		Drake 90hp gas-elect.					2 cars built

ROAD NOS.	BUILDER	DATE	BLDR. NO.	ENGINE & DRIVE	BODY TYPE	LGTH.	WT.	DISPOSITION	NOTES & COMMENTS
PEKIN & PETERSBURG INTERURBAN RY., Pekin to Petersburg, Ill. 8 mi. (Abandoned)									
1		1911		battery elec.	7 win. 4 whl. streetcar	26′			
WESTFIELD MOTOR RY. CO., Kansas to Casey, Ill. 19.5 mi. (Abandoned)									
1	St. Louis Bowen	3/19	1187	Bowen gas	10 win. hood front, 4 whl. lead truck				
WAUKEGAN, ROCKFORD & ELGIN									
(1 car)	White	1914		White 4 cyl. gas	4 win. CE bus body				Ex-Woodstock & Sycamore
WOODSTOCK & SYCAMORE TRACTION CO., Marengo to Sycamore, Ill., 26.5 mi. (Abandoned 1918)									
1	Fair.-Morse	1914		Fair.-Morse 50hp gas.	8 win. 4 whl. wood, bag. 35 pass. cler. roof	34′ 2″	13T		
2	White	1914		White 4 cyl. 40hp gas	4 win. CE bus body			sold to Wau. Rkfd. & Elgin	
707	McKeen	7/11		McKeen, 200hp gas-mech.	8 win. CE bag. 30 pass.	55′	28T	repossessed	Repossessed cars went to the Edmonton, Dunvegan & Brit. Col. and Nor. Albta. Rys.

DERELICT roundhouse is the setting for Jacksonville & Havana M-16, a baggage truck fabricated in 1934 by company forces. It is shown at Jacksonville, Ill., in 1937.
Author's Collection

(Top Photo, Left) STREAMLINED TRAINS were the latest thing in 1938, so the Galesburg & Great Eastern had the *Baby Zephyr,* a Chevrolet station wagon.
Robert Hanft

(Top Photo, Right) HOMELY AS HADES is the Yale Short Line's sole railcar. Is that track, or is this bus-on-flanged-wheels sitting in the weeds? *Jim Buckley Collection*

ROAD NOS.	BUILDER	DATE	BLDR. NO.	ENGINE & DRIVE	BODY TYPE	LGTH.	WT.	DISPOSITION	NOTES & COMMENTS
709	McKeen	12/10		McKeen, 200hp gas-mech.	8 win. CE bag. 30 pass.	55′	28T	burned	May have been rebuilt by McKeen
711	McKeen	7/10		McKeen, 200hp gas-mech.	11 win. CE 44 pass.	70′	35T	repossessed	

YALE SHORT LINE, Casey to Yale, Ill. 13 mi. (Abandoned)

(1 car)				gas	bus body				

Indiana

AREA: 36,291 sq. miles
CAPITAL: Indianapolis
POPULATION (1927): 3,150,000

INDIANA HAD only one short line of any consequence insofar as rail motor cars were concerned, but what a line that was! In its short history (1905 to 1918) the St. Joseph Valley Railway had what must be the most bizarre, outrageous collection of railcars ever assembled.

At one time or another, no less than 17 different cars were used. During this time, six of them were burned in conflagrations. Most of the cars were Fairbanks-Morse built, but there were about four different models used, plus cars from Stover, Hicks, Edison-Beach, and Hall-Scott.

The St. Joseph Valley Railway Co. also operated electric cars as well as steam-operated trains in just under 60 miles of line. All of this was the creation of H.E. Bucklin of Elkhart.

Bucklin had made a fortune in patent medicine and Chicago real estate. For many years this company was known as the "Arnica Salve Line" in honor of his most successful product. It would appear that Bucklin was at heart a rail buff

who could afford to indulge his hobby.

Since the whole organization was closely held by Bucklin, no financial records are available, but it is safe to assume that it was a losing proposition for its entire life because upon Bucklin's death, the whole organization was liquidated in a very short time. One of the surprises of my research on the subject of railcars was to discover that the Hall-Scott gas car ended up on the South Georgia Railway.

Among the other lines, the Chicago Attica & Southern was an attempt to run a redundant branch of the Chicago & Eastern Illinois. The Chicago, Terre Haute & Southeastern was merged into the Milwaukee Road; the Cincinnati Bluffton & Chicago was an interurban that never could afford to electrify and only lasted four years, and all we know in regard to the Ferdinand is that it might have had some kind of a rail motor car in the mid-1920s.

ARNICA SALVE LINE was the nickname of the St. Joseph Valley, and 54-foot Hall-Scott car 204 was the line's largest.
Don Baringer Collection

CITY SERVICE was offered by the St. Joe Valley by cars such as Fairbanks-Morse-Kuhlman No. 173.
Don Baringer Collection

AUTORAILER, built by Evans, was capable of running on rails or highways. It is doing neither in this Chicago Attica & Southern view, taken in 1946 after the line quit.
C.J. DeVilbiss

ROAD NOS.	BUILDER	DATE	BLDR. NO.	ENGINE & DRIVE	BODY TYPE	LGTH.	WT.	DISPOSITION	NOTES & COMMENTS
CHICAGO, ATTICA & SOUTHERN RR CO., La Crosse to West Melcher, Ind. 155 mi. (Abandoned)									
M-1	Evans			Reo gas	2 win. bag.				Autorailer, capable of running on tracks or highways.
CHICAGO, TERRE HAUTE & SOUTHEASTERN RY. CO., Chicago, Ill. to Westport, Ind. 326 mi. (Merged into Milwaukee Road)									
75		1913		gas				to MW serv. 1926 (No. 95)	
CINCINNATI, BLUFFTON & CHICAGO RY. CO., Huntington to Portland, Ind. (Abandoned)									
1-3	Barber	1912		100hp gas	12 win. CE, DE 4 whl. wooden bag. 40 pass.	50'		retired by 1917	(Three cars)
FERDINAND RR CO., Huntingburg to Ferdinand, Ind. 7.58 mi. (In operation)									
One gas car listed in ''Official Ry. Equip. Reg.'' 1928									
ST. JOSEPH VALLEY RY. CO., Elkhart to Angola, Ind., 59.7 mi. (Abandoned 1918) (Motors operated from Bristol to Angola, 50.7 mi.)									
101	Hicks	1905		Marinette 70hp GE	5 win. clere. roof, wood bag.	34'	42½ T	burned 1907	Very small baggage section, used primarily as locomotive
102	St. Louis	1905		Trailer	9 win. deck roof, 44 pass. st.car	48'4"	15T	sold to Nor. Ind. 1907	Nor. Ind. No. 216, was electrified by NI.
130	Stover	1907		Stover 4 cyl 40hp gas	4 win. 4 whl. 20 pass.		4T	out of serv. by 1913	
150	Fair.-Morse Sheffield	1908		Sheffield 25hp gas	4 win. 4 whl. 16 pass.	16'11"	3T	out of serv. by 1913	
151	Fair.-Morse Sheffield	1908		Sheffield 33hp gas	7 win. 4 whl. CE, 24 pass.	22'10"	7½ T	burned 1911	''Orland'' F.M. Model 23
152	Fair.-Morse Sheffield	1908		Sheffield 33hp gas	7 win. 4 whl. CE, 24 pass.	22'10"	7½ T	sold to Bristol Ry. (Vt.)	''Angola'' F.M. Model 23
161	Fair.-Morse Sheffield	1908		Sheffield 25hp gas	4 whl. open, 19 pass.	20'8"	4½ T	burned 1911	F.M. Model 19
162	Fair.-Morse Sheffield	1908		Sheffield 25hp gas	4 whl. open, 19 pass.	20'8"	4½ T	burned 1911	F.M. Model 19
171	Fair.-Morse Brill	1909	16790	Sheffield 50hp gas	8 win. OP, clere. roof, wood, bag. 35 pass.	30'3"	12T	sold 1918	F.M. Model 24
172	Fair.-Morse Brill	1909	16790	Sheffield 50hp gas	8 win. OP, clere. roof, wood, bag. 35 pass.	30'3"	12T	burned 1911	F.M. Model 24
173	Fair.-Morse Kuhlman	1910		Sheffield 50hp gas	8 win. clere. roof, wood, bag. 35 pass.	34'2"	13T	sold 1918	F.M. Model 24 closed rear platform

ROAD NOS.	BUILDER	DATE	BLDR. NO.	ENGINE & DRIVE	BODY TYPE	LGTH.	WT.	DISPOSITION	NOTES & COMMENTS
first 174	Fair.-Morse Kuhlman	1911		Sheffield 50hp gas	8 win. clere. roof, wood, bag. 35 pass.	34′ 2″	13T	burned 1911	F.M. Model 24 closed rear platform
second 174	Fair.-Morse Kuhlman	1911		Sheffield 50hp gas	8 win. clere. roof, wood, bag. 35 pass.	34′ 2″	13T	burned 1914	F.M. Model 24 closed rear platform
third 174	Fair.-Morse Kuhlman	1914		Sheffield 50hp gas	8 win. clere. roof, wood, bag. 35 pass.	34′ 2″	13T	sold 1918	F.M. Model 24 closed rear platform
201	McGuire-Cummings	1912		trailer	11 win. wood, bag. 50 pass.	50′			Ex-elect. interurban 202
203	Edison Beach	1913		Battery-elec. (4) Diehl 30hp motors	10 win. bag. 45 pass.	52′	30½T	sold 1918	
204	Hall-Scott	1914	18	Hall-Scott 150hp GM	9 win. bag. 40 pass.	54′	38T	sold 1918	Eventually used on the South Ga. Ry.

Iowa

AREA: 56,290 sq. miles
CAPITAL: Des Moines
POPULATION (1927): 2,425,000

AS IT WAS crisscrossed from east to west and north to south with the main lines of most of the "granger" railroads, each with many branch lines, Iowa had little room for short lines.

Several railroads that started out as short lines were electrified and became interurbans. The Charles City Western, for instance, began service with a McKeen motor and some motorized horse cars, and the Waterloo, Cedar Falls and Northern interurban had a Stover car.

There were, to be sure, a number of lines that did qualify in the traditional manner. Probably the largest was the Muscatine, Burlington & Southern, which probably should have been an interurban. It was a natural extension of the electrified Clinton, Davenport & Muscatine, and had a pair of very "interurbanish" steam cars built by Bettendorf. They were a "one-of-a-kind" model; Bettendorf was primarily a builder of railway trucks but it was located in the same area as the railroad.

Across the state was the Tabor and Northern. Tabor was one of the few county seats that wasn't on one of the mainline railroads, so it built its own. This line was equipped with some one-of-a-kind models produced by Chicago Motor Vehicle Co.—actually tiny, four-wheeled rail buses—in contrast to the Muscatine, Burlington & Southern's huge interurban-style cars.

Somewhat later in history, the Milwaukee Road decided to abandon a narrow-gauge line. Local interests took it over and installed a very small rail bus based upon the Twin Coach popular "milk wagon" design. Despite the effort, the Bellevue and Cascade, as this line was known, couldn't save itself.

Iowa Southern Utilities purchased a pair of ex-Burlington gas-electric cars when the line de-electrified, but as far as I know they were used as locomotives only.

KNIFE-NOSED McKeen car plied the rails of the Charles City Western, before the short line was electrified as a long-lasting Iowa interurban. Here's a retouched postcard view. *Author's Collection*

ROAD NOS.	BUILDER	DATE	BLDR. NO.	ENGINE & DRIVE	BODY TYPE	LGTH.	WT.	DISPOSITION	NOTES & COMMENTS
ATLANTIC NORTHERN RY., Atlantic to Kimballton, Iowa, 17 mi. (Abandoned 1936)									
MC.1	Co. Shops Brookfield			gas-mech.	4 win. CE, 4 whl. lead trk. bag. 10? pass.	abt. 15'			
CHARLES CITY WESTERN RY., Marble Rock to Colwell, Iowa, 23 mi. (In operation as Iowa Terminal RR)									
1	St. Louis	1892		Hart-Parr 30hp gas	4 win. OP st.car, 4 whl. 32 pass.	24'		conv. to line car	Ex-Peoria Ry. horsecar, acq. 7/10
2	St. Louis	1892		Buda 40hp gas	4 win. OP st.car, 4 whl. 32 pass.	24'		sold Lee Coun. Cen.	Ex-Peoria Ry. horsecar, acq. 7/10
3	St. Louis	1892		Hart-Parr 30hp gas	4 win. OP st.car, 4 whl. 32 pass.	24'		scrapped 1915	Ex-Peoria Ry. horsecar, acq. 7/10
4	St. Louis	1892		Buda 40hp gas	4 win. OP st.car, 4 whl. 32 pass.	24'		sold Bellefonte Cen. (Pa.) 3/15	
5	St. Louis	1892		Hart-Parr 30hp gas	4 win. OP st.car, 4 whl. 32 pass.	24'		sold. Amer. Tract. Int. Falls, Minn. 5/16	
51	McKeen	1910		McKeen 200hp gas-mech.	9 win. CE bag. 75 pass.	55'	30T	sold Mont. Wyo. & Sou. 1917	
MANCHESTER & ONEIDA RY. CO., Manchester to Oneida, Iowa, 8 mi. (Abandoned 1953)									
Goat	Co. Shops			Ford T 4 cyl gas	bus body, 4 whl. lead trk. 2 drive whls. & 4 whl. trail trk. under open bag. sect.				After accident converted for highway use
MUSCATINE, BURLINGTON & SOUTHERN RR CO., Burlington to Muscatine, Iowa, 51.6 mi. (Abandoned 1924)									
212	White			White 4 cyl. gas	6 win. bus 4 whl. lead trk.				
511	Bettendorf	1911		Savant steam	18 win. bag. 56 pass. wood				Interurban style body
611	Bettendorf			Savant steam	18 win. bag. 56 pass. wood				Interurban style body
SOUTHERN INDUSTRIAL RR, Moravia to Mystic, Iowa, 22.5 mi. (Abandoned 1965) (Formerly Iowa Southern Util.)									
9735	EMC Pullman	3/29	343 6203	Hamilton 685A 400hp DE	RPO-Baggage	65'	66T	to Keweenaw Central	Ex-CB&Q 9735, acquired 6/66
9769	EMC Pullman	10/30	460 6390	Hamilton 685A 400hp DE	RPO-Baggage	75'	75T		Ex-CB&Q 9769, acquired 2/66
TABOR & NORTHERN RY. CO., Tabor to Malvern, Iowa, 10 mi. (Abandoned 1933)									
	Chicago Mot. Vehicle Co.	1904		2 cyl. 20hp gas	5 win. clere. roof, 4 wheel, wood, 20 pass.	16' 6"			
	Co. Shops			gas	7 win. bus 4 whl. short hood				Pulled short trailer. "Equip. Reg." 1928, listed 3 motors and one trailer.
WATERLOO, CEDAR FALLS & NORTHERN RY., Waverly-Sumner Branch, 22 mi. (Leased from Chicago Great Western)									
1	Stover	1908		Stover 60hp gas	5 win. CE, 4 whl. short hood, 18 pass.				
BELLEVUE & CASCADE RY., Bellevue to Cascade, Iowa (3 ft. gauge) 35.7 mi. (Abandoned 1936, ex-Milw. Road Branch)									
	Twin Coach	1933		Hercules 34hp gas	"milk wagon" 4 whl. bus body		3T		"Autorailer" type, able to run on rails and highway

Kansas

AREA: 82,264 sq. miles
CAPITAL: Topeka
POPULATION (1927): 1,828,000

BY FAR THE most interesting rail motor car operation in Kansas was also its shortest lived.

When William B. Strang, Jr., of New York, and other investors incorporated the Missouri & Kansas Interurban Railway in 1906, Strang decided to equip it with gasoline-powered cars of his own invention in order to save the cost of electrification. In the next couple of years Strang had Brill build five of these gas-electric cars.

They resembled the classic interurban cars of the era. The first three were wooden, and the last two were remarkable, giant steel cars.

Although these cars included some features that were improvements on other gas cars of the era, as is common with such pioneer designs, they had more than their share of teething problems, so it was decided to electrify the line after all.

The second and third of the five cars, which were twins, were converted to electric cars. The first and last built were sold to the famous "Dan Patch" lines of Minnesota, so that by 1910 they were all gone or converted.

The only other major short line in Kansas, which operated rail motor cars, was the Wichita & Northwestern. It assembled a rather motley collection of home-built cars and modified sedans to serve this Wheat Belt area of Kansas.

Originally the line was called the Anthony & Northern, and was to have built south out of its base city, Pratt. At one time it apparently used the name Nebraska, Kansas & Gulf (its original corporate aim), as a St. Louis Car Co. advertisement shows a car about the size of a Brill type 55 car lettered for the NK&G. This car had a chain drive on the rear truck, and the engine was suspended under the car. This arrangement has never worked very well, so the cars may never have gone into operation. The rest of the short-line operations in Kansas were very limited or of streetcar dimensions.

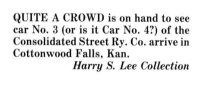

COMPANY SHOPS turned out this round-prow railcar for the Wichita Northwestern. Here we see Ralph Tindle bringing the 300 in from Kinsley, Kan.

Harry S. Lee Collection

QUITE A CROWD is on hand to see car No. 3 (or is it Car No. 4?) of the Consolidated Street Ry. Co. arrive in Cottonwood Falls, Kan.

Harry S. Lee Collection

PACKARD limousine was converted to a railcar which could haul freight trailers on the Wichita Northwestern. Car 403 is at Pratt, Kan., in 1936.
George W. Sisk, Charles E. Winters Collection

ROAD NOS.	BUILDER	DATE	BLDR. NO.	ENGINE & DRIVE	BODY TYPE	LGTH.	WT.	DISPOSITION	NOTES & COMMENTS
ARKANSAS VALLEY RY., INC. Hutchinson to Wichita, Kan. 51 mi. (Abandoned) (Formerly the Arkansas Valley Interurban)									
91	Brill	1927	22590	Brill 250 200 hp GE	15 win. CE bag. 81 pass.		47½ T	sold, Sou. NY Ry. & Pwr. 1941	Ex-Lehigh & New England No. 91, acq. 1940
COLORADO, KANSAS & OKLAHOMA RR, Garden City to Scott City, Kan. 37.08 mi. (Leased by the Santa Fe, 1926)									
One car listed in 1914									
CONSOLIDATED STREET RAILWAY, Cottonwood Falls to Strong City, Kan. 2 mi. (Abandoned)									
(1 car)		1918		gas-mech.	8 win. OP 4 wheel st.car	abt. 30'			Horse cars 3 and 4 spliced and mechanized
LEAVENWORTH, KANSAS & WESTERN RY., Leavenworth to Miltonvale, Kan. 165.8 mi. (Purchased by the Union Pacific)									
(1 car)				gas	open sedan				Also had two 4 wheel trailers, one for passengers, one for freight
LEAVENWORTH & TOPEKA RR CO., Leavenworth to Meriden, Kan. 46.46 mi. (Abandoned)									
(1 car)	White Ry. Specialty	1921		White 4 cyl. gas	8 win. bus body, 4 whl. lead truck. 25 pass.				
MANHATTAN CITY & INTERURBAN RY., MANHATTAN, KAN. (Abandoned)									
1-4	Four Wheel Drive	1921		Wisc. gas	7 win. CE 4 whl., 24 pass.			returned to FWD, 1922	Similar highway buses also built (4 units)
MISSOURI & KANSAS INTERURBAN RY., Kansas City, Mo. to Olathe, Kan. 17 mi., electrified (Abandoned)									
Ogerita	Strang Brill	1906	14184	Strang 100hp gas-elect.	6 win. CE, OP wd. clere. roof, 24 pass.	41' 6"		sold, Dan Patch No. 1	
Mar- guerita	Strang Brill	1906	14877	Strang 100hp gas-elect.	16 win. clere. roof, wood, 41 pass.	52' 9"		rblt. to frt. motor 107	

SAME DESIGN, rail and road. The Manhattan City & Interurban had four Four Wheel Drive gas railcars and four almost identical road units by the same builder. This photo shows both types at the end of track.
Author's Collection

ROAD NOS.	BUILDER	DATE	BLDR. NO.	ENGINE & DRIVE	BODY TYPE	LGTH.	WT.	DISPOSITION	NOTES & COMMENTS
Geral-dine	Strang Brill	1906	14877	Strang 100hp gas-elect.	16 win. clere. roof, wood, 41 pass.	52' 9"		rblt. to pass. mot. 101	
Irene	Strang Brill	1908	15652	Strang 150hp gas-elect.	19 win. clere. roof, obs. plat. 38 pass.	62' 8"	57T	sold to Dan Patch No. 2 1910	
Rosa-mond	Strang Brill	1907	15771	Strang 150hp gas-elect.	19 win.	62' 8"	57T	to Dan Patch	

WESTMORELAND INTERURBAN, Westmoreland to Blaine, Kan. 10 mi. (Abandoned)

ROAD NOS.	BUILDER	DATE	BLDR. NO.	ENGINE & DRIVE	BODY TYPE	LGTH.	WT.	DISPOSITION	NOTES & COMMENTS
(1 car)	White	1907		White 4 cyl. gas-mech.	open touring car, 4 whl. lead truck			lost in a flood	
(1 car)	Mitchell	1912		Mitchell gas-mech.	open touring car, 4 whl. lead truck			body removed, made into loco.	

WICHITA & NORTHWESTERN RY. CO. Pratt to Vaughn, Kan. 100.2 mi. (Abandoned)

ROAD NOS.	BUILDER	DATE	BLDR. NO.	ENGINE & DRIVE	BODY TYPE	LGTH.	WT.	DISPOSITION	NOTES & COMMENTS
100	Co. Shops	acq. 1914		gas-mech.	10 win. OP st.car				Ex-Hutchinson Kan. Street Ry.
101 to 103	St. Louis	2/16	1093	gas-mech.	9 win. bag. pass.			prob. returned to builder	Engine mounted under body, no record of these cars ever being in service
300	Co. Shops			Reo 4 cyl. gas	6 win. CE, 4 whl. 19 pass.				Rebuilt from bus
301	Co. Shops			Reo 4 cyl. gas	6 win. bag. 4 whl. 19 pass.				Bag. door at rear added later
403	Packard Co. Shops			Packard 8 gas	4 door sedan				Also had a number of four wheel open and closed trailers

Kentucky

AREA: 40,395 sq. miles
CAPITAL: Frankfort
POPULATION (1927): 2,538,000

THERE ISN'T too much that can be said about railcar operation in Kentucky except there weren't many lines and they didn't have very much equipment.

The last to run (it lasted long enough to gain a modicum of fame) was the Frankfort & Cincinnati, which ran from Frankfort to Paris. It had two pieces of equipment, one an imposing center-entrance Brill gas-electric that was originally owned by the Lehigh & New England, the other a standard Brill Model 55.

The Flemingsburg and Northern's only equipment was a converted streetcar which was something of a classic.

The Artemus & Jellico's lone car was that rather famous boomer that started out in Pennsylvania on the Lewisburg, Milton & Watsontown Passenger Railway, moved to the Pennsylvania Railroad, then the Artemus-Jellico which dealt it to the Buffalo Creek and Gauley. It finally wound up at the Strasburg Railway Museum, which is close to where it started its checkered career.

NICKNAMED *Queen*, Eastern Kentucky Ry. Co. gas car No. 215 came secondhand from a West Virginia short line in 1929. Alas, the EKS was abandoned in 1933.
F.P. Kutta Collection

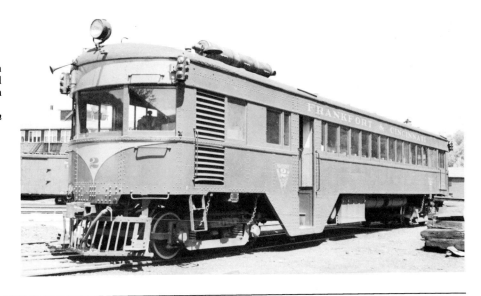

SPIFFY PAINT JOB sparkles on Frankfort & Cincinnati No. 2, a Brill Model 175 acquired from the Lehigh & New England in 1944.
Paul B. Dunn

ROAD NOS.	BUILDER	DATE	BLDR. NO.	ENGINE & DRIVE	BODY TYPE	LGTH.	WT.	DISPOSITION	NOTES & COMMENTS
ARTEMUS-JELLICO RR, Artemus to Wheeler, Ky., 10.4 mi. (Abandoned)									
1	Mack Brill	1921	60005 21368	Mack AC 68hp gas-mech.	7 win. 4 whl. lead truck, bag. 32 pass.	32' 5"	10T	sold to Buffalo Creek 7 Gauly (W. Va.) 1941	Ex-Penn. Ry. 4370, ex-ex-Lewisburg, Milton & Watsontown Pass. Ry., acquired 1930. Now at Straburg Ry. Museum.
(2 units)	Ford Co. Shops			Ford A gas	bus body, 15 pass.				
—				Trailers					Ex-Knoxville St. Ry., ex-horse car?

CADIZ RR, Cadiz to Gracey, Ky., 10 mi. (Abandoned)

Official Guide, 1916, lists two round trips operated by railcars

CARROLLTON RR, Carrollton to Worthville, Ky., 10 mi. in operation

"Automotive Industries" (magazine) 3/22/23 issue reports a gas car in operation.

EASTERN KENTUCKY RY. CO., Riverton to Webbville, Ky., 36.08 mi. (Abandoned)

ROAD NOS.	BUILDER	DATE	BLDR. NO.	ENGINE & DRIVE	BODY TYPE	LGTH.	WT.	DISPOSITION	NOTES & COMMENTS
M1	Co. Shops			gas	4 win. 4 whl. back entrance	abt. 15'			
M2	Co. Shops			Trailer	5 win. 4 whl.	abt. 18'			
215	Mack Brill	6/21	70005 21292	Mack AB 35hp gas-mech.	8 win. 4 whl. lead truck, 25 pass.	28' 8"	5½T	scrapped 1933	Ex-Sewell Valley (West Va.) acq. 1929

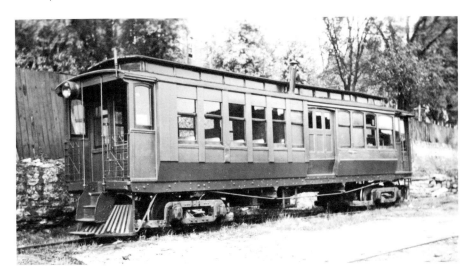

PASSENGER EXIT was in front of this ex-Richmond, Va., streetcar serving as a gas-electric for the Flemingsburg & Northern. The car is of Brill ancestry.
Author's Collection

RUMBLING ONTO the turntable at the company shops is Frankfort & Cincinnati No. M55-1, a Brill Model 55.
Paul B. Dunn

ROAD NOS.	BUILDER	DATE	BLDR. NO.	ENGINE & DRIVE	BODY TYPE	LGTH.	WT.	DISPOSITION	NOTES & COMMENTS
FLEMINGSBURG & NORTHERN RR, Flemingsburg to Flemingsburg Jct., Ky. 5.6 mi. (Abandoned)									
M-1	Co. Shops Brill			gas-elect.	10 win. dbl. truck, wooden streetcar				Ex-Richmond Va. streetcar
FRANKFORT & CINCINNATI RR CO., Frankfort, Ky. 40.1 mi. (Abandoned)									
2	Brill	1926	22275	Brill 175 250hp GE	14 win. CE, DE. bag. 86 pass. bag. door at rear		43T		Ex-Lehigh & New England 90, acq. 1944
M55-1	Brill	1927	22537	Brill 55 68hp GM	10 win. bag. 26 pass.	43′	14½T	to Ky. Ry. Museum	
KENTUCKY & TENNESSEE RY., Stearns to Exodus, Ky., 17 mi. (11 miles in operation)									
1916 "Official Guide" lists train 506, Yamacraw to Exodus, as being motor									
LENOX RR, Redwine to Rush Branch, Ky. (Abandoned 1927)									
(1 car)	Buda			Buda gas	4 whl. Speeder 9 pass.				
MAMMOTH CAVE RR CO., Glasgow Jct. to Mammoth Cave, Ky., 8.7 mi. (Abandoned)									
(1 car)	Stover			Stover 30hp gas	5 win. 2 dr. 4 whl. wood, long hood				Acquired secondhand 1929, possibly from the Tennessee & Cumberland River RR (Tenn.)
MOREHEAD & NORTH FORK RR CO., Morehead to Redwine, Ky., 24.44 mi. (Abandoned)									
200	Edwards	1926		(2) Buda 108hp, gas-mech.	9 win. bag. 36 pass.	43′	17T	sold to Cal. West. (M-100) 1934	

Louisiana

AREA: 48,523 sq. miles
CAPITAL: Baton Rouge
POPULATION (1927): 1,934,000

THE AREA AROUND New Orleans appears to have been a hotbed for four-wheel rail motor cars. One of the first railroads to use them was the St. Tammany & New Orleans Ry. & Ferry Co., which operated from Mandeville, just across Lake Ponchartrain from New Orleans, to Covington, which at the time (around 1908) was something of a resort area.

These cars were among the first of Fairbanks-Morse's type 24 cars, which resembled a small four-wheel streetcar of the period. As a matter of fact, three of the four cars purchased were converted to eight-wheel streetcars when the line was electrified, a thoroughly unprecedented move for its time.

Somewhat later the New Orleans & Lower Coast obtained a three-car train of cars built by the Four Wheel Drive Auto Co. The first car was a motor, the other two were trailers, which featured open platforms and clerestory roofs.

This combination may not have worked too well, but the company ordered a more conventional center-entrance car and trailer. All of these cars had wooden bodies.

In 1924 a nearby railroad—the Louisiana Southern—bought still another FWD motor trailer combination, but with a more modern steel body. It might be noted that none of these roads had to contend with any kind of grades, so they could freely use trailers, which didn't work out so well when grades were encountered.

The largest Louisiana operator of more conventional rail motor cars was the Louisiana & North Western of northern Louisiana. This line owned two Brill Model 75 gas-mechanical cars, and finally an American Car & Foundry "Auto-railer" which was obtained secondhand from the Chicago & Eastern Illinois in 1945.

Louisiana's other rail motor car operators were small and obscure, although the Sibley, Lake Bistineau & Southern had a very rare Russell railcar.

ONE OF TWO railcars owned by Sibley, Lake Bisteneau & Southern was this Russell combine, sporting a Wisconsin 120-hp gasoline engine.
Author's Collection

FOUR WHEEL DRIVE cars made up the entire railcar roster of the New Orleans & Lower Coast. Massive coupler almost dwarfs the radiator of unit No. 1.
Author's Collection

61

THREE THREE CAR GASOLINE TRAIN OPERATED BY NEW ORLEANS AND LOWER COAST RR CO. FOUR WHEEL DRIVE AUTO. CO. CLINTONVILLE WIS USA 622-24-

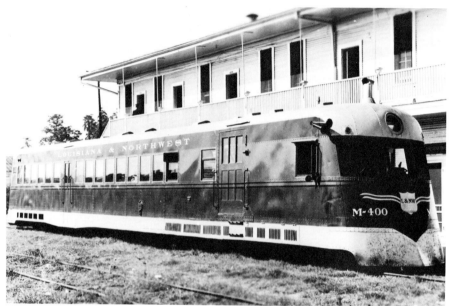

THREE-CAR TRAIN on the New Orleans & Lower Coast forced passengers to enter and leave via open platforms. *Louis Saillard Collection*

ANOTHER example of a late-model, streamlined car gravitating to a short line is the M-400 of the Louisiana & North West at Homer, La., in 1945. This ACF unit was built in 1937 for the Chicago & Eastern Illinois. *Harold K. Vollrath Collection*

ROAD NOS.	BUILDER	DATE	BLDR. NO.	ENGINE & DRIVE	BODY TYPE	LGTH.	WT.	DISPOSITION	NOTES & COMMENTS

ALEXANDRIA & WESTERN RY., Alexandria to McFarland, La., 20.4 mi. (Abandoned 1924)

| 100 | | | | gas | | | | | |
| 102 | | | | Trailer | | | | | |

CHRISTIE & EASTERN RY. CO., Sandel to Pearson, La. 10.17 mi. (Abandoned)

Moody's "Steam Railroads" 1928, lists two railcars.

KENTWOOD & EASTERN RY. CO., Kentwood to Scanlon, La. 15 mi. (Abandoned 1923)

| (1 car) | Fair. Morse Brill | 1911 | | Fair. Morse 50hp gas | 8 win. wood, 4 whl. clere. roof, bag. 35 pass. | 34' 2" | 13T | | |

KINDER & NORTHWESTERN RR CO., Kinder to Timberland, La. abt. 10 mi. (Abandoned 1927)

| 14 | Fair. Morse Brill | | | Fair. Morse 24 50hp gas | 8 win. wood, clere. roof, 4 whl. bag. 35 pass. | 34' 2" | 13T | | |

ROAD NOS.	BUILDER	DATE	BLDR. NO.	ENGINE & DRIVE	BODY TYPE	LGTH.	WT.	DISPOSITION	NOTES & COMMENTS
LOUISIANA & NORTH WEST RR CO., Chestnut, La. to McNeil, Ark. (92.8 mi. in operation)									
M200	Brill	1925	22101	Brill 75 175hp gas-mech.	13 win. bag. 53 pass.	58′	26½T	retired 1946	
M300	Brill	1926	22323	Brill 75 175hp gas-mech.	13 win. bag. 53 pass.	58′	26½T	retired 1948	Ex-Columbus & Greenville M-75, acq. 3/31
M400	Amer. Car & Foundry	1937	1599	Hall-Scott 200hp GM	15 win. CE bag. 61 pass.	75′7″	31T	retired 1948	Ex-Chicago & Eastern Ill. No. 342, acq. 1945
LOUISIANA SOUTHERN RY., New Orleans to Point a la Hache, La. 43.8 mi. (21 miles in operation)									
41	Four Wheel Drive	1924		Wisc. 4 cyl. 42hp gas	4 win. 4 whl. bag. 16 pass.	26′			
51	Four Wheel Drive	1924		Trailer	8 win. 4 whl. 40 pass.	26′			
NEW ORLEANS & LOWER COAST RR, Gretna to Buras, La. 59.7 mi. (Merged in Missouri Pacific)									
01	Four Wheel Drive	1924		Wisc. A 36hp gas-mech.	8 win. CE, wood, short hood, 24 pass. 4 whl.			retired 11/25	
02	Four Wheel Drive	1924		Trailer	6 win. CE, 4 whl. bag. 24 pass.			retired 11/25	
(1 car)	Four Wheel Drive			Wisc. gas-mech.	10 win. 4 whl. deck roof				This motor plus the two following trailers operated as a train. The motor does not seem to have any door except on the rear partition, which leads to the open platform of the trailer behind.
(2 cars)	Four Wheel Drive			Trailer	10 win. 4 whl. OP deck roof				
ST. TAMMANY & NEW ORLEANS RY. & FERRY CO., Mandeville to Covington, La. (Abandoned)									
11	Fair. Morse Brill	1908	16558	Fair. Morse 24 50hp gas	8 win. OP, 4 whl. clere. roof, bag. 35 pass. wood	34′2″	12T	rebuilt to 8 whl. st.car	
17	Fair. Morse Brill	1908	16558	Fair. Morse 24 50hp gas	8 win. OP, 4 whl. clere. roof, bag. 35 pass. wood	34′2″	12T	scrapped	
22	Fair. Morse Brill	1908	16560	Fair. Morse 24 50hp gas	8 win. OP, 4 whl. clere. roof, bag. 35 pass. wood	34′2″	12T	rebuilt to streetcar	
33	Fair. Morse Brill	1908	16560	Fair. Morse 24 50hp gas	8 win. OP, 4 whl. clere. roof, bag. 35 pass. wood	34′2″	12T	rebuilt to streetcar	
(1 car)	Fair. Morse Sheffield			Fair. Morse 19 30hp gas	4 wheel open st.car, wood.		4½T		
SIBLEY, LAKE BISTENEAU & SOUTHERN RY. CO., Sibley to North Station, La., 27.5 mi. (Abandoned)									
Part of the SHREVEPORT, ALEXANDRIA & SOUTHWESTERN RY. SYSTEM									
(1 car)	H.J. Reith	1925		gas	30 pass.				
(1 car)	Russell			Wisc. 120hp gas	10 win. OP, bag. 28 pass. long hood	46′6″	14T		
TREMONT & GULF RY. CO., Tremont to Winnfield, La. with branches 76.6 mi. (Abandoned)									
(1 car)	Chrysler			Chrysler gas	Chrysler sedan, 4 door				"Air flow" may have been for inspection only

Maine

AREA: 33,215 sq. miles
CAPITAL: Augusta
POPULATION (1927): 793,000

MAINE, OF COURSE, was the land of the two-foot-gauge railroads, and insofar as rail motor cars are concerned, their only home in this country.

All except one car was built by, or for, the largest of these lines, the Sandy River and Rangerly Lakes.

The Bridgton & Harrison obtained one of the Sandy River cars on kind of a loan basis, and also built (or modified) a Chevrolet for rail service. The Sandy River shops also modified a Reo bus for the Kennebago Bus Co. for use on an abandoned line of the Maine Central.

This bus, after lying derelict for some time, was beautifully restored and is now in use on the White Mountain Central, a museum railroad in New Hampshire. This unit was, of course, standard gauge, as was the Penobscot Central's lone Patton car.

Patton was one of the real pioneers in the gasoline-electric drive. Although Patton worked very closely with Pullman, these cars apparently had many of the same problems that pioneer cars usually had and only a very few units were built.

TWO-FOOT GAUGE was the remarkable peculiarity of two Maine short lines which operated doodlebugs. Here we see a Bridgton & Harrison unit pulling a four-wheel baggage trailer. The second view gives better detail of the side. It's a Reo Speedwagon on two-foot rails. *(Top Photo) Extra 200 South; (Middle Photo) Bob Leibman Collection*

NARROWNESS of the distance between rails is graphically illustrated in this view of the Bridgton & Harrison's first unit, a sedan towing a two-wheel baggage conveyance. *Author's Collection*

64

A FINE MUSEUM PIECE is this White Mountain Central Museum car, a former highway bus of the Kennebago Bus Co. built by Maine's Sandy River & Rangeley Lakes, a two-foot pike although the car was always standard gauge. Notice the nifty varnish and lettering job. This photo was taken in 1973. *Dan Foley*

ROAD NOS.	BUILDER	DATE	BLDR. NO.	ENGINE & DRIVE	BODY TYPE	LGTH.	WT.	DISPOSITION	NOTES & COMMENTS
BRIDGTON & HARRISON RR CO. (2 ft. gauge) Bridgton Jct. to Harrison, 21.23 mi. (Abandoned)									
(1 car)	Co. Shops			Chevrolet gas	4 door sedan, duel drive whls. at rear				Pulled 2 wheel wooden baggage section
(1 car)	Sand. Riv. & Rang. Lakes Shops	1925		Reo 6 cyl. gas	5 door bus, 4 whl. lead trk.	20' 6"		to Edaville Ry. (Mass.)	Ex-Sandy River & Rangerly Lakes No. 4. Purchased (1936) by Edgar Mead, loaned to the B&H.
KENNEBAGO BUS CO., Oquossoc to Kennebago, Maine, 11 mi. (Using ex-Maine Cen. tracks) (Abandoned)									
(1 car)	S.R.&R.L. Shops, Reo			Reo 6 gas	6 win. hood type bus			now used on White Mtn. Cen. RR (Museum) N.H.	
PENOBSCOT CENTRAL RY., Penobscot, Maine (Abandoned)									
(1 car)	Patton Pullman	1898		Patton, btty. gas-elect.	Cal. type st.car		28T		
SANDY RIVER & RANGELY LAKES RR (2 ft. gauge) Farmington to Berlin Mills, Maine and branches, 96.45 mi. (Abandoned)									
First 1	O.M. Voss	1923		Ford 4 cyl. gas	open 4 wheel			wrecked 1925	Parts used to construct sec. No. 1
Second 1	Co. Shops	5/26		Ford 4 cyl. gas	open 4 wheel			to Edaville 1936, No. 1	Built from parts of first No. 1
First 2	O.M. Voss	1924		Ford 4 cyl, 4	open 4 wh. 4 dr. tour. car, hood front			wrecked 1925	Parts used to build second No. 2
Second 2	Co. Shops	5/26		Ford 4 cyl, 4	open 4 wh. 4 dr. tour. car, hood front			sold to Edaville No. 2	Built from parts of first 2
3	Co. Shops	5/25		Ford 4 cyl, 4	open, 4 rows of seats, hood frt.			wrecked	Got closed body 1926
4	Co. Shops	7/25		Reo 6 cyl. gas	5 door, hood type bus body	20' 6"		sold 1936, loaned to Brig. & Harrison	Built with single front wheel, replaced with 4 wheel truck
5	Co. Shops	6/27		Reo 6 cyl. gas, replaced with Buick "Big 6"	6 door, hood type bus, bag. 18 pass.	29' 2"		wrecked 1936	Orig. 17' 2", baggage sect. added 1928

Maryland

AREA: 10,577 sq. miles
CAPITAL: Annapolis
POPULATION (1927): 1,597,000

BY FAR THE best-known rail motor car operator in this state—indeed one of the best-known short lines in the entire country—was the Maryland & Pennsylvania, known far and wide as the "Ma and Pa."

The most unusual thing about the Ma and Pa cars, at least by short-line standards, was that they were all purchased new. After trying out a couple of cars built by Russell, which were unsatisfactory and returned, two St. Louis-Electro Motive gas-electrics were purchased in 1927 and 1928.

These proved to be very satisfactory,

generally pulling one of the old wooden baggage cars over a rather difficult terrain, and they pretty well took over all the passenger traffic until passenger service was discontinued in 1955.

One other line of some note was the Chesapeake Beach Ry. which ran from the Washington, D.C., area to, as the name suggests, the beaches along Chesapeake Bay, primarily for summer excursionists. It was built by Otto Perry, of Colorado narrow-gauge railroad fame, who named some of his passenger cars after stations on his lines in Colorado.

In 1929, the CB Ry. bought a large

Brill gas-electric. For some reason, perhaps financial, the car was returned to Brill the next year, after which it became a real boomer, serving for a while on the Louisiana, Arkansas & Texas, the Fonda, Johnstown & Gloversville in upstate New York, and finally the Greater Winnipeg Water District of Canada.

Also in the Washington, D.C., area there were some very modest streetcar type operations using battery-electric cars or gasoline-powered cars of the same size as the battery cars.

There also were a few more modest railcar endeavors, mostly on the Delmarva peninsula.

RUNNING ON A short (24-mile) railroad with a long name was No. 10 of the Washington, Brandywine & Point Lookout Railroad, an FWD (Four Wheel Drive) built combo.
Author's Collection

BRILL turned out this snappy motor and trailer combination for the Maryland and Delaware Coast, a 38-mile pike extending across the Maryland-Delaware border.
Author's Collection

ROAD NOS.	BUILDER	DATE	BLDR. NO.	ENGINE & DRIVE	BODY TYPE	LGTH.	WT.	DISPOSITION	NOTES & COMMENTS
BALTIMORE & WASHINGTON TRANSIT CO. OF MARYLAND, Washington, D.C. (Abandoned)									
first 4	Stevenson Brill	1910		Sintz-Wallen 4hp gas	8 win. CE st.car, clere. roof, 30 pass.			repossessed by Brill 1911	Sold to Sioux City Traction, No. 17 as electric car
sec. 4	Federal	1911		Battery-elec.	8 win. 4 whl. deck roof st.car			burned, 9/13	May have been rebuilt to gas car, using a Rutenberg & Davis 60hp gas engine by the Railway Motor Car Co.
5	Federal	1911			8 win. 4 whl. deck roof st.car				
BALTIMORE, CHESAPEAKE & ATLANTIC RY. CO., Ocean City to Claiborne, Md., 87.77 mi. (Merged into Pennsylvania RR)									
(1 car)	Brill White	1923	21857	White 4 cyl, 40hp gas	8 win. bag. 38 pas. 4 whl. lead truck	31'6"	10T		
CHESAPEAKE BEACH RY. CO., Seat Pleasant to Chesapeake Beach, Md. 28.32 mi. (Abandoned)									
300	Brill	1929	22828	Brill 350, 300hp GE	12 win. DE bag. 68 pass.	73'	60T	returned to Brill 1930	Resold to Lou. Ark. & Tex., then to the Fonda, Johnstown & Gloversville and finally to the Great Winn. Water Dist.
CUMBERLAND & PENNSYLVANIA RR CO., Cumberland, Md. to Piedmont, W. Va., 48.41 mi. (Merged into Western Maryland Ry.)									
101	Brill	1928	22601 ?	(2) Brill, 300hp GE	14 win. DE bag. 73 pass.	75' ½"	77T	sold to NY Susq. & West.	May have been a Brill demo, No. 3002, on NYS&W

THE MA AND PA, officially known as the Maryland & Pennsylvania RR, offered these contrasts in railcars: giant No. 61, a St. Louis-Electro Motive rail motor car for mainline passenger service, and this racy, circa 1926 sedan inspection car. Check out that opera window!
(Top Photo) Russ Tipton, Charles E. Winters Collection; (Bottom Photo) W.C. Whittaker Collection

A Small 1800 Pound Battery

That Propels a Street Car

206.8 Miles in 18 Hours, 50 Minutes

continuous running, over heavy grades, MUST NECESSARILY BE AN

Edison Storage Battery

AND THE CAR MUST NECESSARILY BE A

Beach Car

Because no other battery, weighing even three times as much, could possibly perform over such grades and for such great mileage.

Here is the Car.

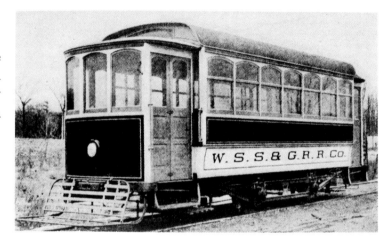

Here is the Profile

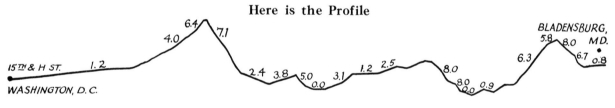

The Edison Storage Battery is guaranteed against depreciation in capacity. The guarantee is not contingent upon the number of miles or the number of grades or the extent of grades over which the battery is worked. On the Washington Spa Springs & Gretta RR. (Washington, D. C.), where the four miles of track consist entirely of grades up to 8%, except for about 800 ft., a Beach Single Truck Car, equipped with the A/6 Edison Battery, is operated over that line, from 144 to 206.8 miles per day, with an average power consumption of only 355 watt hours per car mile, by the following process:—

Charging plugs installed at each end of the line; the Beach Cars operated in conjunction with the trolley cars. All cars necessarily lay over at each end of the line 3 minutes. When the Beach Car reaches a terminal, the charging plug is inserted in the battery circuit, and for 3 minutes the battery is charged at four to five times the normal charging rate, or four to five times faster than the ordinary charge. By the time the car is run to the other end of the line (four miles) the power taken into the battery at this high rate is used, and the battery is given another intermediate charge, at this high charging rate, for another three minutes, and so the process continues throughout the day, as long as desired, without taking the car out of service for charging, and without inconveniencing the schedule arrangements. As a matter of fact, the car goes into the barn, at night, after the long day's work, over the heavy grades, with its battery as "lively" and as fully charged as when it went into service in the morning. Charge any other battery at the high rate and you ruin your battery. Put into your car enough battery, of any other make (which are acid-lead batteries) to perform this mileage per day, and the weight would smash the car structure in the course of a short time. Charge or discharge a lead battery at a high rate, and the lead plates would "buckle," and the battery would be useless. This is not a matter of conversation; it is a matter of performance—A C H I E V E M E N T. By the way, the Washington road has placed another order.

Federal Storage Battery Car Company

Principal Office, 1779 Hudson Terminal, New York City

ROAD NOS.	BUILDER	DATE	BLDR. NO.	ENGINE & DRIVE	BODY TYPE	LGTH.	WT.	DISPOSITION	NOTES & COMMENTS
MARYLAND & DELAWARE COAST RY., West Denton, Md. to Lewes, Del., 38.8 mi. (Abandoned)									
301	Four Whl. Drive	1924		Wisc. 6 cyl. 62hp gas	4 win. 4 whl. bag. 22 pass.	25′6″	9T		
302	Brill	1925	22229	Brill 55, 68hp gas	10 win. bag. 42 pass.	44′5″	15½T		
401	Four Whl. Drive	1924		Trailer	8 win. 4 whl. 32 pass.	25′6″	8T		
402	Brill	1925	22230	Trailer	8 win. rear ent. 34 pass.	29′9″	8T		
MARYLAND & PENNSYLVANIA RR CO., Baltimore, Md. to York, Pa., 80.69 mi. (21 miles in operation)									
51	Russell	1922		Trailer	10 win. 36 pass.	31′3″	9½T		
60	Russell	1922		Wisc. 60hp gas-mech.	4 win. OP bag. 16 pass.	abt. 30′		returned to builder	Long front hood
first 61	Russell	1922		Wisc. 120hp gas-mech.	7 win. bag. 28 pass.	46′6″	14T		Long front hood
second 61	St. Louis EMC	1927	1421 200	Winton 120, 275hp GE	15 win. bag. 56 pass.	59′6″	46T	retired 1955	
62	St. Louis EMC	1928	1480 347	(2) Wint. 106D, 220hp GE	13 win. bag. 52 pass.	59′9″	61T	retired 1955	
TOWSON & COCKEYSVILLE ELECTRIC RY. CO., Towson to Cockeysville, Md. (Abandoned)									
1	Federal	1912		battery-elec.	4 wheel st.car	27′8″			
2	Brill	1916		battery-elec.	7 win. 4 whl. st.car, arch roof	27′8″			
WASHINGTON, BRANDYWINE & POINT LOOKOUT RR CO., Brandywine to Forrest Hall, Md., 24 mi. (Acquired by the Pennsylvania RR)									
10	Four Wheel Drive			Wisc. 62hp gas	5 win. 4 whl. bag. 15 pass.	22′2″	9T	scrapped	
A-1	Brill White	1919		White 4 cyl. gas	7 win. CE bag. 20 pass. 4 whl. lead trk.	18′9″			
WASHINGTON, SPA SPRINGS & GRETTA RR CO., Bladensburg, Md., to Washington, D.C., 4 mi. (Abandoned)									
(1 car)	Federal	1910		battery-elec.	7 win. 4 whl. 20 pass.	25′		returned to builder	

Massachusetts

AREA: 10,577 sq. miles
CAPITAL: Boston
POPULATION (1927): 4,242,000

AN ODD assortment. First of all, there weren't very many short lines to begin with. Two of them were narrow-gauge lines that ran on Nantucket Island that lasted just a short time.

One of them, the Nantucket Railway, built a pair of rail motor cars in its shops in 1906 and retired them in 1908. The other line, the Nantucket Central, also had a pair that even less is known about.

Then there were two lines in the Winthrop Beach area that were streetcar lines; one a standard-gauge branch of the narrow-gauge Boston, Revere Beach and Lynn, which at the time was other-wise steam operated. This two-mile line made do with three battery cars from Manhattan, and as the final irony was abandoned when the rest of the line was electrified in 1929.

The other line was the Port Shirley Street Railway, which obtained a couple of small battery-style cars. These were equipped with gas engines, one of which had an electric drive. Built in 1910 and 1911, they were soon retired.

About the only conventional short-line operation in the state was the Hoosic Tunnel & Wilmington, which did not operate in the Hoosic Tunnel, despite its name. This road purchased in 1923 a motor-trailer set from the Four Wheel Drive Auto Co. of Clintonville, Wis. These tiny units, 25 feet long, about nine tons, were built on the same chassis that was used in the popular FWD truck. The trouble was they rode like a truck, especially on short line-style trackage. The HT&W managed to sell these cars to the nearby West River Railway.

John H. White, Jr.'s *American Railroad Passenger Car* (Johns Hopkins University Press, 1978) mentions a couple of steam cars that were tried in the 19th century. The Boston & Worcester operated a car built by Moore & Parrotts in 1850, and the Worcester & Shrewsbury employed a car built by Remington Arms in 1872. This car is said to have lasted until around 1890. Finally the Plum Island St. Railway got a car in 1888 that was built by Baldwin.

NANTUCKET ISLAND had two railways operating motor cars. One of them, the three-foot-gauge Nantucket Central, boasted this motor-trailer combination.

Al Barker Collection

ROAD NOS.	BUILDER	DATE	BLDR. NO.	ENGINE & DRIVE	BODY TYPE	LGTH.	WT.	DISPOSITION	NOTES & COMMENTS
BOSTON, REVERE BEACH & LYNN RR CO. (standard gauge div.) Winthrop to Shirley, Mass. 2 mi. (Abandoned 1929)									
Gov. Win-throp	Brill	1913		battery-elec.	7 win. 4 whl. wood st.car, 28 pass.			scrapped	Ex-Third Ave. Ry. (NY) No. 1278
Gov. Shirley	Brill	1913		battery-elec.	7 win. 4 whl. wood st.car, 28 pass.			scrapped	Ex-Third Ave. Ry. (NY) No. 1279
101	Federal	1913		battery-elec.	10 win. wood st.car 40 pass.	37' 1"		conv. to work equip. '28. scrap. 1933	Double truck, ex-New York Belt Ry. acquired 1918 (there may have been a similar car numbered 100)
HOOSAC TUNNEL & WILMINGTON RR CO., Hoosac Tunnel to Wilmington, Vt. 24 mi. (Abandoned)									
50	Four Wheel Drive	1923		Wisc. 6 cyl. 95hp gas	5 win. bag. 15 pass.	25' 6"	9T	sold to West River (Vt.)	
60	Four Wheel Drive	1923		trailer	9 win. 40 pass.	25' 9"	8T	sold to West River (Vt.)	
NANTUCKET RY., Nantucket Island, Mass. (Abandoned 1917)									
Glan-conet	Co. Shops	1906		gas	2 win. 4 whl. wood 8 pass.	10' 6"		retired 1908	
Bird Cage	Co. Shops	1906		trailer	4 wheel, open	8'		retired 1908	There is also a record of having had some sort of a 30 pass. gas car
NANTUCKET CENTRAL RY. (3 ft. gauge), Nantucket Island, Mass. (Abandoned)									
Nan-tucket				gas	6 win. OP clere. roof, 4 wheel				
1				trailer	12 win. OP 48 pass. wood				
POINT SHIRLEY STREET RY., Winthrop Beach, Mass. (Abandoned)									
1		1910		gas-elect.					
2	Atlantic Works	1911		6 cyl. 70hp gas	8 win. 4 whl. deck roof st.car		8T		

GASOLINE CAR NO. 2 AT POINT SHIRLEY

In the issue of this paper for Oct. 22, 1910, a description was published of gasoline-electric car No. 1 of the Point Shirley Street Railway, near Winthrop Beach, Mass. Since that time, owing to the large increase in traffic, a

On the truck of this car is installed a six-cylinder gasoline engine, rated at 70 hp at 1500 r.p.m. Energy is transmitted to one axle through a multiple-disk clutch, sliding gear transmission and a bevel gear. This bevel gear is shown in the first engraving. The lever shown in the

End Views of Truck of Point Shirley Gasoline Car

second car has been put into operation. This car differs essentially from the first car in that instead of an electric clutch it has a mechanical clutch.

front right-hand corner is used to reverse the car by engaging one of the two bevel gears contained in the spherical gear box. This illustration also shows the method of sup-

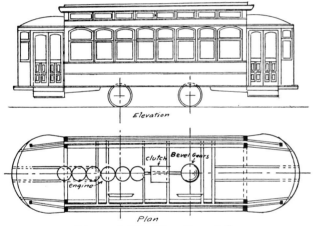

Plan and Side Elevation of Car

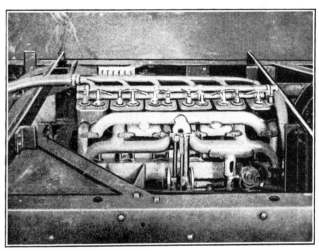

Side View of Motor

porting the engine and the transmission by the use of angle irons dropped from the top of the truck.

The cooling system shown in the second view consists of two radiators, each having a surface of 100 sq. ft. Fans operated by a shaft and bevel gears direct from the crankshaft of the engine maintain the air circulation through the radiators.

The car equipped weighs 8 tons and is capable of a speed of 30 m.p.h. on level track. The car was designed by Herbert N. Ridgeway and was constructed at the Atlantic Works, Boston, Mass. The total cost of the car equipped was $5,500, and the total cost of operation, including fixed and operating costs, is 16.5 cents per car mile when running 95 miles per day.

ARTICLE in a 1911 issue of the *Electric Railway Journal* tells all about the workings of this Point Shirley Street Railway gasoline car.
Author's Collection

Michigan

AREA: 58,216 sq. miles
CAPITAL: Lansing
POPULATION (1927): 4,490,000

MICHIGAN, known as the motor state, was not when it came to rail motor cars.

Six lines, three on each peninsula, boasted a grand total of nine cars. The only substantial operation was on the Detroit and Mackinac, which had two large Brill gas-electrics.

These cars were used in coordination with steam-powered passenger trains in a rather complicated schedule pattern. They lasted as long as passenger traffic did, and were sold to a company which had aspirations of becoming a rival to Sperry in the rail detector business. Known as the Tele-detector Co., one car was rebuilt, and subsequently sold to the Union Pacific System, where it is still in operation.

THE ENGINEER appears to be scratching his chin in anticipation of getting this smart Stover buggy on its way. It's the Wisconsin & Michigan's No. 3, snapped at Nathan, Mich.   *John B. Allen Collection*

MAINLINE passenger service on the Detroit and Mackinac was provided by a pair of heavy Brill RPO-Baggage-Passenger motors, of which No. 201 was the first. It wound up on the Union Pacific.
Jim Buckley Collection

Of the rest of the lines, the Boyne City, Gaylord & Alpena had a used Fairbanks-Morse type 24, probably from the St. Joseph Valley line in Indiana, and two of the very rare Bowen cars, secondhand from the Norwalk & Shelby line in Ohio. The only unusual fact about the East Jordan & Southern's lone Brill 55 was that it was secondhand from the Big 4 (NYC), and was later sold to the Albany Northern Railroad in Georgia, and kept the same number on all three lines, M-1200.

The Escabana & Lake Superior's one car was the only Fairbanks-Morse "Railmobile" sold when F-M tried to get back into the light-rail car business in 1933. Certainly their timing was off, as that year was the very bottom of the Depression.

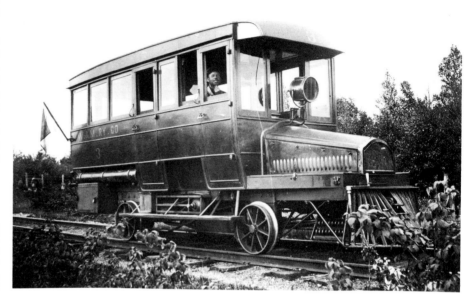

ROAD NOS.	BUILDER	DATE	BLDR. NO.	ENGINE & DRIVE	BODY TYPE	LGTH.	WT.	DISPOSITION	NOTES & COMMENTS
BOYNE CITY, GAYLORD & ALPENA RR, Boyne City to Alpena Jct., Mich. 92.5 mi. (Abandoned)									
1	Glover Brill	1922	21617	36hp gas	10 win. CE bag. 42 pass.		14T	retired 1934	Ex-Norwalk & Shelby 1 (Ohio)
2	Glover Brill	1922	21617	36hp gas	10 win. CE bag. 42 pass.		14T	retired 1934	Ex-Norwalk & Shelby 2 (Ohio)
17	Fair.Morse Brill			F.M. 24 50hp gas	8 win. 4 whl. clere. roof, wood, 35 pass.	34′2″	13T		(Prob. ex-St. Joseph Valley 171, 173 or 174)

ROAD NOS.	BUILDER	DATE	BLDR. NO.	ENGINE & DRIVE	BODY TYPE	LGTH.	WT.	DISPOSITION	NOTES & COMMENTS
DETROIT & MACKINAC RY. CO., Bay City to Cheboygan, Mich., with branches (317.4 miles in operation)									
201	Brill	1928	22749	Hall-Scott 30hp GE	10 win. RPO bag. 38 pass.	75′	59T	sold to Teledetector Co.	Resold by Teledetector to Union Pacific (DC-3)
202	Brill	1928		Hall-Scott 300hp GE	10 win. RPO bag. 38 pass.	75′	58T	sold to Teledetector Co.	Scrapped by Teledetector
EAST JORDAN & SOUTHERN RR CO., East Jordan to Bellaire, Mich. 18.6 mi. (Abandoned)									
M-1200	Brill	1923	22182	Midwest 68hp gas	10 win. bag. 43 pass.	43′	15T	sold to Albany Nor. (Ga.)	Ex-CCC&St.L (Big 4) M-1200, acq. 1931
ESCANABA & LAKE SUPERIOR RR CO., Wells to Channing, Mich., 63.36 mi. (In operation)									
22	Fair.Morse Chrysler	1933		Dodge 65hp gas	3 win. bus 14 pass. bag. sec. in rear	28′	4½T		"Railmobile," had rubber tires
MANISTIQUE & LAKE SUPERIOR RR, Manistique to Shingleton, Mich., 38.7 mi. (Abandoned)									
	Co. Shops Buick	1923		Buick gas	4 door sedan small add. trunk at rear				Small guide wheel ahead of rear wheel, additional wheel under trunk
WISCONSIN & MICHIGAN RR CO., Menominee to Iron Mountain, Mich. 67.2 mi. (Abandoned)									
3	Stover	1906		Stover 30hp gas	5 win. CE, 4 wood, 20 pass. long hood				

Minnesota

AREA: 84,068 sq. miles

CAPITAL: St. Paul

POPULATION (1927): 2,686,000

THE MANY SIMILARITIES of the two most important short lines of Minnesota were such that it is natural to discuss them together, especially since for most of their history they were closely associated, and for a period had common management.

Both of these lines were originally planned as interurban electric lines, a goal which was never achieved. The larger and more prominent of these lines was organized as the Minneapolis, St. Paul, Rochester & Dubuque Electric Traction Co., certainly a name to be reckoned with.

The story of how Col. Marion W. Savage, owner of the famous race horse, *Dan Patch*, conceived of an interurban railway to serve his stock farm as a tourist attraction, and ultimately to be a link in a chain of interurbans that would connect Minneapolis to Chicago, is too well known to need repeating here.

Given the jawbreaker of a name, and serving the attraction that it did, it was soon known as the Dan Patch Line. For financial reasons it was decided to employ gas-electric cars, a relatively new technology at that time, rather than electrify. In order to start operations quickly, some of the Missouri and Kansas Railway's "Strang" cars were purchased.

These cars had been something less than a huge success on the M&K, and they didn't do any better for the Dan Patch, so an order was placed for the cars that were to become intimately associated with the line—the General Electric gas-electric. Although other lines were to have more of these cars, and operate them for a longer period, it was this installation that seems to have caught the public's notice, and for many years these cars were known as the "Dan Patch Cars."

In 1916, *Dan Patch*, the horse, suddenly died. This in turn killed Col. Savage, which in its turn killed Dan Patch, the railroad. The Colonel must have been subsidizing the operation of the railroad, as very soon after his death the railroad went into bankruptcy.

One of the first things done after this occurred was to sell off a large part of the rolling stock, which at the time included 11 gas-electric cars, and about 20 trailers. By 1918 the line had been reorganized as the Minneapolis, Northfield & Southern, a name which certainly more accurately described its operating area.

The line continued to use a few of the gas-electrics up until the time that passenger service was abandoned in 1942. Subsequently the line became part of the Soo Line, and is still in operation.

The other short line was organized in 1908 to build an interurban from Minneapolis to Watertown, South Dakota, and was known as the Electric Short Line. The line was controlled by a prominent Minneapolis family named Luce, and soon the line became known as the Luce Electric.

The company managed only to build as far as Lake Lillian, Minn., and perhaps influenced by the apparent success of the Dan Patch gas-electrics, but more likely for financial reasons, it too was never electrified. A rather interesting roster of gas cars was built up in the next few years.

Included were a McKeen car, a Drake car, and six of the General Electric gas electrics, two of which were demonstrators. In 1924, however, this company was also forced into bankruptcy, and was reorganized as the Minnesota Western Rail*road*, with close ties to the Minneapolis, Northfield & Southern.

This new company, in a rather ill-advised move, pushed the line out another 31 miles to Gluek, Minn. By 1932 the line again was forced to reorganize, to emerge as the Minnesota Western Rail*way*, but still with the common

73

management of the MN&S. In 1940, the only "modern" rail motor car that these lines ever saw was purchased from the Detroit, Toledo & Ironton, built in 1925, when the DT&I was owned by Henry Ford. It was a bit experimental in nature, but it soon caught on fire and was destroyed. In 1956 the Minneapolis and St. Louis Railroad bought the property, which in turn was merged into the Chicago & North Western System. What remains of the road is in the Minneapolis terminal area.

The other short lines of Minnesota were relatively unimportant. The Minnesota Western was owned by the Soo Line for most of its life and the Minnesota International was part of the Northern Pacific.

One other line, the Minneapolis & Northern, was electrified and became the Minneapolis, Anoka & Cuyuna Range. Three of the very small lines that were associated with lumber companies converted old steam coaches to gas drives, in which the engine was slung under the car. Considering Minnesota's severe winters, this idea was not long-lived.

ELECTRIC SHORT LINE also liked GE cars. No. 306 is pictured at the Minneapolis terminal in 1914.
William Hendrick Collection

STRANG CARS with such exotic names as *Ogerita* and *Irene* provided the initial doodlebug service on the Dan Patch Lines (see pages 58-59 of *Interurbans Without Wires*) but soon proved unable to cope. Thereupon the MSPR&D purchased a fleet of General Electric-Wason cars, huge and heavy. Here is No. 9, photographed about 1914.
William Hendrick Collection

ROAD NOS.	BUILDER	DATE	BLDR. NO.	ENGINE & DRIVE	BODY TYPE	LGTH.	WT.	DISPOSITION	NOTES & COMMENTS

AMERICAN TRACTION CO., INTERNATIONAL FALLS, MINN. 6.75 mi. (Abandoned)

ROAD NOS.	BUILDER	DATE	BLDR. NO.	ENGINE & DRIVE	BODY TYPE	LGTH.	WT.	DISPOSITION	NOTES & COMMENTS
(1 car)	St. Louis	1892		Hart-Parr 30hp gas	4 win. OP, 4 whl. st.car, 32 pass.	24'			Ex-Charles City Western (Iowa) No. 5, acquired 5/16

Also reported to have had, in 1918, one other gas car and a storage battery car.

ELECTRIC SHORT LINE RY. CO. (LUCE LINES), Minneapolis to Lake Lillian, Minn., 85 mi. (Reorganized as Minn. Western Ry., 1927)

ROAD NOS.	BUILDER	DATE	BLDR. NO.	ENGINE & DRIVE	BODY TYPE	LGTH.	WT.	DISPOSITION	NOTES & COMMENTS
1	McKeen	3/13	127	McKeen 200hp gas-mech.	14 win. CE bag. 84 pass.	70'	38½T	sold	Ex-Soo Line No. 1, acq. 1920
300	Gen. Elect. Wason	1/12	3703 7317	GE GM16C1, 275hp GE	8 win. CE bag. 45 pass.	50'	38T		Ex-Gen. Elect. demo No. 3, acq. 1914
302	Gen. Elect. Barney & Smith	6/14	3777	GE GM16C1, 275hp GE	12 win. wood, bag. 40 pass. clere. roof	65'	60½T		Ex-Gen. Elect. demo No. 1 (Del. & Hudson No. 1000) rebuilt, orig. built 1905
304	St. Louis Drake	5/13	1004	Drake 90hp gas-elect.	12 win. wood, bag. 44 pass.	56'	32½T		Ex-Missouri, Okla. & Gulf No. 104, wrecked, rebuilt by St. Louis Car
306	Gen. Elect. Wason	8/14	3778 15165	GE GM16C3, 175hp GE	17 win. OP bag. pass.	70'	52T	to Minn. West No. 30	
308	Gen. Elect. Wason	3/15	3779 15165	GE GM16C3, 175hp GE	17 win. OP bag. pass.	70'	52T	to Minn. West No. 32	
310	Gen. Elect. Wason	4/13	3745 12225	GE GM16C1, 175hp GE	17 win. OP bag. pass.	70'	50T		Ex-Gen. Elect. demo No. 24
312	Gen. Elect. Wason	8/16	3792 17965	GE GM16C10, 175hp GE	14 win. bag. 62 pass. rear entr.	70'	52T	sold, Mid. Valley No. 3, 1917	

MINNEAPOLIS, NORTHFIELD & SOUTHERN RY., Minneapolis to Northfield, Minn., 45.2 mi.
Successor to the Minneapolis, St. Paul, Rochester & Dubuque Electric Traction Co. (Dan Patch Lines), (Merged into Soo Line RR)

ROAD NOS.	BUILDER	DATE	BLDR. NO.	ENGINE & DRIVE	BODY TYPE	LGTH.	WT.	DISPOSITION	NOTES & COMMENTS
12	Gen. Elect. Wason	1/16	3791 17275	GE GM16C9 175hp GE	17 win. OP bag. 68 pass.	70'	61T	retired 1942	Ex-Florida East Coast Ry. No. 200, acq. 1919
13	Gen. Elect. Wason	7/15	3789 16500	GE GM16C5 175hp GE	17 win. OP bag. 68 pass.	70'	61T	renumbered 16, 1920	Ex-Dan Patch 13
14	Gen. Elect. Wason	8/15	3790 16500	GE GM16C5 175hp GE	17 win. OP bag. 68 pass.	70'	61T	retired 1942	Ex-Dan Patch 14
15	Gen. Elect. Brill	5/13	3764 17261	GE GM16C1 175hp GE	20 win. clere. roof, 48 pass.	63'	50½T	scrapped 1932	Ex-Dan Patch 15. Rebuild of Strang car "Marion."
16	Gen. Elect. Wason	7/15	3789 16500	GE GM16C5 175hp GE	17 win. OP bag. 68 pass.	70'	61T	retired 1939	Ex-No. 13
55	Wason	6/12	12325	Trailer	19 win. OP 72 pass.	48'6"	22T	retired 1942	Ex-Dan Patch No. 55
59	Wason	4/13	13500	Trailer	19 win. OP 72 pass.	48'6"	22T	retired 1942	Ex-Dan Patch No. 59
A1	Co. Shops White	1918		White 4 cyl. gas	bus body, 31 pass.	20'		sold 1922	

MINNEAPOLIS, ST. PAUL, ROCHESTER & DUBUQUE ELECTRIC TRACTION CO., Minneapolis to Northfield, Minn., 45.2 mi.
(Reorganized as Minn. Northfield & Southern Ry., 1918)

ROAD NOS.	BUILDER	DATE	BLDR. NO.	ENGINE & DRIVE	BODY TYPE	LGTH.	WT.	DISPOSITION	NOTES & COMMENTS
1	Strang Brill	1906 1907	14184 17301	Strang 100hp gas-elect.	6 win. CE, OP wood. clere. roof, bag. 24 pass.	41' 6¼"		retired 1914	Ex-Mo. Kan. "Ogerita," acq. 1908
2	Strang Brill	1908	15652	Strang 150hp gas-elect.	19 win. OP clere. roof 38 pass.	62'8"	57T	rebuilt 5/13 to "Marion" No. 15	Ex-Mo. & Kan., "Irene," acq. 1910
Rosamond	Strang Brill	1907 1910	15771 17301	Strang 150hp gas-elect.	19 win.			burned or retired 1914	Acq. 1910
3	Gen. Elect. Wason	12/10	3706	GE GM10A1 90hp GE	10 win. bag. 44 pass.	49'	34½T	burned 11/19/14	Ex-Gen. Elect. demo 2, reno. 7, acq. 1910
4	Gen. Elect. Wason	5/11	3709 10270	GE GM16A1 175hp GE	12 win. CE bag. 47 pass.	58'	40½T	sold, Okmul. Nor. 1916	
5	Gen. Elect. Wason	5/11	3710 10270	GE GM16A1 175hp GE	12 win. CE bag. 47 pass.	58'	40½T	sold, Okmul. Nor. 1916	Resold by ON to Jonesboro, Lake City & East. 110, 1924, to SL-SF (sec. 2107, 1925)

ROAD NOS.	BUILDER	DATE	BLDR. NO.	ENGINE & DRIVE	BODY TYPE	LGTH.	WT.	DISPOSITION	NOTES & COMMENTS
6	Gen. Elect. Wason	2/11	3704 9780	GE GM10B2 125hp GE	? win. rear ent. bag. 88 pass.	57'	39T	sold, Warren & Ouachita Ry.	W&OV No. 4, rebuilt to trailer
7	Gen. Elect. Wason	7/11	3708 9930	GE GM16A1 175hp GE	? win. rear ent. bag. 75 pass.	57'	40T	wrecked 1914	After collision, rebuilt to RPO-Bag. trailer No. 200
8	Gen. Elect. Wason	3/12	3720 9781	GE GM16B 175hp GE	15 win. OP bag. 88 pass.	67'	45T	sold, Spokane, Port. & Seattle	SP&S No. 1102, sold 4/17, resold to W&OV
9	Gen. Elect. Wason	5/12	3735 12050	GE GM16A5 175hp GE	17 win. OP bag. 91 pass.	70'	49T	sold, Visalia El. No. 450, 1916	Resold to Nor. West Pac. No. 902, 6/21, SP Ry (San Fran.-Oak. Bay Bridge, 12/39) scrap. 1948
10	Gen. Elect. Wason	5/12	3736 12050	GE GM16A5 175hp GE	17 win. OP bag. 91 pass.	70'	49T	sold, Okla. New Mex. & Pacific	
11	Gen. Elect. Wason	8/13	3766 13700	GE GM16C1 175hp GE	17 win. OP bag. 91 pass.	70'	49T	sold, San Diego Sou. East, 12/16	San Diego & Sou. Eastern and San Diego, Arizona & Eastern No. 41, scrapped 1939
12	Gen. Elect. Wason	8/13	3767 13700	GE GM16C1 175hp GE	17 win. OP bag. 91 pass.	70'	49T	sold, San Diego Sou. East, 12/16	SD&SE, SDA&E No. 42, scrapped 1939
13	Gen. Elect. Wason	7/15	3789 16500	GE GM16C5 175hp GE	17 win. OP bag. 69 pass.	70'	51T	to Minn. Norfld. & Sou. 16, 1918	Scrapped 1939
14	Gen. Elect. Wason	8/15	3790 16500	GE GM16C5 175hp GE	17 win. OP bag. 69 pass.	70'	51T	to MN&S, 14 1918	Scrapped 1942
15	Gen. Elect. Brill	5/13	3764 17261	GE GM16C1 175hp GE	19 win. OP 38 pass.	62'8"	50½T	to MN&S No. 15 1918	Ex-Strang car "Irene" (No. 2) rebuilt and renamed "Marion," retired 1932
50 to 53				trailers					Ex-New York City El cars
54-55	Wason	6/12	12335	trailers	19 win. OP 104 pass.	48'6"	22T	54 sold Nev. Nor. 1916	55 to MN&S 55, 1918
56 to 59	Wason	4/13	13500	trailers	19 win OP 104 pass.	48'6"	22T	56 burned 11/14, 59 to MN&S 1918	
60 to 62	Wason	5/13	13500	trailers	19 win. OP 104 pass.	48'6"	22T	62 burned 11/14, 60-62 sold 1918	
63 to 74	Brill	7/15	19602	trailers	19 win. OP 104 pass.	57'4"		sold 1918	
200	Co. Shops Wason	1914 7/11	9930		trailer RPO-baggage	57'			Ex-Motor No. 7 (wrecked and rebuilt 1914)

MINNESOTA WESTERN RY. CO., Minneapolis to Gluek, Minn., 115 mi. successor to the Electric Short Line Ry. Co. Merged into Minn. & St. Louis Ry., to Chi. Norwest Syst. (44 miles in operation, sold to Burlington Northern)

ROAD NOS.	BUILDER	DATE	BLDR. NO.	ENGINE & DRIVE	BODY TYPE	LGTH.	WT.	DISPOSITION	NOTES & COMMENTS
30	Gen. Elect. Wason	8/14	3778 15165	GE GM16C3 175hp GE	17 win. OP bag. pass.	70'	52T	retired 1936	Ex-Elect. Short Line 306
32	Gen. Elect. Wason	3/15	3779 15165	GE GM16C3 175hp GE	17 win. OP bag. pass.	70'	52T	retired 1936	Ex-Elect. Short Line 308
34	McKeen	3/13	127	McKeen 200hp gas-mech.	14 win. CE bag. 84 pass.	70'	38½T	sold, CGW ?	Ex-Elect. Short Line 1, ex-ex-Soo Line No. 1
36	Gen. Elect. Wason	5/13	3743 12225	GE GM16C1 175hp GE	12 win. OP RPO bag. pass.	70'	49T	retired 1942	Ex-Okla. Kan. & Mo. 106, ex-ex-Chi. Peoria & St. Louis 103, acq. 1924
38	Gen. Elect. Wason	4/13	3746 12226	GE GM16C1 175hp GE	12 win. OP RPO bag. pass.	70'	49T	retired 1942	Ex-Okla. Kan. & Mo. 107, ex-ex-CP&SL 102, acq. 1924
39	Pullman	1925	4926	(2) Hall-Scott 150hp GE	12 win. RPO bag. 48 pass. clere. roof	72'6"	66T	burned	Ex-Detroit, Toledo & Ironton No. 36, acquired 1940

MINNEAPOLIS & NORTHERN RY. CO., Minneapolis to Anoka, Minn. (Became Minn. Anoka & Cuyuna Range (elect.) (Abandoned)

ROAD NOS.	BUILDER	DATE	BLDR. NO.	ENGINE & DRIVE	BODY TYPE	LGTH.	WT.	DISPOSITION	NOTES & COMMENTS
Minneapolis	McKeen	1913	128	McKeen 200hp gas-mech.	13 win. CE bag. 50 pass.	55'	35T	repossessed, to Un. Pac. M-27	
Anoka	McKeen	1913	127	McKeen 200hp gas-mech.	13 win. CE bag. 50 pass.	55'	35T	repossessed, to U.P. M-28	
(1 car)	McKeen	7/13		McKeen 200hp gas-mech.	4 win. OP bag. freight	49'	28T	repossessed	

ROAD NOS.	BUILDER	DATE	BLDR. NO.	ENGINE & DRIVE	BODY TYPE	LGTH.	WT.	DISPOSITION	NOTES & COMMENTS
MINNEAPOLIS, RED LAKE & MANITOBA RY. CO., Bemidji to Redby, Minn., 32.99 mi. (Abandoned)									
M-1	Railway Motors	1925		(2) Cont. 104hp gas	15 win. OP bag. 40 pass. wood, clere. roof	60'	35T		Ex-steam coach
MINNESOTA, DAKOTA & WESTERN RY. CO., International Falls to Loman, Minn., 20.43 mi. (Abandoned)									
1	Oneida	1923		(2) Cont. 6B 70hp gas	16 win. wood, 38 pass. OP clere. roof	68'	37½T		Ex-steam coach, secondhand
2	Oneida	1924		(2) Cont. 6B 70hp gas	16 win. wood, 38 pass. OP clere. roof	68'	37½T		
8	Fairmont			Fairmont gas	3 win. 4 whl. bag. pass.		7T		
9	Fairmont			Fairmont gas	3 win. 4 whl. bag. pass.		7T		
M-8				trailer					
MINNESOTA & INTERNATIONAL RY. CO., Brainerd to International Falls, Minn., 202 mi. (Merged into Nor. Pacific)									
M-1	Stand. Steel EMC	1/29	328 344	Winton 120 275hp GE	2 win. RPO bag.	70'	55T	to Nor. Pac. sec. B-6	
MINNESOTA & NORTHWESTERN ELECTRIC RY. CO., Thief River Falls to Goodridge, Minn., 18.67 mi. (Merged into Soo Line)									
101	Gen. Elect. Wason	11/13	3776	GE GM16C3 175hp GE	17 win. OP bag. 91 pass.	70'	49T	sold 12/40 Steel Prod. Co.	Built for Elect. Short Line, not used.
VIRGINIA & RAINY LAKE RY., Virginia, Minn. (Abandoned)									
(1 car)	Oneida	1924		Cont. 45hp gas	14 pass.	14'	3½T		

LAST RAILCAR acquisition by the Minnesota Western was Pullman No. 39, purchased in 1940 from the DT&I. *Al Barker Collection*

ZEBRA STRIPES adorned General Electric car 101 of the Minnesota & Northwestern. It was built for the Electric Short Line. *Author's Collection*

Mississippi

AREA: 47,716 sq. miles
CAPITAL: Jackson
POPULATION (1927): 1,290,000

IT MIGHT BE NOTED that we have not included the Columbus & Greenville Railroad in our rosters of short lines, as it long has been a Class I railroad back in the days when a million dollars in revenue qualified a line as such.

This despite the fact that it has been a member of the Short Line Association,

and the general operation of the line was more in the short line tradition. However for those who are interested its roster appears in our book *Doodlebug Country*.

Other than the cars on the C&G, the rail motor cars in Mississippi all were small. Not an electric drive was to be found, and the incidence of converted buses and other extremely lightweight equipment was high.

The most unusual piece of equipment was car No. M-4 of the Fernwood, Columbia & Gulf. This home-built unit,

now owned by a well-known author o. rail lines of the South, Louis Saillard was an almost exact copy of a Kalama zoo-built car that the FC&G had gotte in 1936. If anything the M-4 looks bette built than that predecessor, the M-3, an the M-4 is in operation!

Recently, Mississippi has become th home base for a number of "new" shor lines, mostly remnants of various Ill nois Central Gulf Lines. The only re maining "old" short line is the Missis sippi & Skuna Valley, the subsidiary of a large lumber company.

ZIPPY FRONT lends glamor to rail-bus M-3 of the Fernwood, Columbia & Gulf, a Kalamazoo product photographed at Columbia, Miss., in 1952.
M.H. Ferrell,
Louis A. Marre Collection

KALAMAZOO bus also operated on the Mississippi & Skuna Valley, shown here in a 1937 view.
Author's Collection

HIGHWAY BUS built by Mack was adapted for rail use by the Okalona, Houston & Calhoun City. Data indicates that it was secondhand from the St. Louis & Hannibal.
Author's Collection

ROAD NOS.	BUILDER	DATE	BLDR. NO.	ENGINE & DRIVE	BODY TYPE	LGTH.	WT.	DISPOSITION	NOTES & COMMENTS
BATESVILLE & SOUTHWESTERN RR, Batesville to Crowder, Miss., 16.9 mi. (Abandoned 1931)									
01	Ford	1924		Ford T 4 cyl. gas	Mod. T truck 20 pass. bus	24'	3T		
02 Darnell	Weller Kissel	1926		Kissel 50hp gas	bus body, 50 pass.		10T	burned	
DE KALB & WESTERN RR CO., De Kalb to Electric Mills, Miss., 13 mi. (Abandoned)									
(1 car)	Brill White	1922	21367	White 45 40hp gas	8 win. CE, 4 whl. lead truck, bag. 41 pass.	30'11"	10T		Ex-Aberdeen & Rockfish 101, ex- ex-Union Trans. (NJ) Model 43
FERNWOOD, COLUMBIA & GULF RR, Fernwood to Columbia, 41.44 mi. (Merged into Ill. Cen. Gulf)									
M-1	Brill	1929	22829	Brill 40hp gas	30 pass.	22'11"	6½T		Model 30
M-3	Kalamazoo	1936	C-58373	Ford V-8 85hp gas	6 win. bag. 17 pass.	27'6"	6½T		
M-4	Co. Shops	1937		Ford V-8 85hp gas	6 win. bag. 17 pass.	27'6"	6½T		Owned by Lewis Saillard, on Reader RR

KOSIUSKO & SOUTHEASTERN RR CO., Kosiusco to Zama, Miss., 16.3 mi. (Abandoned)

1928 ''Equipment Register'' lists three railcars.

MOTOR AND TRAILER built by Four Wheel Drive burnished the rails of the Mississippi Central.
Charles P. Harrington

79

ROAD NOS.	BUILDER	DATE	BLDR. NO.	ENGINE & DRIVE	BODY TYPE	LGTH.	WT.	DISPOSITION	NOTES & COMMENTS
LIBERTY-WHITE RR, McComb to Tylertown, Miss., 49 mi. (Abandoned 1920)									
100	Fair. Morse	1910		Fair. Morse 50hp gas	8 win. OP, wood, clere. roof, bag. 35 pass.	34' 2"	13T		4 wheel, pulled 4 wheel home-buil trailer
MISSISSIPPI & ALABAMA RR, Leakesville, Miss. to Vinegar Bend, Ala., 17.2 mi. (Abandoned)									
303	Ford Co. Shops			Ford Model A gas	Ford chassis, 8 win. home-built body				
MISSISSIPPI & SKUNA VALLEY RR, Bruce to Bruce Jct., Miss. 21 mi. (In operation)									
2	Kalamazoo	abt. 1935		Ford V-8 85hp gas	6 win. rear bag. 28 pass.				
4	Superior International	1948		International gas-mech.	10 win. hood, front school bus, mail sect.	27' 8"			
MISSISSIPPI CENTRAL RR CO., Natchez to Hattiesburg, Miss., 150.99 mi. (Merged into Ill. Cen. Gulf)									
1	Fair. Morse	1909		Fair. Morse 50hp gas	8 win. OP, clere. roof, 4 whl. bag. 35 pass.	35'	13T	retired by 1912	
300	Four Wheel Drive Boston	1923		Wisc. 6 cyl. 94hp gas	6 win. 4 whl. bag. 24 pass.	25' 5"	9T	scrapped 1945	
400	Boston	1923		Trailer	10 win. 4 whl. 34 pass.	25' 5"	8T	scrapped 1945	
OKALONA, HOUSTON & CALHOUN CITY RR, Okalona to Calhoun City, Miss. 38 mi. (Abandoned)									
139	Mack			Mack AD gas	5 win. hood type bus, 4 whl. lead truck				Prob. ex-St. Louis & Hannibal

Missouri

AREA: 69,686 sq. miles
CAPITAL: Jefferson City
POPULATION (1927): 3,510,000

MOST OF the short lines of Missouri were concentrated in the southeast corner of the state. This area, along with the adjacent northeast corner of Arkansas, was a very active scene of rail motor car operation during the 1920s and 1930s.

In addition to short line activity, the Cotton Belt and Frisco operated numerous, if short, branch line runs, most of them equipped with big General Electric

MARGINAL PHOTO of this Southwest Missouri Railroad railbus must be included because of its rarity. This is one of two such units crafted in company shops for service after cessation of electric interurban service. *Earl E. McMechan Collection*

gas-electric cars. Most of the cars on the short lines were small, however.

The Butler County, which became part of the Frisco, had a secondhand McKeen car, which was converted to a trailer, and the Deering and Southwestern had the one-of-a-kind Cincinnati Car Co. railcar, based on the Cincinnati lightweight streetcar body. When this line became part of the Cotton Belt, the car became Cotton Belt No. 22, and eventually wound up on the Paris & Mt. Pleasant line in Texas.

The only short line of any consequence outside of this area was the St. Louis & Hannibal, which was owned by the Ringling Circus interests. The SL&H operated three rail buses built with Mack chassis. One of these eventually migrated to another Ringling road, the White Sulphur Springs and Yellowstone Park railroad in Montana.

Two other cars of some interest were a pair of home-built rail buses built by the Southwest Missouri Interurban. When electric interurban service ceased, the rail buses were used for a short time on a segment of the line.

PORTLY GENTLEMAN is not trying to push Stover car No. 1 of the Cape Girardeau & Chester (later the CG Northern). He's just holding on to the tailgate chain.
Author's Collection

SUPPORT POLE almost spoils picture of St. Louis & Hannibal homebuilt railbus No. 55, but the rakish car architecture is too good to leave out. Company emblem also is too good to miss.
Jim Buckley Collection

ROAD NOS.	BUILDER	DATE	BLDR. NO.	ENGINE & DRIVE	BODY TYPE	LGTH.	WT.	DISPOSITION	NOTES & COMMENTS
BUTLER COUNTY RR CO., Poplar Bluff, Mo. to Tipparary, Ark., 50.93 mi. (Merged into SL-SF, 9/27)									
10	McKeen	1914		McKeen 200hp gas-mech.	11 win. CE bag. 55 pass.	55'	30T	rblt. to coach, 1924, length 50'	Renumbered to 33, was secondhand, possibly Jamestown, Chat. & Lake Erie. Frisco No. 33.
15	Laconia Unit	1919		Unit steam	11 win. bag. 46 pass.	50' 6"		re-eng. with a Buda eng. 1925	Re-eng. by Edwards, renumbered 25, became No. 3002 on the Frisco
CAPE GIRARDEAU NORTHERN RY., Ancell to Farmington, Mo. and branches 104.2 mi. (Largely abandoned by 1924, Perryville to Perryville Jct. until '30s)									
1	Stover			Stover 30hp gas	5 win. CE, 4 whl. 15 pass. long hood, wooden				Orig. owned by predecessor co., Cape Girardeau & Salem

Moody's Steam Railroads (1928) lists 3 motor passenger cars and 2 motor car trailers.

DEERING & SOUTHWESTERN RR CO., Caruthersville to Hornersville, Mo., 31 mi. (Merged into Cotton Belt)									
82	Cincinnati Car	1922	2610	International gas	10 win. "Cinn. Lt. Wt. St.Car" body, 40 pass.	39' 6"		to SSW No. 22	Sold by SSW to Paris & Mt. Pleasant No. 22

HOMELY is the word for this Shelby
County car, but it must have done its
job. The camera captured it at Shel-
bina, Mo., in 1938.
Paul Stringham,
R.R. Wallin Collection

SLEEK is a good word to descri
St. Louis & Hannibal motor coa
52, a Mack gas-mechanical with
nifty job of lettering and striping.

ROAD NOS.	BUILDER	DATE	BLDR. NO.	ENGINE & DRIVE	BODY TYPE	LGTH.	WT.	DISPOSITION	NOTES & COMMENTS
MISSISSIPPI RIVER & BONNE TERRE RY., Riverside to Doe Run, Mo., 72.69 mi. (Abandoned)									
50	Pierce-Arrow	1922		Pierce 6 cyl. 66hp gas	4 door sedan, 4 whl. lead truck	146" wheel base			
100	Buick	1919		Buick 6 cyl. gas	4 door open touring car, 4 whl. lead trk.				
SALEM, WINONA & SOUTHERN RR CO., Angeline to Winona, Mo., 21.5 mi. (Abandoned 1927)									
(1 car)	Ford	1926		Ford T gas	mail & exp. truck				
MISSOURI SOUTHERN RR CO., Leeper to Bunker, Mo., 54.22 mi. (Abandoned)									
M-100	Brill	1924	22113	Midwest 68hp gas	10 win. bag. 38 pass.	43'	14½T	sold, Nat. de Mexico, 1941	
CASSVILLE & EXETER RY., Cassville to Exeter, Mo. 5 mi. (Abandoned)									
200	Federal			Battery El.	8 win. bag. pass. OP	38' 11"		body sold, used as antique shop	Probably used as a trailer only. Ex-Kan. City and Memphis No. 200 (Ark.)
2124	St. Louis EMC	11/28 11/33	1474 314 & 507	(2) Winton 148 200hp GE	RPO baggage	74'	73½T	returned to SL-SF ?	Ex-SL-SF 2124, wreck and rebuilt, used for a short time in 1953 (too heavy)

ROAD NOS.	BUILDER	DATE	BLDR. NO.	ENGINE & DRIVE	BODY TYPE	LGTH.	WT.	DISPOSITION	NOTES & COMMENTS
ST. LOUIS & HANNIBAL RR CO., Hannibal to Gilmore, Mo., 85.6 mi. (Abandoned 1944)									
40		1925		gas-mech.	bag. pass.			gone by 1929	
52	Mack	1930		Mack gas-mech.	7 win. hood type bus, 4 whl. lead truck			see notes	Of the three Mack buses, one was rebuilt to No. 55, one went to the White Sulphur Springs and Yellowstone Park, another ''Ringling Road'' (Mont.) and the last probably to the Oklahoma, Houston & Calhoun City (Miss.)
53	Mack	1930		Mack gas-mech.	7 win. hood type bus, 4 whl. lead truck			see notes	
54	Mack	1930		Mack gas-mech.	7 win. hood type bus, 4 whl. lead truck			see notes	
55	Co. Shops			Mack gas-mech.	5 win. bag. 12 pass. 4 whl. lead truck				
SHELBY COUNTY RY., Shelbina to Shelbyville, Mo., 9 mi. (Abandoned)									
(1 car)	White Co. Shops			White 4 cyl. 40hp gas	5 win. wood bag. 12 pass. 4 whl. lead trk.				
SOUTHWEST MISSOURI RR, Baxter Springs, Kan. to Picher, Okla. 7 miles after cessation of elect. service (mostly in Mo.) 1938 (Abandoned)									
(2 units)	Co. Shops	1938			5 win. 4 whl. bus	abt. 15'			

Montana

AREA: 147,138 sq. miles
CAPITAL: Helena
POPULATION (1927): 714,000

JUST ABOUT the only unusual thing that occurs to me about Montana is that all of the rail motor cars used in that state (all four of them) were secondhand. About the only other bit of information that I can add is that the Billings Traction Co. had six battery cars at one time.

MONTANA WESTERN No. 31 was an early St. Louis-EMC motor, acquired secondhand from the Great Northern and eventually donated to the Mid-Continent Railway Museum in Wisconsin.
Harold K. Vollrath Collection

WIDE-OPEN SPACES stretch out behind this down-at-the-heels Mack railbus of the White Sulphur Springs & Yellowstone Park. Note steering wheel still in place.

Author's Collection

ROAD NOS.	BUILDER	DATE	BLDR. NO.	ENGINE & DRIVE	BODY TYPE	LGTH.	WT.	DISPOSITION	NOTES & COMMENTS
MONTANA WESTERN RY. CO., Valier to Conrad, Mont., 20.13 mi. (Abandoned)									
20	White Eklund	1921		White 4 cyl. 39hp gas	7 win. CE 36 pass. 4 whl. lead truck		11½T		Ex-Great Nor. 2307, acq. 1929
31	St. Louis EMC	6/25	1368C 130	Winton 106 175hp GE	12 win. DE bag. 52 pass.	59'	36T	traded back to GN	Ex-GN 2313, acq. 1/40. GN donated car to Mid-Cont. Ry. Mus. 8/66
MONTANA, WYOMING & SOUTHERN RY. CO., Bridger to Washoe, Mont., 23.65 mi. (Abandoned)									
Bear Creek	McKeen	1910		McKeen 200hp gas-mech.	9 win. CE bag. 75 pass.	55'	30T		Ex-Charles City Western, acquired 1917
WHITE SULPHUR SPRINGS & YELLOWSTONE PARK RY., White Sulphur Springs to Ringling, Mont., 23 mi. (Abandoned) (Ringling Road)									
10	Mack	1930		Mack AD gas	4 win. 4 whl. lead truck, bus body				Ex-St. Louis & Hannibal

Nebraska

AREA: 77,217 sq. miles
CAPITAL: Lincoln
POPULATION (1927): 1,396,000

NEBRASKA WAS in the very heart of "doodlebug country," but surprisingly was almost completely devoid of short lines. The only one that ever operated—the Sioux City, Crystal Lake & Homer—started out using some Omaha Line tracks and operated what apparently was the only car produced by a short-lived organization known as Prouty-Pierce.

This company built a rather large interurbanish-looking car using a St. Louis carbody, with a drive of its own devising, which in common with many such experimental cars was a mechanical failure.

After a reorganization, a couple of small four-wheeled gas cars with small four-cylinder engines were tried. These were not much more satisfactory, and after a time the line was taken over by the local transit line in Sioux City and electrified. Thus ended (in 1910) Nebraska's only short line railroad.

ROAD NOS.	BUILDER	DATE	BLDR. NO.	ENGINE & DRIVE	BODY TYPE	LGTH.	WT.	DISPOSITION	NOTES & COMMENTS
SIOUX CITY, CRYSTAL LAKE & HOMER RY., Sou. Sioux City to Dakota City, Nebr., 5½ mi. (road electrified 1910) (Abandoned)									
(1 car)	Prouty-Pierce St. Louis	1904	482	gas, orig. eng. replaced 11/04, 120hp	16 win. clere. roof, wood int. type car, 42 pass.			demotorized, used as trailer	
(2 cars)	P.H. Batten & Co.	1907		Whiting 4 cyl. gas	4 whl. wood st.car, 30 pass.	26'	10T		Brill trucks

Nevada

AREA: 110,540 sq. miles
CAPITAL: Carson City
POPULATION (1927): 77,000

FOR A STATE rather lacking in railroad mileage and in population, at least during the railcar era, Nevada was well supplied with short lines, most of which had rail motor cars in operation, both standard gauge and narrow.

A goodly variety of builders was represented: Meister, Northwestern, Fairbanks-Morse, Hall-Scott, McKeen, Brookville, White, and Brill, plus some home-built units.

An Electro-Motive St. Louis-built car also operated in the state on the California-based Tonopah & Tidewater, and the Nevada Northern—which didn't have any motors—had some ex-Dan Patch motor trailers built by Wason.

It might be noted that the Virginia & Truckee's McKeen was the last "pure" McKeen to operate; all the other McKeens that operated longer than the V&T's car had been converted to electric drives. The last Hall-Scott car in existence came from the Nevada Copper Belt Railway.

The only short line still hanging on is the Nevada Northern, but its fate depends on a proposed tourist operation, and on the possibility of a large coal-burning power plant that might be built in the Ely area.

BELIEVE IT OR NOT, there are two complete arch-bar trucks under Meister car 23 of the Eureka Nevada. The diminutive railcritter suns itself at the Southern Pacific depot in Palisade, Nev. *Author's Collection*

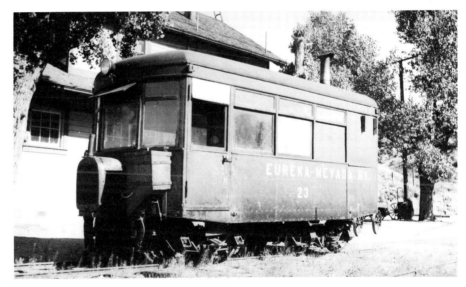

HALL-SCOTT motor 21 of the Nevada Copper Belt is now at the Western Railway Museum at Rio Vista Junction, Calif. A color photo of this car appears on the back dust jacket of *Interurbans Without Wires*. *Author's Collection*

PINT-SIZED Fairbanks-Morse "streetcar" motor was taken out for a jaunt on the Nevada Copper Belt one fine day, and these scenic shots were the result.
Both: Randolph Brandt Collection

BOTH MEISTER cars pause during an inspection trip on the Nevada, California & Oregon shortly after the cars were delivered in 1923.
Randolph Brandt Collection

FABLED Virginia & Truckee ran this contrast in railcars: ponderous knife-nosed McKeen 22 and White Thomson-Graf-Elder 99, both shown at the V&T depot in Carson City. The 99 was photographed on June 6, 1938. *Author's Collection, Tom Gray*

ROAD NOS.	BUILDER	DATE	BLDR. NO.	ENGINE & DRIVE	BODY TYPE	LGTH.	WT.	DISPOSITION	NOTES & COMMENTS
EUREKA NEVADA RY. CO. (3 ft. gauge) Palisade to Eureka, Nev., 84.6 mi. (Abandoned)									
21	Meister			gas	6 win. CE 12 pass.	abt. 30'			Baggage section added to rear in later years, 2 arch bar trucks
22	Northwestern Car			Ford 4 gas	2 win. 4 whl. wood 4 pass.	abt. 15'			
23	Meister			Ford 4 gas	4 win. rear bag. 8 pass.	abt. 25'			2 arch bar trucks
NEVADA-CALIFORNIA-OREGON RY., Reno, Nev. to Lakeview, Ore., 236 mi. (3 ft. gauge) (Merged into Southern Pacific; part sold to WP)									
15 Helen		2/17		gas	stretch open touring car				
16 Martha				gas	stretch open touring car				

ROAD NOS.	BUILDER	DATE	BLDR. NO.	ENGINE & DRIVE	BODY TYPE	LGTH.	WT.	DISPOSITION	NOTES & COMMENTS
101	Meister	1923		White 4 cyl. gas	8 win. CE, 4 whl. lead truck, 22 pass. eng. in rear	32'	7½T	returned to builder	
102	Meister	1923		White 4 cyl. gas	8 win. CE, 4 whl. lead truck, 22 pass. eng. in rear	32'	7½T	returned to builder	

NEVADA CENTRAL RR CO., Battle Mountain to Austin, Nev. 93.2 mi. (3 ft. gauge) (Abandoned)

ROAD NOS.	BUILDER	DATE	BLDR. NO.	ENGINE & DRIVE	BODY TYPE	LGTH.	WT.	DISPOSITION	NOTES & COMMENTS
3	Co. Shops ?			Ford 4 cyl. gas	3 win. 4 whl. bag.				May have come from the Nevada Short Line
104	Co. Shops ?			gas	10 win. CE, pass. 4 whl. rear bag. sec.				5 window front
105	Meister			Buda 60hp gas	3 win., bag. 20 pass., 4 whl. lead truck, rear bag. sect.				
106	Meister			Buda 60hp gas	3 win., bag. 20 pass., 4 whl. lead truck, rear bag. sect.				

NEVADA COPPER BELT RR CO., Thompson to Ludwig, Nev., 39.93 mi. (Abandoned)

ROAD NOS.	BUILDER	DATE	BLDR. NO.	ENGINE & DRIVE	BODY TYPE	LGTH.	WT.	DISPOSITION	NOTES & COMMENTS
20	Fair. Morse			Fair. Morse 50hp gas	8 win. clere. roof, 4 whl. wood, bag. 35 pass.	34' 2"	12½T	burned	
21	Hall-Scott Holman	1910	5	Hall-Scott 100hp gas	12 win. wood, bag. 69 pass.			now at Rio Vista Ry. Mus.	
22	Hall-Scott	1913	13	Hall-Scott 150hp gas	13 win. bag. pass.			scrapped	Ex-Salt Lake & Utah No. 503

SILVER PEAK RY., Silver Peak, Nev.

ROAD NOS.	BUILDER	DATE	BLDR. NO.	ENGINE & DRIVE	BODY TYPE	LGTH.	WT.	DISPOSITION	NOTES & COMMENTS
12 Mary	McKeen	1908		McKeen 200hp gas-mech.	9 win. CE bag. pass.	55'	34T	sold to the Red River Lbr. Co. (Cal.)	

TONOPAH & GOLDFIELD RR CO., Mina to Goldfield, Nev., 102.99 mi. (Abandoned)

ROAD NOS.	BUILDER	DATE	BLDR. NO.	ENGINE & DRIVE	BODY TYPE	LGTH.	WT.	DISPOSITION	NOTES & COMMENTS
1	Ford Brookfield			Ford gas	pickup truck body				
99	White Thom. Graf-Edler	1921		White 4 cyl gas	7 win. CE bag. 16 pass. 4 whl. lead truck			sold 1926 to Va. & Truckee	V&T No. 99
M-102	Brill	1927	22438	Brill 250 250hp GE	4 win. RPO-bag. 18 pass.	60'	46T	scrapped	Ex-Wheeling & Lake Erie M-102, acq. 8/35
M-103	Brill	1927	22438	Brill 250 250hp GE	4 win. RPO-bag. 18 pass.	60'	46T	scrapped	Ex-Wheeling & Lake Erie M-103, acq. 10/34

VIRGINIA & TRUCKEE RY., Reno to Virginia City, Nev. 67.48 mi. (Abandoned 1950)

ROAD NOS.	BUILDER	DATE	BLDR. NO.	ENGINE & DRIVE	BODY TYPE	LGTH.	WT.	DISPOSITION	NOTES & COMMENTS
22	McKeen	1910		McKeen 200hp gas-mech.	11 win. CE RPO bag. 20 pass.	70'	34T	scrapped	Had extra bag sect. & door at rear, body still in use as storage bldg.
23	White Thom. Graf-Edler	1917		White 4 cyl. gas	4 door open bus body				
99	White Thom. Graf-Edler	1921		White 4 cyl. gas	7 win. CE, bag. 16 pass. 4 whl. lead truck, rear bag.			retired 1941	Ex-Tonopah & Goldfield No. 99, acq. 1926

New Hampshire

AREA: 9,304 sq. miles
CAPITAL: Concord
POPULATION (1927): 455,000

IN A SOMEWHAT strange turn-about, the only short lines in New Hampshire that had rail motor cars weren't formed until recent times, both utilizing abandoned branches of the Boston & Maine.

The Claremont & Concord wasn't organized until 1954, and used two ex-Boston & Maine cars, as well as ex-B&M track.

The Wolfboro Railway also used discarded B&M track, and operated on it that well-traveled ex-Grasse Valley, ex-ex-Lincoln, Oxford & Southern car that eventually wound up at the Strasburg Railway Museum. This operation didn't get started until the early 1970s.

Neither short line survived very long.

The city of Concord apparently had some battery-powered streetcars early in the century.

CLASSIC EDISON-BEACH car was this Concord Street Railway unit, but no further data was found by the author.
Stephen D. Maguire Collection

ENTIRE doodlebug roster of New Hampshire's Claremont & Concord pauses at the depot in Claremont one wintry day. Both motor and trailer were sent down from the Boston & Maine. *P. Kutta Collection*

ROAD NOS.	BUILDER	DATE	BLDR. NO.	ENGINE & DRIVE	BODY TYPE	LGTH.	WT.	DISPOSITION	NOTES & COMMENTS
CLAREMONT & CONCORD RY., Claremont to Concord, N.H., 59 mi. (Abandoned; used ex-Boston & Maine branch) (Formed 1954)									
100	Osgood Bradley EMC	8/26	8795 164	Winton 120 275hp GE	10 win. bag. 44 pass.	64'	47T		Ex-B&M 1181, acq. 12/54
101	Brill	7/25	22274	Trailer	14 win. bag. 50 pass.		21T		Ex-B&M 1081, acq. 12/54

New Jersey

AREA: 7,836 sq. miles
CAPITAL: Trenton
POPULATION (1927): 3,749,000

RAIL OFFICIALS and guests try out the brand-new White rail motor on the Union Transportation Co. The moment was captured on April 25, 1922, at the New Egypt, N.J., depot.
White, Author's Collection

PERHAPS the most interesting rail motor car operation in New Jersey wasn't exactly on a "short" line railroad. Rather, it was on a short segment of the far-flung Public Service Corporation trolley system.

In 1930 Public Service de-electrified the southern segment of its Trenton Fast Line, south of New Brunswick, in a misguided attempt to economize the operation of an interurban with falling traffic and rising expenses.

The "Fast Line" was anything but, compared to the nearby race track of the main line of the Pennsylvania Railroad. It was, however, cheap: cheaply built, cheaply operated, and cheaply priced to its dwindling patronage.

To provide service for this interurban-

without-wires, three heavyweight 1916 Brill streetcars were converted to gas-electric drive, a concept that Public Service applied much more successfully to its large fleet of buses.

The heavy ex-streetcars were too slow and sluggish for this type of service, and in 1934 were replaced by buses-on-flanged wheels: Yellow Coaches adapted for rail/highway use.

But traffic still didn't pick up, and in 1937 Public Service abandoned the rail line entirely and turned the route over to buses operating on the public highways, as it had already done over much of the remainder of its system.

Otherwise, almost all of the rail motor cars of note in the Garden State operated on the mainline railways.

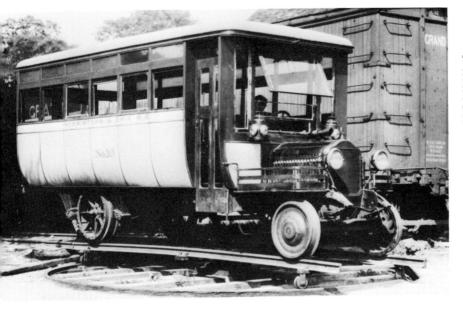

TINY TURNTABLE turns this diminutive White railcar No. 10 on the Morristown and Erie at Whippany, N.J., in 1921. Note the details on the Grand Trunk boxcar at rear—cars like these are not around nowadays.
Author's Collection

BIG TROLLEY operator Public Service of New Jersey de-electrified part of its Trenton Fast Line and installed a small fleet of motorized streetcars including the 6500, pictured here. *Al Barker; Motor Bus Society; NJ-NRHS*

Such crowd-swallowers proved to be too big, and PSNJ then tried a couple of buses with flanged guide wheels including the 1001. The idea did not work, and the operation was replaced by regular buses on public highways in 1937. *Al Barker; Motor Bus Society; NJ-NRHS*

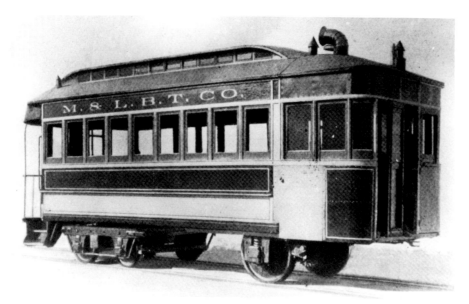

STEAM CAR, acquired possibly before the turn of the century, served on the Manahawken & Long Beach.

Stephen D. Maguire Collection

ROAD NOS.	BUILDER	DATE	BLDR. NO.	ENGINE & DRIVE	BODY TYPE	LGTH.	WT.	DISPOSITION	NOTES & COMMENTS
CAPE MAY, DELAWARE BAY & SEWELLS POINT RY.									
In 1912, two storage battery cars (18' 3") were ordered; in 1913 one more was ordered from St. Louis Car (21')									
MORRISTOWN & ERIE RR CO., Morristown to Essex Falls, N.J., 12.96 mi. (In operation)									
10	White	8/18		White 4 cyl. 30hp gas	6 win. mot. bus, hood front			out of serv. 4/28/28	
50	Four Whl. Dr.	1922		Wisc. gas	hood front bus			conv. to MW service	Converted from truck
MANAHAWKEN & LONG BEACH TRANSPORTATION CO., Manahawken to Barnegat City and Bonds, N.J. (Abandoned)									
(1 car)	Grice & Long	18 ?		2 cyl. uprt. steam	9 win. OP, clere. roof, sing frnt. driver, 4 whl. trail truck, wooden, 36 pass.				Acquired second (or third) hand
PUBLIC SERVICE CORP. OF NEW JERSEY, New Brunswick to Trenton, N.J., 27.3 mi. (de-electrified line) (Abandoned 1937)									
883	Mack Co. Shops			Mack AD gas	7 win. hood type bus			converted to line car	
1001 to 1002	Yellow Co. Shops			Yellow gas	5 win. hood type bus				Had guide wheels for use on rails
6500 to 6502	Brill Co. Shops	1916 1930		(2) 150hp gas-elect.	12 win. st.car, 32 pass.			scrapped 1938	Ex-2622, 2623, 2629
STONE HARBOR RR CO., Cape May Court House to Stone Harbor, N.J., 4.53 mi. (Abandoned)									
101	Mack Brill	1920	70003 21285	Mack AB 30hp gas	8 win. 25 pass. hood type bus, 4 whl. lead trk.	28' 8"	5½ T	scrapped 1936	
102	Mack Brill	1920	70004 21285	Mack AB 30hp gas	8 win. 25 pass. hood type bus, 4 whl. lead trk.	28' 8"	5½ T	scrapped 1936	
UNION TRANSPORTATION CO., Hightstown to Pemberton, N.J., 25 mi. (Abandoned)									
20	Brill White	1922	21367	White 45 40hp gas	8 win. CE 4 whl. lead trk. bag. 41 pass.	30' 11"	10T	sold to Aberdeen & Rockfish (No. 101)	Resold to DeKalb & Western (Miss.)
Used a Chevrolet truck conversion with a four wheel flatcar trailer during the '30s.									

New Mexico

AREA: 121,666 sq. miles
CAPITAL: Santa Fe
POPULATION (1927): 392,000

THERE JUST ISN'T much that can be said about short lines or their rail motor cars in the state of New Mexico. There were only two lines, and they had one car each.

The New Mexico Central (Santa Fe to Torrance) was taken over by the Santa Fe in 1926, and was abandoned piecemeal over several years. Its one car went to the Santa Fe and became AT&SF second M.101, before it was sold to a lumber company.

The Arizona & New Mexico was taken over by the Southern Pacific (through ownership of the El Paso & Southwestern). The one railcar had been sold previously to the Magma Arizona Railroad of Arizona.

COMB. PASSENGER AND BAGGAGE GASOLINE RAIL CAR

SAGEBRUSH east of Albuquerque was served by the New Mexico Central and its lone railcritter, Brill-built 101 shown in a builder's photo.
Author's Collection

WHITE-built car 301 provided the passenger service on the Arizona & New Mexico, a line eventually sold to the Southern Pacific.
Author's Collection

ROAD NOS.	BUILDER	DATE	BLDR. NO.	ENGINE & DRIVE	BODY TYPE	LGTH.	WT.	DISPOSITION	NOTES & COMMENTS
ARIZONA & NEW MEXICO RY. CO., Hachita, N.M. to Clifton, Ariz., 108.84 mi. (Merged into Southern Pacific)									
301	White			White gas	11 win. CE bag pass.			sold to Magma Ariz. 1923	
NEW MEXICO CENTRAL RY. CO., Santa Fe to Torrance, N.M., 115.75 mi. (Merged into AT&SF)									
101	Mack Brill	8/21	70010 21372	Mack AB 30hp gas	6 win. bag. 25 pass. bag. dr. at rear	28′8″	5½T	to AT&SF, '26 No. M.101	

New York

AREA: 49,576 sq. miles
CAPITAL: Albany
POPULATION (1927): 11,423,000

NEW YORK had more self-propelled railcars than any other state in the Union; in fact, Manhattan Island could also make this boast.

Of course the reason for this was the large number of battery electric cars owned by the Third Ave. and the New York Railways. Between the two of them they owned 206 cars, plus a gas-electric car on the Third Ave. line.

Neither of these lines qualifies as short line railroads. But then, they were short, and were railways, so they deserve mention, if not further coverage.

New York was, however, well blessed with many of the more conventional lines. In fact, it's the furthest north of a chain of short lines that followed the Appalachian Mountains down through to Georgia. Starting up in the Adirondacks with the Grasse Valley Railroad, the Lowville & Beaver River, and the Deer River, we encounter such lines as the Unadilla Valley, Delaware Northern, Dansville & Mt. Morris, and sweeping into Pennsylvania on the Pittsburgh, Shawmut & Northern.

These roads all had the usual, unusual mix of equipment that so characterize short line operations. In the New York City area there also were a number of very weak short lines (many of them built to serve real estate promotions) that utilized cast-off battery cars from Manhattan.

(Top Photo) "LATEST THING in Railroad Transportation," reads the postcard caption of McKeen motor No. 101 of the Central New York Southern. This might have been a true statement in 1914, but the McKeen proved unreliable for most short lines in the long run.
Author's Collection

INTERURBAN Fonda, Johnstown & Gloversville also was a big user of doodlebugs. Here's a big bruiser of a Brill, unit 340, acquired used in 1938.   *Author's Collection*

CLASSIC early White railbus poses at Dansville, N.Y., one fine day shortly after its 1915 delivery.
Harold K. Vollrath Collection

LONG BEACH RAILWAY No. 13, a Reo, fed into the busy Long Island Rail Road commuter station back in the early 1920s.
Stephen D. Maguire Collection

ROAD NOS.	BUILDER	DATE	BLDR. NO.	ENGINE & DRIVE	BODY TYPE	LGTH.	WT.	DISPOSITION	NOTES & COMMENTS
ARCADE AND ATTICA RR CORP., Arcade to Attica, N.Y., 32 mi. (In operation)									
1	Hewlett-Ludlow	1917		Wisc. D 4 cyl. 70hp ags	10 win. CE 32 pass. door one side only	25'	10T		Ex-San Diego & Arizona Eastern, acq. 1920
102	Evans	1937		Reo 6 cyl. 70hp gas	6 win. CE 23 pass. bus	25'	5T	sold	Ex-Arlington & Fairfax 102 "Autorailer"
108	Evans	1937		Reo 6 cyl. 70hp gas	6 win. CE 23 pass. bus	25'	5T	sold	Ex-Arlington & Fairfax 108 "Autorailer"
109	Evans	1937		Reo 6 cyl. 70hp gas	6 win. CE 23 pass. bus	25'	5T	sold to Chi. Sou. Shore & Sou Bend	Ex-Arlington & Fairfax 109, used for a time as sect. gang car. Line car on CSS&SB "Autorailer."

Predecessor company, Buffalo, Arcade & Attica, reportedly had a Federal-built battery car.

ROAD NOS.	BUILDER	DATE	BLDR. NO.	ENGINE & DRIVE	BODY TYPE	LGTH.	WT.	DISPOSITION	NOTES & COMMENTS
CENTRAL NEW YORK SOUTHERN RY., Auburn to Ithaca, N.Y. (Abandoned 1925)									
101	McKeen	1914		McKeen 200hp gas-mech.	14 win. CE bag. 56 pass.	70'	37T	scrapped 1925	
102	McKeen	1914		McKeen 200hp gas-mech.	14 win. CE bag. 56 pass.	70'	37T	scrapped 1925	
DANSVILLE & MT. MORRIS RR CO., Dansville to Mt. Morris, N.Y., 15.54 mi. (In operation)									
300	White	1915		White 4 cyl. gas	6 win. hood type bus, 4 whl. lead truck, 30 pass.			scrapped 1937	Re-engined with Buick 6
(1 car)	Edwards	1924		Buda 108hp gas	11 win. bag. 50 pass.	51'	24T		(Some question about this one)
FONDA, JOHNSTOWN & GLOVERSVILLE RR CO., Fonda to Northville, N.Y. (steam div.) 25.47 mi. (In operation)									
200	Brill	1922	21488	Midwest 68hp gas	10 win. bag. 43 pass.	43'	14T	sold to Cuba	
201	Brill	1922	21488	Midwest 68hp gas	10 win. bag. 43 pass.	43'	14T	sold to Pitt. Lisbon & Western	
202	Brill	1923	21727	Midwest 68hp gas	10 win. 43 pass. bag. conv. to RPO express	43'	14T	scrapped 1957	
340	Brill	1929	22828	Brill 275 300hp GE	12 win. 2 bag. doors, bag. exp. pass. sect. removed	73'	60T	sold to Gt. Winn Water Dist. '50	Ex-La. Ark. & Tex., ex-ex-Chesapeake Beach Ry., acquired 1938

EDISON-BEACH battery car bounced along the rails of the 28th & 29th Street Crosstown RR in Manhattan early in the century. Though not from a short line railroad, we include this photo to illustrate one of the interesting uses for self-propelled railcars.
George E. Votava Collection

ROAD NOS.	BUILDER	DATE	BLDR. NO.	ENGINE & DRIVE	BODY TYPE	LGTH.	WT.	DISPOSITION	NOTES & COMMENTS
GRASSE RIVER RR CORP., Chilwold Station to Cranberry Lake, N.Y., 16 mi. (Abandoned)									
11	Co. Shops Pierce			Pierce gas	2 win. 2 door 8 pass. bus, bag. door at rear, 4 whl. lead trk.				
12	Lanc. Oxford & Sou. Co. Shops	1889 1913		gas	10 win. CE, wood, clere. roof, bag. 36 pass.			to Wolfboro Ry. Strasburg Ry. 1961	Built by Lancaster, Oxford & Sou. from narrow gauge coach, acq. 1918
	Evans	1937		Reo 6 cyl. 70hp gas	6 win. CE 23 pass. bus	25′	5T		Ex-Arlington & Fairfax, "Autorailer"
GREENWICH & JOHNSONVILLE RY. CO., Johnsonville to Northumberland, N.Y., 21.46 mi. (17 miles in operation as Batten Kill RR)									
10	Brill	1923	21814	Midwest 68hp gas	10 win. bag. 43 pass.	43′	14½T		
JAMESTOWN, CHATAUQUA & LAKE ERIE RR, Jamestown to Westfield, N.Y., 32 mi. (Abandoned)									
1	McKeen			McKeen 200hp gas-mech.	10 win. CE bag. pass.	55′	35T	sold, poss. to Butler County	Possibly secondhand
LONG BEACH RY., Long Beach, N.Y. (Abandoned)									
16	Reo			Reo gas	7 win. hood type bus, 4 whl. lead truck				
LOWVILLE & BEAVER RIVER RR CO., Lowville to Croghan, N.Y., 10.4 mi. (Abandoned)									
1	Hall-Scott	1913	12	Hall-Scott 150hp gas	13 win. bag. 50 pass.			de-motorized, used as coach	Ex-Salt Lake & Utah No. 502
MANHATTAN BEACH RR, Manhattan Beach, N.Y. (Abandoned)									
1	Federal	1913		battery el.	6 win. 4 whl. wood st.car	27′ 6″			
2	Federal	1913		battery el.	6 win. 4 whl. wood st.car	27′ 6″			

REMINGTON ARMS unit M-1 (what else could they call it?) is pictured at Middletown, N.Y., on the Middletown & Unionville.
Louis A. Marre Collection

GRASSE RIVER Railroad had two interesting cars. No. 12 dated originally from 1889 and eventually had several owners. No. 11 was rebuilt in company shops from a Pierce highway bus. Notice the homemade pilot (slightly askew) and the little brooms for sweeping the rails. The first photo was taken in 1958; the second in 1946, both at Conifer, N.Y.
George Votava; C.A. Brown

ROAD NOS.	BUILDER	DATE	BLDR. NO.	ENGINE & DRIVE	BODY TYPE	LGTH.	WT.	DISPOSITION	NOTES & COMMENTS
THE MARINE RY. CO., Manhattan Beach to Sheepshead Bay, N.Y., 1.36 mi. (Abandoned)									
3	Brill	1913	18921	battery el.	7 win. 4 whl. wood st.car				In 1918 three battery cars listed
MIDDLETOWN & UNIONVILLE RR CO., Middletown to Unionville, N.Y., 14.3 mi. (Abandoned)									
(1 car)	Reo, J. Blaine Worcester	3/21		Reo 4 cyl. 27hp gas	4 win. hood type bus, 19 pass.	12′2″	5T	sold	
(1 car)	Gramm-Bern-stein, J. Blaine Worces.	11/22		Hinkley 4 cyl. 29hp gas	7 win. hood type bus, 31 pass. 4 whl. lead truck	19′3″	5¼T		Reported to have replaced earlier rail buses
M-55	Brill	1926	22472	Brill 55 68hp gas	10 win. bag. 38 pass.	43′	14½T		Parts from this car may have been used to construct M-1
M-1	Co. Shops				Baggage, clere. roof, Brill front				
PRATTSBURGH RY. CORP., Kanona to Prattsburgh, N.Y., 11.44 mi. (Abandoned)									
Modified Model T Ford									
SUFFOLK TRACTION CO., Holtsville to Sayville, N.Y. (Abandoned 1919)									
1 & 2	Brill El. Stor. Btty.	1911	19317	4 mot. btty. elect.	7 win. 4 whl. st.car, wood		7T		
3	Brill El. Stor. Btty.	1911	18849	4 mot. btty. elect.	7 win. 4 whl. st.car, wood		7T		
4	Brill El. Stor. Btty.	1911	19315	4 mot. btty. elect.	7 win. 4 whl. st.car, wood		7T		
UNADILLA VALLEY RY. CO., Bridgewater to New Berlin Jct., N.Y., 42 mi. (Abandoned)									
M-1	Brill	1923	21914	Midwest 68hp	7 win. 28 pass.	43′	14½T	wrecked, 6/20/24	

North Carolina

AREA: 52,712 sq. miles
CAPITAL: Raleigh
POPULATION (1927): 2,987,000

NORTH CAROLINA was at the very heart of the Appalachian chain of short lines, and at the very center of this heartland was the city of Sanford.

Sanford was the headquarters of the Atlantic & Western Railway and the Edwards Car Co. These two organizations were very much intertwined in the early part of the 1920s, did more to promote the use of railcars in the South than any other agency.

Edwards, using the Atlantic & Western as a test ground, demonstrated the potential of the lightweight rail motor car. Soon after, rail motor cars came into regular use in that section of the country.

Another pioneer builder in this area was the Watson Car Co. of Tarboro. Watson used "rebel ingenuity" to construct some wild and wonderful cars, mostly from old streetcars.

Another offbeat organization was the New Holland, Higginsport & Mt. Vernon Railway. Even to find where this line had operated was a task. I was surprised to find it, according to my map, ending in the middle of a lake.

With the help of Prof. Michael J. Dunn, a specialist in North Carolina railroad history, I learned that this was a part of a project to drain Lake Mattamuskee, a shallow lake in the Pamlico Sound area of the North Carolina coast, with the idea of reclaiming it for agriculture land. To this end a large pumping plant was built in the middle of the lake. The railroad served the pumping plant with the coal needed to run the pumps, and hopefully to take out the rich bounty of agricultural products expected.

To encourage investment in this scheme, the company took out some full-page listings in the *Official Guide* with instructions on how to get there by rail from New York and other population centers. This railroad's only outside connection was via an obscure branch of the Norfolk Southern, not one of the premier passenger railroads of the South.

If a potential investor managed to make it that far, he was greeted with an open Model T Ford from which to inspect the line.

As might be expected, this scheme failed. As a matter of fact, this area was eventually designated as a wilderness area, and the headquarters for this agency uses the old pumping plant!

Many of the short lines in North Carolina were owned by lumbering interests and as the areas were logged out the lines were abandoned. But several lines like the Aberdeen & Rockfish, and the Cape Fear Railway, and even a small portion of the Atlantic and Western are still in operation.

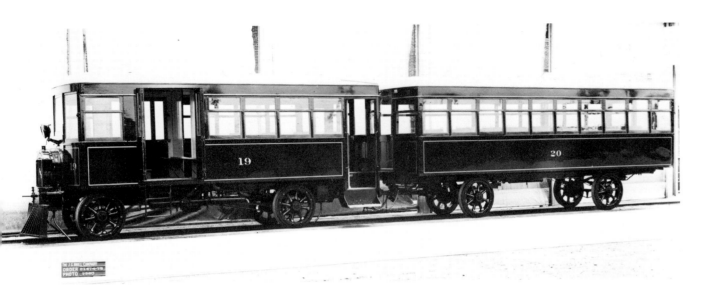

UTILITARIAN is the only word to describe Elkin & Allegheny No. 1. The creature was created in company shops and sported a Ford gasoline engine. *Author's Collection*

EDWARDS CARS were often seen in the South. An example is Virginia & Carolina Southern 304 at St. Pauls, N.C., in 1938. *John B. Allen*

(Top Photo) MOTOR 19 and trailer 20 of the Cape Fear Rails get their picture taken at the Brill plant in 1922.
Historical Society of Pennsylvania

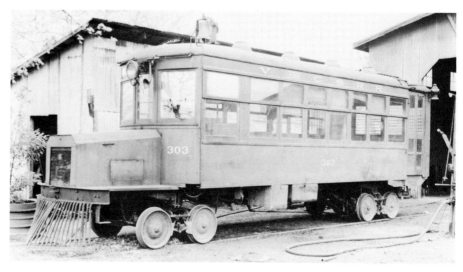

RECOGNIZE THE BIRNEY CAR?
Virginia & Carolina Southern 303
was made from a Birney, yes indeed.
Edwards did the job in 1923. New
snout on the front housed a 75-hp
Buda engine.

John B. Allen Collection

ROAD NOS.	BUILDER	DATE	BLDR. NO.	ENGINE & DRIVE	BODY TYPE	LGTH.	WT.	DISPOSITION	NOTES & COMMENTS
ABERDEEN & ROCKFISH RR CO., Aberdeen to Fayetteville, N.C., 44.9 mi. (In operation)									
100	Mack Brill	6/21	70006 21311	Mack AB 45hp gas	8 win. 4 whl. lead trk. 25 pass. hood frt.	27'	5½T		AB model
101	Brill White	1922	21367	White 45 40hp gas	8 win. CE, 41 pass. 4 whl. lead truck, hood front	30' 11"	9½T	sold to DeKalb & West. 1941	Ex-Union Transportation Co. No. 20
103	Brill	1933	23084	Brill 65 6 cyl. gas	10 win., bag. 41 pass.	44' 5"	15½T	wrecked, rebuilt as No. 107	
105	Chevrolet			Chevrolet 6 gas	2 door sedan				
106	American Car & Foundry	1935	1432	Hall-Scott 175hp gas-mech.	14 win. CE, 57 pass. baggage	61' 7"	26T	sold to Salt Lake Garfield & Western	Ex-Seaboard Air Line No. 2026, acq. ca. 1944
107	Brill Co. Shops	1933	23084	Stirling 125hp gas-mech.	10 win. 38 pass. baggage	55'	20T	scrapped	Rebuilt with "shovel nose" front
APPALACHIAN RY., Elna to Parsons Jct., N.C., 18 mi. (Abandoned)									
One motor car listed in 1926 and 1928 issues of "Equipment Registers."									
ATLANTIC & CAROLINA RR CO., Kenansville to Warsaw, N.C., 9 mi. (Abandoned)									
100	Watson Car Co.	—		Wisc. ? gas	6 win. 4 whl. OP deck roof, ex-st.car				Body ex-Capital Traction Co.
200	Watson Car Co.			trailer	6 win. 4 whl. OP deck roof, ex-st.car				Body ex-Capital Traction Co.
ATLANTIC & WESTERN RY. CO., Sanford to Lillington, N.C., 24 mi. (3 miles in operation)									
1	Co. Shops	1917		Kelly-Spring. gas	bus type, bonnet style hood			scrapped 1921	
2	Co. Shops	1920		Kelly-Spring. gas	bus type, bonnet style hood				
3	Edwards	1923		Buda gas					
4	Edwards	1923		Buda gas					
5	Edwards	1924		Buda GL-6 108hp gas-mech.	8 win. OP 30 pass. baggage	31' 9"	10T		
6	Edwards	1924		Buda GL-6 108hp gas-mech.	6 win. OP 30 pass. baggage	31' 9"	10T		
7	Brill	1927		Brill 68hp gas	10 win. 43 pass. baggage	43'	14½T	retired, body may still exist	Ex-Long Island Ry., No. 1134, acq. 12/39
?	Edwards	1926		trailer	8 win. 30 pass.		8T		

ROAD NOS.	BUILDER	DATE	BLDR. NO.	ENGINE & DRIVE	BODY TYPE	LGTH.	WT.	DISPOSITION	NOTES & COMMENTS

BLACK MOUNTAIN RY. CO., Kona to Burnsville, N.C., 11.59 mi. (Merged into Clinchfield Ry.)

| (1 car) | Brill | 1922 | 21406 | White 4 cyl. gas | 8 win. 28 pass. 4 whl. lead trk. bag. door at rear | | | | |

BONLEE & WESTERN RY. CO., Bonlee to Bennett, N.C., 10.37 mi. (Abandoned)

| (1 car) | Edwards | 1926 | | Buda 108hp gas | 8 win. OP 25 pass. baggage | 31′6″ | 9T | | |

CAPE FEAR RYS., INC., Fort Bragg to Skibo, N.C., 9 mi. (In operation)

18	Brill, Four Wheel Drive	1922	21474	Wisc. 40hp gas	4 win., 4 wheel bag. pass., rear train door				
19	Brill, Four Wheel Drive	1922	21474	Wisc. 40hp gas	4 win., 4 wheel bag. pass., rear train door				
20	Brill	1922	21475	trailer	10 win. 4 whl. 36 pass., no doors except frnt. tr. door				
?	Edwards	1924		Buda 108hp gas	8 win. CE bag. 30 pass.	30′	9½T	sold to Win. & West.	May have been more than one of these

CHARLOTTE RAPID TRANSIT CO., Charlotte, N.C. (Abandoned)

| (two cars) | Federal | 1911 | | battery-elect. 200 cell | 7 win. 4 whl. st.car, 20 pass. | 18′ | | sold, Mex. & San Diego Ry. 1912 | Mex & S.D. 1 and 2 |

CAROLINA & NORTHEASTERN RR, Gumberry to Lasker, N.C., 15 mi. (Abandoned)

Motor train listed in 1928 to 1933 ''Official Guides.''

CAROLINA & NORTHWESTERN RY. CO., Lenoir, N.C. to Chester, S.C., 133.5 mi. (Merged into Southern System)

| 2 cars | Edwards Thomas | 1923 | 113 & 114 | Buda 108hp gas-mech. | 8 win., OP 30 pass. bag. | 32′ | 10T | | |

EAST CAROLINA RY., Tarboro to Hookerton, N.C., 38.2 mi. (Merged into Atlantic Coast Line)

14	Watson Car Co.	1910		2 cyl. gas	closed ''speeder''				
501	Watson Car Co.	1912		Buda gas	6 win. 4 whl. OP streetcar				Ex-Washington D.C. streetcar
502	Watson Car Co.	1915			7 win. 8 whl. ex-streetcar				Ex-Washington D.C. streetcar
600-602	Brill ?			trailers	7 win. OP 4 whl. ex-cable car trailers	abt. 18′			Ex-Washington D.C. streetcar
G-17	Watson Car Co.	1922		Packard	3 win. OP bag. loco.				Had drivers from an old steam loco., 4 wheel lead truck

ELKIN & ALLEGHENY RR, Elkin to Veneer, N.C., 15 mi. (Abandoned)

| 1 | Co. Shops | 1925 ? | | Ford T gas | 5 win. CE wood 4 whl. lead truck | | | | |

FAYETTEVILLE STREET RAILWAY & POWER CO., Fayetteville, N.C. (Abandoned)

1917 Federal census listed one gas car.

HENDERSONVILLE TRACTION CO., Hendersonville, N.C. (Abandoned)

| 113 | Federal | 1911 | | battery-elect. | 8 win. 4 whl. st.car, clere. roof wooden | 18′ | | | |

LAURINBERG & SOUTHERN RR CO., Johns to Raeford, N.C., 30 mi. (Abandoned)

| 4 | Edwards | 1923 | | Midwest gas | 8 win. 25 pass. bag. | 30′ | 9T | | |
| ? | Edwards | 1923 | | trailer | 10 win. 36 pass. | 30′ | 8T | | |

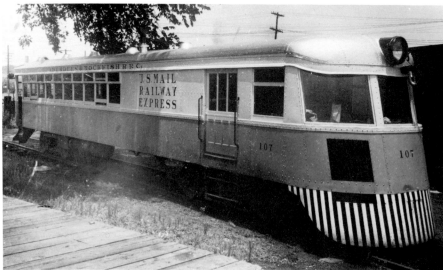

CONDUCTOR seems to be taking a break on the pilot of Aberdeen & Rockfish No. 100 at Aberdeen, N.C., in 1927. But to show that it was in step with the times, the A&R rebuilt Brill 55-footer 107 with a shovel front and this unit provided service in later years.
M.B. Connery Collection; Author's Collection

ROAD NOS.	BUILDER	DATE	BLDR. NO.	ENGINE & DRIVE	BODY TYPE	LGTH.	WT.	DISPOSITION	NOTES & COMMENTS
MAXTON, ALMA & SOUTHBOUND RR, Alma to Rowlands, N.C., 15.8 mi. (Abandoned)									
(1 car)	Atlantic & Western	1920 ?		Kelly-Springfield gas	bus type body, "bonnet" hood, 25 pass.				
(1 car)	Pierce ?			gas	open touring car, 4 whl. lead truck				
NEW BERN-GHENT STREET RAILWAY, New Bern, N.C. (Abandoned)									
(1 car)	Cinn. Car Co.	1913		battery-elect.	4 wheel streetcar	18' 2"			
NEW HOLLAND, HIGGINSPORT & MT. VERNON RR, Wenona to New Holland, N.C. (Abandoned)									
(1 car)	Ford	1920		Ford 4 cyl.	open truck				Pulled 4 wheel open trailer

TENNESSEE & NORTH CAROLINA RY. CO., Spruce to West Canton, N.C., 17 mi., and Crestmont, N.C. to Newport Jct., Tenn. 21 mi. (Abandoned 1941, two divisions)
Had a small bus type car on each division, operated from ca. 1922 until 1934.

TOWNSVILLE RR CO., Manson to Townsville, N.C., 10 mi. (Abandoned)
1928 "Moodys" listed one motor car in 1928. Predecessor Roanoke River Ry., had a 1918 Corbett truck equipped for rail operation.

SMOKEY MOUNTAIN RAILWAY CO., Ritter to Proctor, N.C., 4 mi. (Abandoned 1927) (Do not confuse with Smokey Mountain Railroad [Tenn.])

(1 car)	Edwards	1923		Buda 108hp gas	8 win., OP bag. 30 pass.	32'	10T		

ROAD NOS.	BUILDER	DATE	BLDR. NO.	ENGINE & DRIVE	BODY TYPE	LGTH.	WT.	DISPOSITION	NOTES & COMMENTS
TUCKOSEEGEE & SOUTH EASTERN RY., Sylva to East La Porte, N.C., 12 mi. (Abandoned)									
(1 car)	Brill	1923							
VIRGINIA & CAROLINA SOUTHERN RR CO., Hope Mills to Lumberton, 25.23 mi., and St. Pauls to Elizabethtown, N.C., 27.72 mi. (Merged into ACL)									
300-301	Edwards	1923		Buda 75hp gas	8 win. 32 pass. bag.	32'	9½T	301 burned	
302-303	Edwards	1923, 24		Buda 75hp gas	8 win. 34 pass. bag.	32'	9½T		
304	Edwards	1934		Buda 108hp gas	11 win. 40 pass.	45'	17T	sold 1941	Model 20
	Chevrolet	1940		Chev. 6 gas	van truck				
WILMINGTON, BRUNSWICK & SOUTHERN RR CO., Navassa to Southport, N.C., 30.2 mi. (Abandoned)									
11	Edwards	1924		Buda 75hp gas	7 win. OP 28 pass. baggage	32'	10T		
(1 car)	Edwards	1924		trailer	10 win. OP 40 pass.	34'	8T		
(1 car)	Edwards	1924		trailer	bag.-exp.	25'	6T		

North Dakota

AREA: 70,665 sq. miles
CAPITAL: Bismarck
POPULATION (1927): 641,000

NORTH DAKOTA had one claim to fame in regard to its short lines; every one of them had rail motor cars. The fact that there was only one line in the state perhaps had a good deal to do with this.

That one line, the Midland Continental, was intended to be the first section of a line that was to extend all the way from Canada to the Gulf of Mexico, hence the rather high-flown name. Only about 68 miles were ever built, however.

The rail motor car was one of the few White Ecklund cars ever built and probably was secondhand from the La Crosse and Southeastern line in Wisconsin.

ROAD NOS.	BUILDER	DATE	BLDR. NO.	ENGINE & DRIVE	BODY TYPE	LGTH.	WT.	DISPOSITION	NOTES & COMMENTS
MIDLAND CONTINENTAL RR, Edgeley to Wimbleton, N.D., 67.77 mi. (Abandoned)									
(1 car)	Ford	ca 1920		Ford 4 cyl GM	2-door sedan			ret. ca. 1932	
A-1	White Ecklund	1922		White 4 cyl gas	7 win. CE, 4 wh. lead truck			ret. ca 1934	Prob. ex-La Crosse & Sou. East. No. 400
A-2	Indiana	ca 1934		Ind. gas-mech.	4 wh, home blt			ret. 1957	Rubber tired flanged wheels
B-1	Co. Shops	ca 1920		trailer	open 4 wheel				

South Dakota

AREA: 77,047 sq. miles
CAPITAL: Pierre
POPULATION (1927): 696,000

SOUTH DAKOTA shared with its sister state, North Dakota, the distinction of having its only short line employing rail motor cars. The operation on the Rapid City, Black Hills and Western was a good deal more extensive than on the line in North Dakota.

In the years from about 1905 until 1927 some six units were used, five motors and one trailer, on what was basically a tourist operation.

There was one other operation, in the city of Mitchell, where a streetcar line was operated with an open Fairbanks-Morse type 19 motor car. Riding in this car during South Dakota's minus 20-degree winters must have been a bit of a thrill, to say the least.

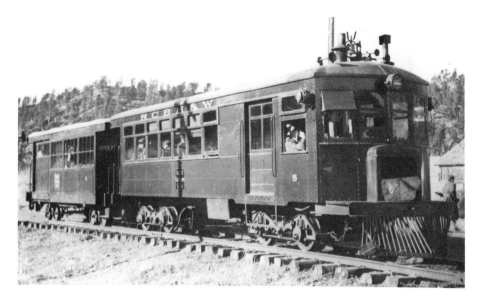

Rapid City, Black Hills & Western No. 5, with trailer, is at Portola, S.D., on July 1, 1943.
Stephen D. Maguire

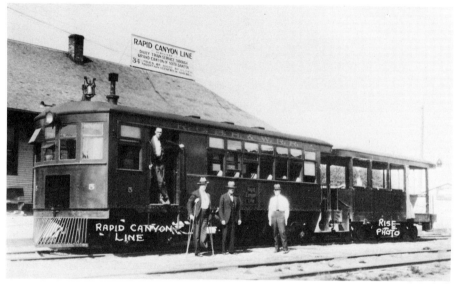

THE BLACK HILLS of South Dakota were a tourist magnet in railroad days, too. Here are Edwards motor 5 and trailer 6 standing at the Rapid City station with some officials. The Rapid City, Black Hills & Western was known as the Rapid Canyon Line. *Author's Collection*

ROAD NOS.	BUILDER	DATE	BLDR. NO.	ENGINE & DRIVE	BODY TYPE	LGTH.	WT.	DISPOSITION	NOTES & COMMENTS

RAPID CITY, BLACK HILLS & WESTERN RR CO., Rapid City to Mystic, S.D., 33.5 mi. (Abandoned)

ROAD NOS.	BUILDER	DATE	BLDR. NO.	ENGINE & DRIVE	BODY TYPE	LGTH.	WT.	DISPOSITION	NOTES & COMMENTS
2	Fair. Morse Sheffield	1905		Fair. Morse 19 30hp gas	4 wheel, open st.car, wooden		4½T	wrecked 1907	
3	Fair. Morse Brill	1910		Fair. Morse 24 50hp gas	8 win. 4 whl. bag. 35 pass. clere. roof, wood	34′ 2″	12½T		
4	Fair. Morse Brill	1911		Fair. Morse 24 50hp gas	8 win. 4 whl. bag. 35 pass. clere. roof, wood	34′ 2″	12½T		
5	Edwards	1928		Buda 123hp gas	7 win. OP 30 pass. baggage	31′ 9″	12T	burned 1947	
6	Edwards	1928		trailer	open, 8 wheel pass. car			scrapped	
8	Mack McGuire-Cummings	4/22	60009	Mack AC 45hp gas	7 win. 29 pass. 4 whl. lead truck, hood front	34′ 7″	10T	resold to CB&Q 9/33	Ex-CB&Q No. 501, acq. 3/28

MITCHELL STREET & INTERURBAN RY., Mitchell, S.D. (Abandoned)

ROAD NOS.	BUILDER	DATE	BLDR. NO.	ENGINE & DRIVE	BODY TYPE	LGTH.	WT.	DISPOSITION	NOTES & COMMENTS
(1 car)	Fair. Morse Sheffield			Fair. Morse 19 30hp gas	4 wheel open streetcar				Ex-Lewiston Terminal (Idaho)

Ohio

AREA: 41,222 sq. miles
CAPITAL: Columbus
POPULATION (1927): 6,710,000

I T WOULD SEEM that Ohio has no particular distinction in the use of rail motor cars on short lines. There weren't too many to start with, and those that had them didn't use them for long.

For instance, the Akron, Canton & Youngstown bought two used General Electric gas electrics from the Bangor & Aroostook in 1920, and sold them to the Houston & Brazos Valley by 1923.

The Lakeside and Marblehead did have one of the last McKeen cars in existence—it wasn't sold until 1947. The McKeen was used as a stationary diner until 1962, when this treasure was destroyed by fire.

DROP-CENTER Bowen car served the Norwalk & Shelby. It was built by American Railway Motors in 1923. *Author's Collection*

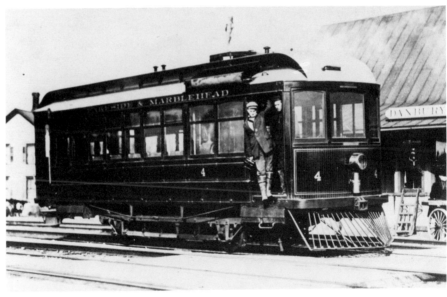

TYPICAL Fairbanks-Morse unit was Lakeside & Marblehead No. 4; this one had a Brill body. It is shown at Danbury, Ohio, in 1910. *Bob Lorenz Collection*

ROAD NOS.	BUILDER	DATE	BLDR. NO.	ENGINE & DRIVE	BODY TYPE	LGTH.	WT.	DISPOSITION	NOTES & COMMENTS
AKRON, CANTON & YOUNGSTOWN RY. CO., Mogadore to Copley Jct., Ohio, 10 mi. (Merged into Norfolk & Western)									
51									Listed in "Equipment Reg." 1922
55	Gen. Elect. Wason	8/11	3717 9931	GE GM16 175hp gas-elec.	18 win. CE, bag. 97 pass.	66′	47T	sold, Houston & Brazos, Vy. 12/22	Ex-Bangor & Aroostook No. 5, acq. 6/20
56	Gen. Elect. Wason	1/12	3722 9931	GE GM 16A5 175hp gas-elec.	14 win. CE, bag. 91 pass.	68′	48T	sold, H&BV 2/23	Ex-Bangor & Aroostook No. 6, acq. 6/20
GALLIPOLIS & NORTHERN TRACTION CO., Gallipolis, Ohio (Abandoned)									
(1 car)	Indiana Truck	1922		Hercules gas	7 win. hood type bus, abt. 28 pass.				
HOCKING & SUNDAY CREEK TRACTION CO., Nelsonville to Athens, Ohio, 14 mi., electrified									
1	McKeen			McKeen 200hp gas-mech.	12 win. CE 60 pass.	55′	37T	sold, poss. to Chat. & Lake Erie	

ROAD NOS.	BUILDER	DATE	BLDR. NO.	ENGINE & DRIVE	BODY TYPE	LGTH.	WT.	DISPOSITION	NOTES & COMMENTS

KANAUGA TRACTION CO., Gallipolis, Ohio (Became Gallipolis & Northern Traction Co., see above)

ROAD NOS.	BUILDER	DATE	BLDR. NO.	ENGINE & DRIVE	BODY TYPE	LGTH.	WT.	DISPOSITION	NOTES & COMMENTS
1	Fair. Morse Sheffield			Fair. Morse 25hp gas	4 wheel wood, open car 19 pass.	20'8"	4½T		Model 19
2	Fair. Morse Sheffield			Fair. Morse 25hp gas	6 win. CE 4 whl. wood, 19 pass.	20'8"	4½T		Closed Model 19

LAKESIDE & MARBLEHEAD RR, Marblehead to Danbury, Ohio, 6.88 mi. (Abandoned)

ROAD NOS.	BUILDER	DATE	BLDR. NO.	ENGINE & DRIVE	BODY TYPE	LGTH.	WT.	DISPOSITION	NOTES & COMMENTS
4	Fair. Morse Brill	5/10		Fair. Morse 24 50hp gas	8 win. 4 whl. 30 pass., bag. clere. roof, wood	34'2"	13T	sold 8/31/17	
5	McKeen	1916	152	McKeen 200hp gas-mech.	9 win. CE bag. 56 pass.	55'2"	30T	sold 5/19/47	Used as a diner at Bono, Ohio, burned 1962

LIMA & DEFIANCE RR CO., Lima to Defiance, Ohio, 40 mi. (Abandoned 1929) (Started as a steam road, electrified [Ohio Elect.] then de-electrified)

Had some sort of a gas car about 1925

LORAIN, ASHLAND & SOUTHERN RR, Lorain to Custaloga, Ohio, 68 mi. (Abandoned 1926)

ROAD NOS.	BUILDER	DATE	BLDR. NO.	ENGINE & DRIVE	BODY TYPE	LGTH.	WT.	DISPOSITION	NOTES & COMMENTS
15 (1)	Ry. Stor. Btty.	1914		Edison batty. elect.	10 win. 42 pass. bag.	57'3"			
20 (2)	Ry. Stor. Btty.	1914		Edison batty. elect.	10 win. 42 pass. bag.	57'3"			Road also had gas car or cars

MARIETTA, COLUMBUS & CLEVELAND RR, Marietta to Palos, Ohio, 44.6 mi. (Abandoned)

Circa 1926 used a motor car on the Curtice Jct.-Sharpsburg branch (2.8 mi.), four round trips daily.

NORWALK & SHELBY RR CO., Norwalk to Shelby, Ohio (Abandoned)

ROAD NOS.	BUILDER	DATE	BLDR. NO.	ENGINE & DRIVE	BODY TYPE	LGTH.	WT.	DISPOSITION	NOTES & COMMENTS
1 & 2	Amer. Ry. Motors Glover Car Co.	1923		Midwest 36hp gas	10 win. CE bag. 42 pass.	36'	14½T	sold to Boyne City, Gaylord & Alpena, 1924	"Bowen" car

McKEEN METAMORPHOSIS: Lakeside & Marblehead No. 5 was a 1916 McKeen, one of the last built. It was reincarnated as a diner at Bono, Ohio, with its "U.S. Mail" signage intact. *Both: Bob Lorenz Collection*

Oklahoma

AREA: 69,918 sq. miles
CAPITAL: Oklahoma City
POPULATION (1927): 2,384,000

IN THE LATE TEENS and the early twenties, Oklahoma became the happy hunting ground for used General Electric gas-electric cars.

At this time a number of railroads that had invested in these cars went bankrupt, among them the Dan Patch and the Chicago, Peoria and St. Louis. Cars from these roads wound up on the Northeast Oklahoma; Oklahoma, New Mexico & Pacific; and the Okmulgee Northern. In some cases the boomer cars were resold after a relatively short time.

There were also two lines using McKeen cars. The famous Sand Springs Railway, which is still in operation, started out with two of these cars. The rather obscure Peoples Electric of Muskogee ordered two McKeens, the first of which was so unsatisfactory that Peoples wouldn't pay for it and the car was repossessed. The other was never delivered. Each of these cars eventually wound up on the Union Pacific.

The Sand Springs also got rid of their McKeens in a short time, probably to the relief of the mechanical department.

A number of other Sooner State lines operated gas cars, but generally for a short time.

Oklahoma was of course in the heart of "Mainline Doodlebug Country," with the Santa Fe, Frisco, Katy, and the Muskogee Group all operating numerous schedules.

SECOND CAREER on the Warner & Webbers Falls brought this Chalmers touring car a measure of fame. It was driven 20,000 miles on the highways before being fitted with flanged wheels. As a locomotive, it was able to pull two small freight cars up a 2½ percent grade. The photo was taken in 1917.

Author's Collection

ROAD NOS.	BUILDER	DATE	BLDR. NO.	ENGINE & DRIVE	BODY TYPE	LGTH.	WT.	DISPOSITION	NOTES & COMMENTS
CLINTON & OKLAHOMA WESTERN RR CO., Clinton to Cheyenne, Okla., 58.99 mi. Merged into Santa Fe									
100	Brill	1924	21994	Brill 55 68hp gas	10 win. 40 pass. baggage	43'	14½T	to AT&SF, then Va. Cent.	Ran as second M.100 on Santa Fe
CLINTON STREET RAILWAY, Clinton, Okla. (Abandoned)									
1	Fair. Morse Sheffield			Fair. Morse 30hp gas	4 wheel open streetcar	22'	4½T		
NORTHEAST OKLAHOMA RR CO. (ex-Oklahoma, Kansas & Missouri) Miami, Okla. to Columbus, Kan. 24.32 mi. (Abandoned)									
106	Gen. Elect. Wason	5/13	3743 12225	GE GM 16C1 175hp gas-el.	17 win. OP bagg. 91 pass.	70'	49T	sold, Elect. Sht. Line No. 36, 1922	Ex-Chi. Peoria & St. Louis 103 (OK&M 106)
107	Gen. Elect. Wason	4/13	3746 12225	GE GM 16C1 175hp gas-el.	17 win. OP bagg. 91 pass.	70'	49T	sold, ESL No. 38, 1922	Ex-Chi. Peoria & St. Louis 102 (OK&M 107)
108	Gen. Elect. Wason	2/13	3747 12225	GE GM 16C1 175hp gas-el.	17 win. OP bagg. 91 pass.	70'	49T	sold 1923	Ex-Chi. Peoria & St. Louis 101 (OK&M 108)
OIL FIELDS SHORTLINE RR. Dilworth to Clifford, Okla. 4½ mi. (Abandoned)									
(1 car)	Four Wheel Drive			Wisconsin gas 62hp	8 win. 4 wheel CE, wood, 24 pass.	25'	8T		

ROAD NOS.	BUILDER	DATE	BLDR. NO.	ENGINE & DRIVE	BODY TYPE	LGTH.	WT.	DISPOSITION	NOTES & COMMENTS

OKLAHOMA & ARKANSAS RY. CO., Salina, Okla. (Abandoned 1926)

One gas motor listed in 1924 ''Official Register''

OKLAHOMA, NEW MEXICO & PACIFIC RY. CO., Ardmore to Ringling, Okla., 29.79 mi. Merged into Santa Fe (a Ringling road)

ROAD NOS.	BUILDER	DATE	BLDR. NO.	ENGINE & DRIVE	BODY TYPE	LGTH.	WT.	DISPOSITION	NOTES & COMMENTS
1	Curtiss			gas mechanical	48 pass.	60'		leased 1919	
5	Gen. Elect. Wason	5/12	3736 12050	GE GM16A5 175hp gas-el.	14 win. OP bagg. 80 pass.	70'	49T	sold to Midland Vy. (No. 4) 1923	Ex-Dan Patch No. 10, leased 191?
6	Wason	4/13	13500	trailer	19 win. OP 104 pass.	48'6"	22T	to Mid. Vy. (T-4) 1923	Ex-Dan Patch No. 57?, leased 1916
7	Wason	4/13	13500	trailer	19 win. OP 104 pass.	48'6"	22T	to Mid. Vy. (T-4) 1923	Ex-Dan Patch No. 58?, leased 1916
10	Co. Shops Four Whl. Drive	1923		Wisconsin gas				burned 12/25	

OKLAHOMA & SOUTHWESTERN RY. CO., Bristow to Nuyoka, Okla., 23.85 mi. (Abandoned)

ROAD NOS.	BUILDER	DATE	BLDR. NO.	ENGINE & DRIVE	BODY TYPE	LGTH.	WT.	DISPOSITION	NOTES & COMMENTS
200	St. Louis Car 4 Whl. Drive	5/20	1275	Wisc. 6 cyl. 60hp gas	4 win. 4 wheel bag., 16 pass.	25'	9T		Arched paired windows
201	St. Louis Car	5/20	1276	trailer	9 win. 4 wheel, 36 pass.	25'	8T		Arched paired windows

PEOPLES ELECTRIC RY. CO., Muskogee, Okla. (Abandoned)

ROAD NOS.	BUILDER	DATE	BLDR. NO.	ENGINE & DRIVE	BODY TYPE	LGTH.	WT.	DISPOSITION	NOTES & COMMENTS
1	Federal Stg.	1911		4 12½hp battery electric	10 win. 4 wheel bag., 40 pass.	40'6"	9T	sold, Webber Falls, Shawnee & Western	
Joe Haskell	McKeen	11/11	121	150hp Samet gas-mech.	15 win. CE, bag. 38 pass.	70'	39½T	reposs. by McKeen	Became Saratoga & Encampment Valley M-1, then Union Pacific second M-9
Maj. Patterson	McKeen	1911	122	200hp McKeen gas-mech.	15 win. CE, bag. 48 pass.	70'	38T	refused, not delivered	Became Union Pacific M-26

OKMULGEE NORTHERN RY. Deep Fork to Okmulgee, Okla., 9.9 mi. (Abandoned)

ROAD NOS.	BUILDER	DATE	BLDR. NO.	ENGINE & DRIVE	BODY TYPE	LGTH.	WT.	DISPOSITION	NOTES & COMMENTS
109	General Elect. Wason	5/11	3709 10270	GE GM10A1 175hp gas-el.	12 win. CE bag. 47 pass.	58'	40T		Ex-Dan Patch No. 4, acq. 1912.
110	General Elect. Wason	5/11	3710 10270	GE GM10A1 175hp gas-el.	12 win. CE bag. 47 pass.	58'	40T	to Jones. Lake Cy. & East No. 110	Became SL-SF second 2117 ex-Dan Patch No. 5. Acq. 1916.
111	General Elect. Wason	5/13	3744 12226	GE GM16C1 175hp gas-elec.	17 win. OP, bag. 91 pass.	70'	49T	to JLC&E No. 111, SL-SF sec. 2111	Ex-Chicago, Peoria & St. Louis 104, acq. 3/16

ST. LOUIS, EL RENO & WESTERN RY. CO., Guthrie to El Reno, Okla., 42 mi. (Abandoned 1923)

Had a battery-electric car in the teens.

SAND SPRINGS INTERURBAN RY., Tulsa to Sand Springs, Okla., 10 mi. (In operation)

ROAD NOS.	BUILDER	DATE	BLDR. NO.	ENGINE & DRIVE	BODY TYPE	LGTH.	WT.	DISPOSITION	NOTES & COMMENTS
1 & 2	McKeen	6/11	102 & 104	McKeen 200hp gas-mech.	15 win. CE bag. 38 pass.	70'	40T	sold 1912	1 sold to Rivera Beach & Nor., 2 to Midland Vy.
101	American Car	1912		trailer	4 win. wood, bag.	41'			
102	American Car	1912		trailer	15 win. wood, 56 pass. clere. roof	45'			

WEBBER FALLS, SHAWNEE & WESTERN RY. and WARNER & WEBBER FALLS RY., Webber Falls to Checotah, Okla. (Abandoned)

ROAD NOS.	BUILDER	DATE	BLDR. NO.	ENGINE & DRIVE	BODY TYPE	LGTH.	WT.	DISPOSITION	NOTES & COMMENTS
(1 car)	Federal	1914		Thomas 6 cyl. gas	40 pass. 10 win. streetcar	40'6"	8T		Ex-Peoples Elect. Ry. (Muskogee) battery car converted to gas car
(1 car)	Chalmers	1917		Chalmers 6 gas	7 pass. touring car				(Warner & Webber Falls)

Oregon

AREA: 96,981 sq. miles
CAPITAL: Salem
POPULATION (1927): 890,000

THE BIG INDUSTRY in Oregon was, and continues to be, lumbering. As many lumbering operations (at least up until the very recent past) operated a railroad in conjunction with the logging operation, it will come as no surprise that many of the short lines of Oregon were owned by lumber companies.

Most of the cars used on these lines tended to be light in weight and often home-built.

However, one line, the Valley and Siletz, had two of the large Hall-Scott gas cars, in addition to a lightweight Hofius-built car and a couple of home-builts, thus touching all bases for variety.

A glance at the accompanying rosters will reveal a real variety of equipment, everything from McKeens to battery cars.

Two roads merit some additional re-marks. One is the City of Prineville Rail-road, one of the very few city-owned rail-roads in the United States which is still in operation. At one time, its profits paid enough to underwrite the entire budget of the city government.

The other is the Oregon Pacific and Eastern, which also is still in operation, perhaps more as a tourist attraction than anything else. It had the only Budd RDC car operated by a working short line. The ex-SP-NWP car was resold to the Moody Foundation of Galveston, Texas, in 1978.

McKEEN CAR No. 1 bears the Salem, Falls City & Western name but seems to be hooked up to two other McKeens owned by Southern Pacific. The SP took over this short line and the photo (made at Salem) may have been taken about that time. *Author's Collection*

A RARE CASE was the ownership of a Budd RDC car by a short line, but it happened on the Oregon, Pacific & Eastern. The ex-Southern Pacific unit is shown at Cottage Grove, much the worse for wear.
*Tom Gray,
W.C. Whittaker Collection*

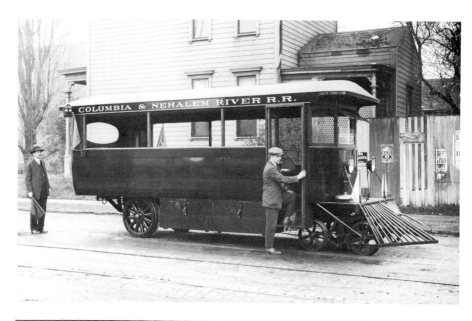

FLAGMAN keeps a wary eye for the photographer, who is recording this breezy White railbus, circa 1920, on the Columbia & Nehalem River. Windows were later installed.
Randolph Brandt Collection

ROAD NOS.	BUILDER	DATE	BLDR. NO.	ENGINE & DRIVE	BODY TYPE	LGTH.	WT.	DISPOSITION	NOTES & COMMENTS
CALIFORNIA & OREGON COAST RR CO., Grants Pass to Waters Creek, Ore., 14.61 mi. (Abandoned)									
(1 car)	Fair. Morse ? Co. Shops			Fair. Morse gas	4 win. 4 whl. CE, wood. "speeder" chassis with home-built body				
CITY OF PRINEVILLE RY., Prineville to Prineville Jct., Ore., 18.3 mi. (In operation)									
1	White, New Haven Car	1919		White 4 cyl. gas	5 win. CE, 4 whl. lead truck, wood			sold 1928	Originally open, later windows installed
2	Buda, Skagit	1928		Buda gas	1 win. CE, bag.	25′		sold 1941	
COLUMBIA & NEHALEM RIVER RR (Abandoned)									
	New Haven Carr., White	1918		White 4 cyl. gas	open, wood bus, 4 whl. lead trk.				Windows installed at a later date
CONDON, KINZUA & SOUTHERN RR CO., Condon to Kinzua, Ore. 24 mi. (Abandoned)									
5	White			White 4 cyl. gas	bag. doors only, 4 whl. lead truck			on display, Fossil, Ore.	
10	Kuhlman Mack	1922	70014	Mack AB 30hp gas	7 win. hood type bus, 4 whl. lead truck, 28 pass.	27′	5½ T		Ex-Mt. Hood Ry., No. 10
INDEPENDENCE & MONMOUTH RY., Independence to Monmouth, Ore., 2.5 mi. (Abandoned)									
(1 car)	Co. Shops			gas	4 win. 4 whl. CE wood, 10 pass.	abt. 15′			
MOUNT HOOD RR CO., Hood River to Parkdale, Ore., 22.2 mi. (16 miles in operation)									
1	White, New Haven Carr.	1916		White 6-60 60hp gas	hood type open bus, 2 whl. lead truck			retired 11/24	
2	White, New Haven Carr.	1917		White 4-40 40hp gas	hood type open bus, 2 whl. lead truck			retired 11/29	
10	Cummings Mack	4/22	70014	Mack AB 30hp gas	7 win. hood type bus, 4 whl. lead truck	28′ 8″	5½ T	sold, Con. Kin. & Sou. 1941	

ROGUE RIVER VALLEY had two
'critters, and here are both of them.
The little Fairbanks-Morse is really
a speeder with a roof for passenger
comfort. Bigger No. 2 has a demure
deck roof and a fancy paint job.
(Top Photo) Ted Wurm Collection;
(Bottom Photo) Randolph Brandt
Collection

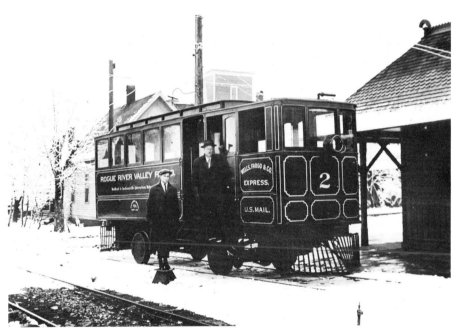

ROAD NOS.	BUILDER	DATE	BLDR. NO.	ENGINE & DRIVE	BODY TYPE	LGTH.	WT.	DISPOSITION	NOTES & COMMENTS
OREGON, PACIFIC & EASTERN RY. CO., Cottage Grove to Disston, Ore., 23.63 mi. (Abandoned)									
1	Co. Shops	1917		gas-mech.	old streetcar body, RPO sect.?			retired by 1927	
2	(no info)								
100	Budd	1953	5917	2 GM 628, 275hp dies.-hydr.	16 win. 76 pass. sing. end	73'	83½T	sold, Moody Foundation, 1978	Ex-Sou. Pac. SP-10, acq. 7/71, now on display Cen. Trans. & Comm., Galveston, Texas
PACIFIC & EASTERN RY., Medford area, Ore. (Abandoned)									
(1 car)	Pierce ?			Pierce gas ?	4 whl. 3 win. open bus, 8 pass.				
PORTLAND & OREGON CITY RY. CO., Portland to Carver, Ore. (Abandoned)									
(1 car)	White			White 4 cyl. gas	3 win. CE, 4 whl. lead truck, bus			rebuilt into highway bus	Ex-highway bus

CITY OF PRINEVILLE No. 1, a White railbus, disappeared from the property early. However, the city-owned railroad in Central Oregon endured well into the 1980s.
Author's Collection

BAGGAGE AND FREIGHT only were carried by White-built No. 5 of the Condon, Kinzua & Southern. She's at Kinzua in 1947.
Ken Kidder,
W.C. Whittaker Collection

NO-NONSENSE Mt. Hood Mack No. 10 plied between Hood River and Parkdale, Ore., not far from Portland on the Columbia River.
W.C. Whittaker Collection

ROAD NOS.	BUILDER	DATE	BLDR. NO.	ENGINE & DRIVE	BODY TYPE	LGTH.	WT.	DISPOSITION	NOTES & COMMENTS
PORTLAND & SOUTHWESTERN RR									
(1 car)	Co. Shops			Mack gas	4 win. hood type bus, 4 whl. lead truck, wood body				
ROGUE RIVER VALLEY RY. CO., Medford to Jacksonville, Ore., 6 mi. (Abandoned)									
1	Fair. Morse			Fair. Morse gas	open 4 whl. "speeder" type body				
2	Ferry Garage	1910		Brennan 4 cyl. 70hp gas	6 win. CE 4 whl. wood bag. 28 pass. deck roof				
SUMPTER VALLEY RY. CO. (3' gauge) Baker to Prairie City, Ore., 79.63 mi. (Abandoned)									
Motor No. 1	White Co. Shops	1918		White 4 40hp gas	open 27 pass. hood type bus			wrecked after 30 days of service	
SALEM, FALLS CITY & WESTERN RY., Salem to Falls City, Ore. (Merged into Southern Pacific)									
1	McKeen	1909	56	McKeen 200hp gas-mech.	12 win. CE bag. 80 pass.	70'	34T	to SP 7/1/15 (No. 67)	
UNION RAILROAD OF OREGON, Union to Union Jct., Ore., 2.5 mi. (Abandoned)									
(1 car)	Pierce			Pierce gas	4 win. 4 wheel open wood				
VALLEY & SILETZ RR CO., Independence to Valsetz, Ore. 40.6 mi. (Abandoned)									
5	Hofius	1916		Wisc. 125hp gas	7 win. OP bag. 30 pass.		15T	scrapped 1945	Ex-Hartford & Eastern No. 3, acq. 1918, lengthened in 1923
9	Hall-Scott	1913	7	Hall-Scott 150hp gas-mech.	11 win. bag. pass.	60'			Ex-Holton Int. No. 5
10	Hall-Scott	1913	11	Hall-Scott 150hp gas-mech.	13 win. bag. pass.	60'			Ex-Salt Lake & Utah 501
35	Cobb & Mitchell Lumber Co.			Hercules gas	2 win. 4 whl. wood "speeder"			rebuilt to maint of way	
40	Skagit			Buda YBO gas	3 win. CE bag-pass. "speeder" wooden				
WILLAMETTE PACIFIC (Merged into SP)									
(1 car)	McKeen	1914		McKeen 200hp	12 win CE	55'	35T		
WILLAMETTE VALLEY & COAST RR CO., Cherry Grove to Patton, Ore., 5 mi. (Abandoned)									
1	Edwards	1923		Buda 108hp gas	7 win. OP bag. 25 pass.	30'	8½T		
10	Ry. Stor. Btty.			battery-elect.					
WILLAMINA & GRANDE RONDE RY.									
(1 car)	Mack Brill	12/21	70012	Mack AB 30hp gas	8 win. 25 pass. hood type bus, 4 whl. lead trk.	28'8"	6½T		
(1 car)	Mack Cummings	11/22	70016	Mack AB 30hp gas	8 win. 25 pass. hood type bus, 4 whl. lead trk.				

Pennsylvania

AREA: 45,333
CAPITAL: Harrisburg
POPULATION (1927): 9,730,000

OUTSIDE OF THE SOUTH, Pennsylvania had the greatest number of short lines operating rail motor cars in the United States. At the upper end of the Appalachian chain of short lines, many of these roads were associated with the coal-mining industry, but inasmuch as there were short lines in all areas of the state, just about all phases of short line railroading were represented; from local transit-type lines to heavy almost mainline-type operation.

Among the most interesting was the famous three-foot-gauge East Broad Top, with its home-built gas-electric car. The Ligonier Valley had one of the very early (1862) Grice and Long steam cars, and in later years a modest fleet of Brill gas cars and Electro-Motive gas-electrics, which were all secondhand.

The Huntington & Broad Top Mountain was one of the few short lines that operated one of the "last-generation" really big gas-electric cars. Purchased in 1929, it was one of the 600-hp dual Hall-Scott engined Brills, and weighed out at 75 tons.

Although none of the lines bought any of the first-generation heavy cars (McKeen, General Electric, Hall-Scott) there were some rare models to be seen.

The Pittsburgh & Shawmut had three of the very few Bowen cars, and the Susquehanna and New York had the only Smalley car ever built.

This car was not successful and was demotorized which was thought to have been the end of its story. However, further research uncovered evidence lead to the conclusion that this car was sold to the Live Oak, Perry and Gulf Railroad in Florida, where it was repowered and used for a number of years. It also probably ran on the affiliated South Georgia Railway.

One wonders how many other deals of this sort have not yet been uncovered.

EAST BROAD TOP was prepared to haul any size load, or crowd, on its motor cars. The large M-1 was assembled in company shops from a Brill kit, while the tiny M-3 was really a speeder with room for passengers.
(Top Photo) Author's Collection
(Middle Photo) Bob Leibman Collection

AWAITING ITS CALL to duty is Lake Erie Franklin & Clarion Brill Model 55 at Clarion, Pa., in 1935.
William Monypeny Photo; Louis Saillard Collection

ROAD NOS.	BUILDER	DATE	BLDR. NO.	ENGINE & DRIVE	BODY TYPE	LGTH.	WT.	DISPOSITION	NOTES & COMMENTS

BELLEFONTE CENTRAL RR CO., Bellefonte to State College, Pa. 3.64 mi. (Abandoned)

ROAD NOS.	BUILDER	DATE	BLDR. NO.	ENGINE & DRIVE	BODY TYPE	LGTH.	WT.	DISPOSITION	NOTES & COMMENTS
first 1	Wason, New York & New England Ry.	1894 1897		Amer. Loco. 2 cyl. steam	10 win. OP bag. pass.	64'			Built as diner for NYNH&H (No. 271), transferred to NY&NE (No. 198) and rebuilt to steam drive. Sold to Bell. Cen. in 1909, but was too long.
second 1	St. Louis Car Charles City Western Ry.	1892 1910		Buda 4 cyl. 40hp gas	6 win. OP, 4 whl. streetcar	24'			Built as horse car for Peoria Ry., sold to CCW who motorized the car, sold to Bell. Cen. 3/24/15.

CAMBRIA & INDIANA RR CO., Manver to Revloc, Pa. and branches 60.43 mi. (Abandoned)

ROAD NOS.	BUILDER	DATE	BLDR. NO.	ENGINE & DRIVE	BODY TYPE	LGTH.	WT.	DISPOSITION	NOTES & COMMENTS
14 140	Brill, Ry. Store. Btty.	1914	19431	Edison 250 cell batt.-elect.	13 window bag. 48 pass.	49'	30T	sold to Can. Nat. (No. 15802) 1922	Had trolley pole for use on a steep grade
15 150	Brill, Ry. Store. Btty.	1916	19904	Edison 210 cell batt.-elect.	8 win. 4 whl. bag. 32 pass.	36'6"	23T	sold to Can. Nat. (No. 15803) 1922	Had trolley pole for use on a steep grade
98	Brill Service	10/22	21874	Midwest 68hp gas-mech.	10 win. bag. 43 pass.	43'	15T	sold, 4/42	
99	Brill Service	10/22	21874	Midwest 68hp gas-mech.	10 win. bag. 43 pass.	43'	15T	sold, 4/42	

CHESTNUT RIDGE RY. CO., Kunkletown to Palmerton and Lehigh Gap, Pa., 11.54 mi. (Abandoned)

ROAD NOS.	BUILDER	DATE	BLDR. NO.	ENGINE & DRIVE	BODY TYPE	LGTH.	WT.	DISPOSITION	NOTES & COMMENTS
51	Mack Brill	1922	70013 21468	Mack AB 30hp gas	8 win. hood type bus body, 4 whl. lead truck, 25 pass.	27'	5½T	later used as gang car	Ex-Pittsburgh, Lisbon & Western No. 51, acq. 1924
99	Ford			Ford 4 cyl. gas	truck body			scrapped 1935	

CORNWALL & LEBANON RR, Lebanon to Conewago, Pa. 22 mi. (Merged into Penn. RR)

ROAD NOS.	BUILDER	DATE	BLDR. NO.	ENGINE & DRIVE	BODY TYPE	LGTH.	WT.	DISPOSITION	NOTES & COMMENTS
"Gretna"	Fair. Morse Sheffield			Fair. Morse 30hp gas	6 bench, 4 wheel, wood, open st.car	22'	4½T		

COUDERSPORT & PORT ALLEGHENY RR CO., Port Allegheny to Newfield Jct., 32.36 mi. (Abandoned)

ROAD NOS.	BUILDER	DATE	BLDR. NO.	ENGINE & DRIVE	BODY TYPE	LGTH.	WT.	DISPOSITION	NOTES & COMMENTS
20	Brill	1922	21500	Midwest 40hp gas	8 win. 4 whl. ld. trk. bag. 30 pass.	31'6"	10T	scrapped 1943	
107	Evans	1937		Reo gas 6 cyl. 70hp	5 win. CE bus 23 pass.	25'	5T		Ex-Arlington & Fairfax 107, acq. 11/40

DENTS RUN RR, Dents Run to Wilmere, Pa., 6 mi. (Abandoned 1936)

ROAD NOS.	BUILDER	DATE	BLDR. NO.	ENGINE & DRIVE	BODY TYPE	LGTH.	WT.	DISPOSITION	NOTES & COMMENTS
(1 car)	Brookville			Ford gas ?	open truck ?				

EAST BROAD TOP RR & COAL CO., Mt. Union to Alvan, Pa., 32.62 mi. (Partly open as tourist attraction)

ROAD NOS.	BUILDER	DATE	BLDR. NO.	ENGINE & DRIVE	BODY TYPE	LGTH.	WT.	DISPOSITION	NOTES & COMMENTS
M-1	Brill Co. Shops	1926	22416	Brill gas-elect.	4 win. bag. 12 pass.		46T	in service	Car assembled by the EBT shops
M-2	Co. Shops	1927			7 win. OP wood deck roof st.car				Ex-Johnson City, Tenn. streetcar
M-3	Co. Shops			Nash gas	3 win. rear door "speeder" with hood				

EPHRATA & LEBANON ST. RY., Ephrata to Lebanon, Pa., abt. 15 mi. (Electrified and then abandoned)

ROAD NOS.	BUILDER	DATE	BLDR. NO.	ENGINE & DRIVE	BODY TYPE	LGTH.	WT.	DISPOSITION	NOTES & COMMENTS
1	Federal	3/12		190 cell btty. (2) 12hp el.mot.	9 win. bag. 34 pass. st.car	35'1"		returned to builder	Used on Wilmington, New Castle & Dela. City for a short time
2 & 3	Federal	3/12		190 cell btty. (2) 12hp el.mot.	9 win. 4 whl. st.car	27'6"			
4				battery-elect.	9 win. 4 whl. st.car				Used car

HUNTINGTON & BROAD TOP MOUNTAIN RR & COAL CO., Huntington to Bedford, Pa., 74.2 mi. (Abandoned)

ROAD NOS.	BUILDER	DATE	BLDR. NO.	ENGINE & DRIVE	BODY TYPE	LGTH.	WT.	DISPOSITION	NOTES & COMMENTS
26	Brill	1929	22830	trailer	RPO bag., 2 bag. doors	55'	28T	wrecked 1957	Ex-San Francisco & Napa Valley 56, orig. built for Wichita Falls & Nor. as motor, canceled

ROAD NOS.	BUILDER	DATE	BLDR. NO.	ENGINE & DRIVE	BODY TYPE	LGTH.	WT.	DISPOSITION	NOTES & COMMENTS
27	Brill Co. Shops	1929	22761	trailer		73'		at Ry. Cy. Mus.	Rebuild of motor M-39 (next)
M-39	Brill	1929	22761	(2) Hall-Scott 275, 300hp GE	bag. 54 pass.	73'	75T	wrecked 5/5/42	Rebuilt to trailer 27 (see above)

LAKE ERIE, FRANKLIN & CLARION RR, Clarion to Summerville and Sutton, Pa., 32.92 mi. (Abandoned)

ROAD NOS.	BUILDER	DATE	BLDR. NO.	ENGINE & DRIVE	BODY TYPE	LGTH.	WT.	DISPOSITION	NOTES & COMMENTS
10	Brill	1925		Brill 55 70hp gas	10 win. bag. 38 pass.	43'	15T	sold 1942	

LANCASTER, OXFORD & SOUTHERN RY. (3 foot gauge) Quarryville to Oxford & Peachbottom, Pa. (Abandoned)

ROAD NOS.	BUILDER	DATE	BLDR. NO.	ENGINE & DRIVE	BODY TYPE	LGTH.	WT.	DISPOSITION	NOTES & COMMENTS
(1 car)	Co. Shops Jack. & Sharp	1913 1889		gas-mech.	10 win. CE. clere. roof, wood bag. 36 pass.			sold to Grasse Riv. Ry. 1918	Ex-steam road combine

LEWISBURG, MILTON & WATSONTOWN PASSENGER RY. (Merged into Pennsylvania RR)

ROAD NOS.	BUILDER	DATE	BLDR. NO.	ENGINE & DRIVE	BODY TYPE	LGTH.	WT.	DISPOSITION	NOTES & COMMENTS
12	Brill Federal	1910	18217	(4) 12hp GE el. mot. 190 cell battery	10 win. 40 pass. wood st.car	36' 3"	15T	retired 1922	
14	Brill Federal	7/12	18331	(4) 12hp GE el. mot. 190 cell battery	8 win. bag. 32 pass. st.car	39' 8"	16T	retired 1922	
20	Mack Brill	11/21	60005 21368	Mack AC 64hp gas	7 win. bag. 32 pass. 4 whl. lead truck	34' 7"	10T	to PRR No. 4738	Subsequently to Artemus & Jellico Ry., Buffalo Creek & Gauley RR, Strasburg Ry.

LIGONIER VALLEY RR CO., Latrobe to Ligonier, Pa., 10.3 mi. (Abandoned)

ROAD NOS.	BUILDER	DATE	BLDR. NO.	ENGINE & DRIVE	BODY TYPE	LGTH.	WT.	DISPOSITION	NOTES & COMMENTS
M-10	Brill	1924	22097	Brill 55 68hp gas	10 win. bag. 43 pass.	43'	14½T	rebuilt to a trailer	Ex-Punxatawney Coal Co., M-10
M-21	Brill	1929	22751	Brill 55 68hp gas	8 win. bag. 40 pass.	43'	14½T		Ex-St. Louis Sou. Western M-21
1150	St. Louis Car EMC	1/26	1368D 127	Winton 220hp gas-elect.	12 win. bag. 44 pass.	59' 7"	39½T		Ex-Boston & Maine 1150, acq. 1943
1152	St. Louis Car EMC	2/26	1368D 129	Winton 220hp gas-elect.	12 win. bag. 44 pass.	59' 7"	39½T		Ex-Boston & Maine 1152, acq. 1943
(1 car)	Grice & Long	1862	17	steam, (2) 6x10 cyl.	13 win. wood abt. 40 pass.			sold 1883 to Cam. Glou. & Mt. Ephraim Ry. (NJ)	

MONONGAHELA RY. CO., Brownsville Jct., Pa. to Fairmont, W. Va., 69.3 mi., total operated (leased and trackage rights) 171.56 mi. (In operation)

ROAD NOS.	BUILDER	DATE	BLDR. NO.	ENGINE & DRIVE	BODY TYPE	LGTH.	WT.	DISPOSITION	NOTES & COMMENTS
M-70	Mack Pullman	1928	162001	(3) Mack AP 120hp gas-elect.	14 win. bag. 72 pass.	74'	57½T	scrapped 7/51	Built as Mack demo M2001, sold to Pitt. & Lake Erie (M-70) to Mon. Ry. 1/40

MT. JEWETT, KINZUA & RITERSVILLE RR CO., Mt. Jewett to Kushequa, Pa., and branches, about 22 mi. (Abandoned)

ROAD NOS.	BUILDER	DATE	BLDR. NO.	ENGINE & DRIVE	BODY TYPE	LGTH.	WT.	DISPOSITION	NOTES & COMMENTS
first 10		1899		steam	8 win. OP, clere. roof, 4 whl. st.car body			wrecked ?	Prob. secondhand
second 10	Brill White	1923	21531	White 40hp gas	8 win. CE, bag. 30 pass.	31' 11"	9½T		There are also records of Edwards supplying a car at this time, which car was used, unknown.
11				steam	9 win. OP, 4 whl. "Bombay" roof, st.car body				Prob. secondhand

NEW BERLIN & WINFIELD RR, New Berlin to Winfield, Pa., 8 mi. (3 foot gauge) (Abandoned 1916)

ROAD NOS.	BUILDER	DATE	BLDR. NO.	ENGINE & DRIVE	BODY TYPE	LGTH.	WT.	DISPOSITION	NOTES & COMMENTS
	Mitchell			Mitchell gas	open sedan, 4 whl. lead truck				Side seats in rear, open back door, abt. 6 pass.

PITTSBURGH, LISBON & WESTERN RR CO., New Galilee, Pa., to Lisbon, Ohio, 23.3 mi. (Merged into Youngstown & Southern)

ROAD NOS.	BUILDER	DATE	BLDR. NO.	ENGINE & DRIVE	BODY TYPE	LGTH.	WT.	DISPOSITION	NOTES & COMMENTS
21 and 22	Brill	1924	21993	Brill 55 68hp gas	10 win. bag. 24 pass.	43'	15T		
51	Mack Brill	1/22	70013 21468	Mack AB 30hp gas-mech.	8 win. hood type bus, 25 pass. 4 whl. lead truck	28' 8"	5½T	sold to Chestnut Ridge Ry. '24	

ROVER CAR: Panama Traction
later the Youngsville & Sugar Grove
t. Ry.) operated this White railbus
f classic dimensions. A painting of
his car by Larry Fisher adorns the
ust jacket of this book. Meander-
ng, rickety track was pretty typical
f many such short lines.
Author's Collection

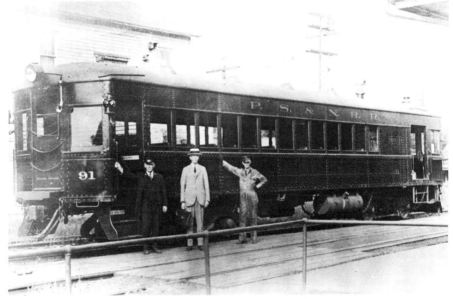

LONE PASSENGER is bracketed by
the two-man crew of Pittsburgh,
Shawmut & Northern 55-foot Brill
No. 91. Short line penetrated into
New York State and this view was
taken at Olean, N.Y., in 1935.
Harold K. Vollrath Collection

AFTER THE WIRES came down, Wilkes-Barre & Hazleton operated three Mack railbuses, including No. 204, pictured at Wilkes-Barre, Pa., in February 1933.
George Votava Collection

(Opposite Page) BULLDOG MAC front adorned Lewisburg, Milton Watsontown railbus No. 20. Th unit was sold to the mighty Pennsy vania RR and later to three oth short lines. *Author's Collectio*

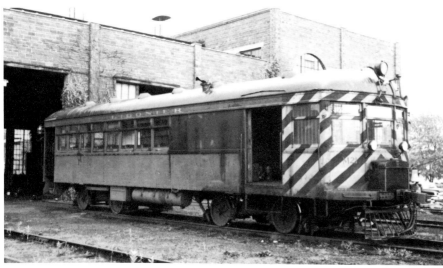

IN NEED OF PAINT, Ligonier Valley M-21 Brill combine waits patiently outside company shops for its next call to duty. *Paul B. Dunn*

ROAD NOS.	BUILDER	DATE	BLDR. NO.	ENGINE & DRIVE	BODY TYPE	LGTH.	WT.	DISPOSITION	NOTES & COMMENTS
PITTSBURGH & SHAWMUT RR CO., Erie Jct. to Freeport, Pa., 88.01 mi. (In operation)									
400-402	Bowen Barny & Smith	8/21		Midwest 62hp gas	9 win. CE, bag. 39 pass.	39'5"	16T	retired, 1936 to 1941	
403 & 404	Brill			Brill 55 68hp gas-mech.	10 win. bag. 40 pass.	43'	14½T	retired by 1940	Acq. secondhand about 1935 (the photo stated the cars were Tuscan Red, ex-Pennsy?)
PITTSBURGH, SHAWMUT & NORTHERN RR CO., Hyde, Pa., to Wayland Jct., NY, 144.5 mi. (Abandoned)									
90	Brill	1925	22190	Winton 110 185hp gas-mech.	13 win. bag. 56 pass.	55'	28T	sold, Con. Ry. of Cuba 1/39	
91	Brill	1926	22391	Winton 110 185hp gas-mech.	13 win. bag. 54 pass.	55'	27½T	sold 1936	
PITTSBURGH & SUSQUEHANNA RR CO., Wigton to Fernwood, Pa., 15.4 mi. (Abandoned)									
	Republic truck			Cont. ''Red Seal'' gas	hood type 26 bus body		4½T		

QUAKERTOWN & DELAWARE RIVER TRACTION CO., Quakertown, Pa. (Abandoned)

Obtained 4 ex-Capitol Traction Co. 4 wheel horse car trailers (Nos. 1556, 1501, 1517, 1297), converted 2 of them (1501 & 1517) to gas cars.

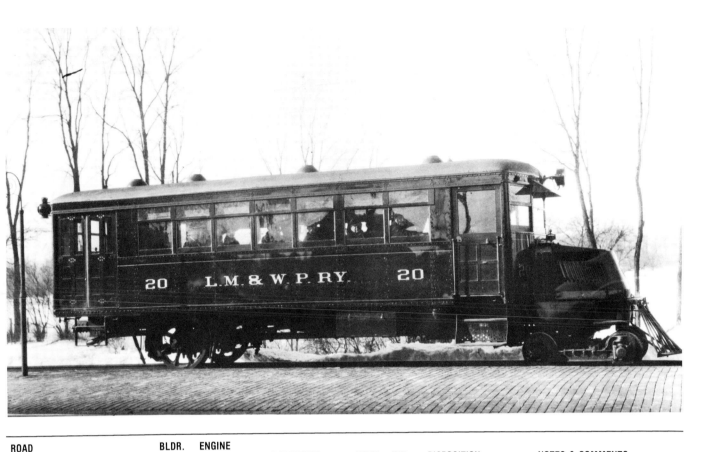

ROAD NOS.	BUILDER	DATE	BLDR. NO.	ENGINE & DRIVE	BODY TYPE	LGTH.	WT.	DISPOSITION	NOTES & COMMENTS
SCHUYKILL & DAUPHINE TRACTION CO., Williamsport, Pa. (Abandoned)									
(1 car)	Ry. Motor Car Brill	1910 ?		Rutenberg & Davis 60hp gas	8 win. 4 whl. 30 pass. st.car, deck roof	32'	10½T		Brill 21E truck
STEWARTSTOWN RR CO., Stewartstown to New Freedom, Pa. 7.2 mi. (In operation)									
7	Brill	1923	21740	White 4 cyl. 40hp gas	8 win. 4 whl. lead truck, bag. 27 pass.	31'6"	10T		Model 43
SUSQUEHANNA & NEW YORK RR CO., Towanda to West Williamsport, Pa., 67.72 mi. (Abandoned)									
M-251	Smalley	1925		(2) Climax 75hp gas-mech.	15 win. bag. 50 pass.	60'	30½T	rebuilt to coach No. 206	To Live Oak, Poplar & Gulf
TIONESTA VALLEY RY. CO., Clarendon Jct. to Halton, Pa., 36.6 mi. (Abandoned)									
M-55	Co. Shops Chevrolet			Chevrolet 6 gas	2 win. van type truck body, 4 whl. lead truck				
(1 car)	Co. Shops Chevrolet			Chevrolet 6 gas	2 win. van type truck body, 4 whl. lead truck				Narrow gauge
WAYNESBURG & WASHINGTON RR CO., Waynesburg to Washington, Pa., 28.19 mi., 3 foot gauge (Abandoned 1975)									
1	Co. Shops	1938		Ford V-8 gas	4 whl. hood frt. panel truck			sold or scrap. 1958	Orig. narrow gauge. Standard gauged 1943.
6590	Fairmont ?	1933		gas	4 whl. open "speeder"				
WILKES-BARRE & HAZELTON RR, Wilkes-Barre to Hazelton, Pa., ex-interurban railway									
204	Mack	8/32		Mack AD gas	6 win. hood type bus, 4 whl. lead truck			sold Lehigh Vy. Tract. 1933 (125), rblt to bus	
206 & 208	Mack	8/32		Mack AD gas	7 win. bus, 4 whl. lead truck			sold LVT 1933, Nos. 126 & 127, rblt to bus	

ROAD NOS.	BUILDER	DATE	BLDR. NO.	ENGINE & DRIVE	BODY TYPE	LGTH.	WT.	DISPOSITION	NOTES & COMMENTS
WILLIAMSPORT & NORTH BRANCH RY. CO., Halls to Saterfield, Pa., 44.4 mi. (Abandoned)									
1		1880		vert. steam	9 win. 4 whl. clere. roof, wood				
(1 car)	Ford	1924		Ford 4 cyl gas	Model T 4 pass. wooden sta. wag.				Orig. used for inspection, later used for express and perishables.
YOUNGSVILLE & SUGAR GROVE ST. RY., Youngsville to Sugar Grove, Pa. (Abandoned) (ex-Panama Traction Co.)									
(1 car)	White	1919		White 4 40hp gas	4 wheel open bus, abt. 20 pass.				

Rhode Island

AREA: 1,214 sq. miles
CAPITAL: Providence
POPULATION (1927): 704,000

MEETING the New Haven Railroad at Kingston, R.I., was the duty of Narragansett Pier railbus which had both tires and flanged wheels.
P. Kutta Collection

WITH ITS TINY SIZE and the number of trolley car lines that Rhode Island had, it is only natural that there wasn't much room for even short, short lines.

But there was one—the Narragansett Pier Railroad was only eight miles long. It managed to accumulate a fair-sized fleet, having at one time or another six cars, and they were all different.

The NPRR started out on the wrong foot, however, buying a secondhand, 70-foot McKeen car. This car was just too long for such a short line, and the story goes that it didn't even complete one round trip.

After this fiasco, short cars for a short line became the byword.

Two Mack rail buses were purchased in the early 1920s. These were replaced by two tiny Evans Auto-Railers, and finally an International-powered school bus-type unit that took the place of one of the Evans cars after it caught fire in 1945.

The other Auto-Railer and the school bus continued to provide service till the end of passenger service, which came in 1953. It was a colorful little short line, and a favorite among its passengers and admirers for many years.

MACK RAILBUS (either No. 9 or 10) rounds the bend on one of its daily trips from the Pier to the Kingston connection. This photo was taken on May 29, 1937.
George E. Votava Collection

(Below) A LONG CAREER on the Hampton & Branchville was the fortune of Edwards-built motor M-200. It was bought in 1926 and ran until 1951.   *M.B. Connery Collection*

ROAD NOS.	BUILDER	DATE	BLDR. NO.	ENGINE & DRIVE	BODY TYPE	LGTH.	WT.	DISPOSITION	NOTES & COMMENTS
NARRAGANSETT PIER RR CO., Narragansett Pier to Kingston, R.I., 8.03 mi. (Abandoned)									
8	McKeen	1910	90	McKeen 200hp gas-mech.	CE, bag. pass.	70'	37½T	scrapped 1930	Ex-Deer River, ex-ex-Buff. Roch. & Pitt. 1001, never used (too long)
9	Mack Brill	6/21	70007 21323	Mack AB 30hp gas	6 win. bag. 31 pass. hood type bus	28'8"	5½T	scrapped 1940	
10	Mack Brill	6/22	60001	Mack AC 64hp gas	7 win. hood type bus, bag. 40 pass.	34'7"	10T	scrapped 1940	
32	Evans			Reo gas	5 win. CE, 24 pass. bus			burned 1945	Ex-Arlington & Fairfax (Va.)
34	Evans			Reo gas	5 win. CE, 35 pass. bus			scrapped 1953	Ex-Arlington & Fairfax (Va.)
36	Intl. Harvester			Int. gas	6 win. school bus			sold 1953	

South Carolina

AREA: 31,055 sq. miles

CAPITAL: Columbia

POPULATION (1927): 1,845,000

RIGHT IN THE MIDST of our Appalachain belt of short lines comes South Carolina, which rather upsets our theory.

It did have a fair number of short lines, to be sure, but only five of them (and one of these was a local traction line) invested in rail motor cars, and even then in a very modest way.

About the most unusual fact about any of these lines is that the Hampton & Branchville is still in operation, and *still* has its Edwards car on the property. We hear they are willing to sell it.

AUGUSTA NORTHERN RY., Ward to Saluda, S.C., 12 mi. (Abandoned)

1940 "Official Register" listed one passenger motor and one combination (Pass., Mail, Exp.)

BAMBERG, EHRHARDT & WALTERBORO RY. CO., Bamberg to Ehrhardt, S.C., 14.4 mi. (Abandoned)

Official Registers in 1922, 23 and 24 listed one car (No. 711) as a gas car.

BLUE RIDGE RY., Walhalla to Belton, S.C., 44 mi. (Merged into Southern Ry.)

ROAD NOS.	BUILDER	DATE	BLDR. NO.	ENGINE & DRIVE	BODY TYPE	LGTH.	WT.	DISPOSITION	NOTES & COMMENTS
(2 cars)	Edwards	1924		Buda gas	7 win. OP bag. 30 pass.	31'	10T		

CAROLINA TRACTION CO., Rock Hill, S.C., 2.7 mi. (Abandoned)

ROAD NOS.	BUILDER	DATE	BLDR. NO.	ENGINE & DRIVE	BODY TYPE	LGTH.	WT.	DISPOSITION	NOTES & COMMENTS
(2 cars)	Federal	1911		battery-elect.	4 wheel st.car, 7 win. 28 pass.	27'8"		sold 1918	Arch roof
(1 car)	Federal	1912		battery-elect.	4 wheel st.car, 7 win. 28 pass.			sold 1918	Arch roof

HAMPTON & BRANCHVILLE RR CO., Hampton to Cottageville, S.C., 47.6 mi. (17 mi. in operation)

ROAD NOS.	BUILDER	DATE	BLDR. NO.	ENGINE & DRIVE	BODY TYPE	LGTH.	WT.	DISPOSITION	NOTES & COMMENTS
M-200	Edwards	1926		(2) Buda 108hp gas	10 win. bag. 42 pass.	43'	17T	used up until 11/51, stored on property	

Tennessee

AREA: 42,244 sq. miles

CAPITAL: Nashville

POPULATION (1927): 2,485,000

MOST OF THE important short lines of Tennessee were associated with the coal-mining industry, and were very much off the beaten track in the mountainous area of the state.

Of these the only one still in operation is the Tennessee Railroad.

Except for one notable exception, the cars used on these lines ranged from small to tiny. This exception was on the Tennessee, Kentucky & Northern, which purchased a huge McKeen from the Southern Railway in 1914. Given the fact that the car was only four years old when the Southern sold it, it is safe to say that the operating quality of the car left a bit to be desired.

What the little TK&N could have done with this unwieldy beast is hard to imagine. It is sufficient to say that in a few years the road purchased a White rail bus which weighed 4½ tons as contrasted to the McKeen's 40 tons.

OPEN-PLATFORM TRAILER 16 served the Tennessee Railroad Co. The body may have been made by Edwards but not much is known of the origin of the lightweight trucks. It is pictured in 1946.

S.P. Guthrie;
Charles E. Winters Collection

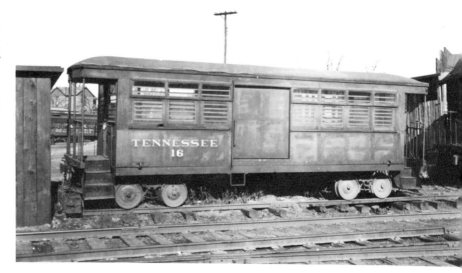

STUDEBAKER autobus No. 26 ran on the Little River with flanged wheels. *W.A. Cannon Collection*

MAIL CONTRACT was often what kept short line doodlebug runs going. This Tennessee Railroad Brill carries U.S. mail, baggage, parcels and passengers (at least a few). *Author's Collection*

ROAD NOS.	BUILDER	DATE	BLDR. NO.	ENGINE & DRIVE	BODY TYPE	LGTH.	WT.	DISPOSITION	NOTES & COMMENTS
LITTLE RIVER RR CO., Walland to Elkmont, Tenn., 8 mi. (Abandoned 1940)									
1	Co. Shops			gas-mech.	4 win. 4 whl. OP wood, door in back wall	abt. 15'			Probably built on "speeder" chassis
26	Studebaker Auto Body Co.	1926		Studebaker "Big Six" 75hp gas	5 win. hood type bus, 4 whl. lead truck	20'		ran until aban.	Was only piece of equipment at time of abandonment
MEMPHIS & RUGBY RY. CO. (Abandoned)									
200	Brill	1916	19437	battery-elect.	7 win., 4 whl. streetcar, arch roof	27'			
201	Brill		20110	battery-elect.	7 win., 4 whl. streetcar, arch roof				
MIDDLE TENNESSEE RR CO., Franklin to Mt. Pleasant, Tenn., 41.5 mi. (Leased to Nashville Interurban Ry., 1922-1928) (Abandoned 1928)									
28				White 4 cyl. 40hp gas	9 win. CE, rear bag. door, 4 whl. lead truck	abt. 30'			Said to have been purchased from the Tenn. Ky. & Nor. in 1923 by the Nashville Int. Ry.
NASHVILLE INTERURBAN RY. (Operated Middle Tenn. RR 1923-1928, see above)									

ROAD NOS.	BUILDER	DATE	BLDR. NO.	ENGINE & DRIVE	BODY TYPE	LGTH.	WT.	DISPOSITION	NOTES & COMMENTS
ONEIDA & WESTERN RR CO., Oneida to Louvain, Tenn., 30.15 mi. (Abandoned)									
M-3	Chevrolet Co. Shops			Chevrolet gas	5 win. hood type bus, 4 whl. lead truck				
M-4	Brill			Brill 55 68hp gas	10 win. bag. 40 pass.	43'	19½ T	retired 1953	
TENNESSEE & NORTH CAROLINA RY. CO., Newport Jct., Tenn. to Crestmont, N.C., 21 mi. and Spruce to West Canton, Tenn., 17 mi. (Abandoned)									
200	Brill	1922	21486	Midwest 68hp gas	10 win. bag. 40 pass.	43'	14½ T		
(1 car)	White			White 4 cyl. 40 hp gas	6 win. hood type bus, 4 whl. lead truck			retired 6/34	
TENNESSEE RR CO., Oneida to Fork Mountain, Tenn., 45 mi. (In operation)									
M-2	Brill	1923	21877	Midwest 68hp gas-mech.	10 win. bag. 43 pass.	43'	15T	scrapped	Ex-West River Ry., ex-ex-Lehigh Valley Ry. No. 3
16	Edwards ?			trailer	7 win. OP, cen. bag. door, bag.	abt. 30'			
TENNESSEE & CUMBERLAND RIVER RR, Tennessee Ridge to Bear Springs, Tenn., 14 mi. (Abandoned 1917)									
(1 car)	Stover	1908		Stover 30hp gas	5 win. 4 whl. wood, long hood			sold, poss. went to Mamm. Cave RR	
TENNESSEE KENTUCKY & NORTHERN RR CO., Algood to Livingston, Tenn., 19 mi. (Abandoned)									
7	McKeen	1910	60	McKeen 200hp gas-mech.	14 win. cen. & rear door, bag. 60 pass.	70'	40T		Ex-Sou. Ry. No. 3, acq. 1914
101	White St. Bernard Body	7/19		White 4 40hp gas	6 win. hood type bus, 20 pass. 4 whl. lead truck	14' 10" (body)	4½ T		
(1 car)	Edwards	1923		Buda 75hp gas	8 win. OP bag. 36 pass.	32'	10T		
	Edwards	1924		Buda 75hp gas	7 win. OP bag. 30 pass.	32'	9½ T		

Texas

AREA: 267,339 sq. miles

CAPITAL: Austin

POPULATION (1927): 5,397,000

THE STORIES of Texas's size and diversity are legion. Certainly the same thing can be said about its short lines. There were more of them than any other state, and the fact that state law required all railroads in Texas be incorporated and have headquarters in Texas led to some large operations by short line standards.

The explosive growth in the early part of the century led to the building of many tiny lines to serve boom towns that were off the main line by a few miles. There were even some mini-empires put together by some of the wheeler-dealers of the era.

And so it remains to this day—the land of boom and bust, which went from good to bad for marginal operations such as short lines.

During the boom period of the 1920s, most of the bigger short lines were grabbed up by the major lines of the area, particularly the Texas & New Orleans (Southern Pacific) and the Gulf Coast Lines (Missouri Pacific), with the Frisco also acquiring a few that were left over.

Among the larger roads that were absorbed were the Gulf, Texas & Western (Frisco), San Antonio & Aransas Pass, Texas Midland (Southern Pacific), San Antonio, Uvalde & Gulf; San Benito & Rio Grande Valley (Missouri Pacific).

The Frisco also had some very small operations in the Brownsville area, left over from the days when that line controlled the Gulf Coast Lines. They were essentially non-electrified streetcar

lines, plus a very odd three-foot, six-inch gauge line called the Rio Grande Railway whose chief function was to carry water from Brownsville to a Coast Guard installation at Port Isabel. This line was later renamed the Port Isabel & Rio Grande Valley and standard gauged.

There were a small number of small railroads in the Rio Grande Valley, most of which incorporated "Rio Grande" in their names. Among them, in addition to those already mentioned were the Rio Grande & Eagle Pass; the Rio Grande City Railway; and the Ft. Worth & Rio Grande. With all the other Rio Grande-named railroads in the nation—including the Colorado Rio Grandes—things could get confusing!

Equipment tended to be small. In the early days the Fairbanks-Morse type 24 car (which looked like a little four-wheel streetcar) was a great favorite. Later on the ubiquitous Brill 55 served no less than seven different lines.

One short line abnormality was the complete lack of Electro-Motive and Brill gas-electric cars. In fact, except for a number of General Electric gas-electrics (and a semi-experimental diesel-electric the Texas American Railway acquired from the Boston & Maine), electric drive was not used on Texas short lines.

CURVED-SIDER from Cincinnati Car Co. was converted into a motor for the Cotton Belt and later found its way to the Paris & Mt. Pleasant. Eventually it became a trailer.
Author's Collection

POSTCARD VIEW of Texas City Terminal McKeen 22 has the whole crew looking at the photographer. The car burned in 1923.
Author's Collection

MR. McKEEN made several sales to Texas railroads, and two of them wound up on the Weatherford, Mineral Wells & Northwestern. This view dates from around 1913.
Author's Collection

TEXAS MIDLAND operated this General Electric car and mate 5002; both went to the Southern Pacific in a merger. This photo was taken at the Wason plant in Massachusetts.
George E. Votava Collection

PLAIN JANE: What could be simpler than this wooden box on wheels lettered for the San Benito & Rio Grande Valley? It was a homemade express and baggage van.
R.H. Carlson Collection

IT TAKES TWO photos to do justice to this silver Twin Coach transit bus converted into a railcar for the Wichita Falls & Southern. That enormous protrusion in front certainly is interesting. No one is certain if the bus ever ran in revenue service. *Both: Author's Collection*

ROAD NOS.	BUILDER	DATE	BLDR. NO.	ENGINE & DRIVE	BODY TYPE	LGTH.	WT.	DISPOSITION	NOTES & COMMENTS
ABILENE & SOUTHERN RY., Abilene to Ballinger, Texas, 96.76 mi. (Merged into Missouri Pacific)									
900	Brill	1923	21864	Midwest 68hp gas	10 win. bag. 43 pass.	43′	14½T		
ASHERTON & GULF RY., Asherton to Bart, Texas, 32 mi. (Merged into Missouri Pacific)									
"La Foresta"		1915		gas	open sedan			retired 1921	
(1 car)				gas	bag. 4 pass.			retired 1927	
103	Brill	1924	22121	Brill 55 68hp gas	10 win., bag. 40 pass.	43′	14½T	to Mo. Pac. No. 536	
AMARILLO TRACTION CO., Amarillo, Texas, electrified 7/11									
One gas car put in service 1910, either a Buda or McGuire-Cummings									
BARTLETT & WESTERN RY. CO., Bartlett to Florence, Texas, 23.2 mi. (Abandoned 1935)									
(1 car)	Ford			Ford 4 cyl. gas	Model "T" truck				
ANGELINA & NECHES RIVER RR CO., Keltys to Chirino, Texas, 31 mi. (9 miles in operation)									
300	Brill	1923	21898	Midwest 68hp gas	10 win. bag. 40 pass.	43′	14½T		Ex-Gulf, Mobile & Northern No. 300
BROWNSVILLE & MATAMOROS BRIDGE CO., Brownsville, Texas, 1.6 mi. (Abandoned)									
(1 car)	Fair. Morse Sheffield			Fair. Morse 30 gas	4 wheel open st.car, 25 pass.	22′	4½T		May have been more than one
BROWNSVILLE STREET & INTERURBAN RY., Brownsville, Texas (Abandoned)									
2117-2118	Barber	1912	15 & 16	Knight 30hp gas	10 win. CE 4 whl. wooden, 40 pass.	33′	11T	retired 1914 & 1913	
BRYAN & CENTRAL TEXAS INTERURBAN RY., Bryan to Stone City, Texas, 23.3 mi. (Abandoned)									
300	Hall-Scott	1914	16	Hall-Scott 100hp gas-mech.	14 win. bag. 56 pass.				Baggage door right-hand side only
BRYAN & COLLEGE INTERURBAN RY. CO., Bryan to College Station, Texas, 6.75 mi. (Abandoned 1923)									
201-202	Fair. Morse Brill	9/10	17485	Fair. Morse 24 50hp gas	8 win. 4 whl. 35 pass. bag. wood clere. roof	28′8″	13T		
203	Brill			trailer					
(2 cars)	Fair. Morse Sheffield			Fair. Morse 19 30hp gas	4 whl. open, wood, 25 pass.	20′4″	4½T		
CARO NORTHERN RY. CO., Caro to Mt. Enterprise, Texas, 16.5 mi. (Abandoned 1934)									
	Edwards	1924		Buda 75hp gas	8 win. bag. 28 pass.	31′6″	10T		
CRYSTAL CITY & UVALDE RY., Corpus Christi to Crystal City, Texas, with branches 316 miles, name changed to San Antonio, Uvalde & Gulf (Merged into Missouri Pacific)									
100	St. Louis Kobusch-Wagenthals	1908	793	Kob.-Wag. steam	8 win. bag. 30 pass. wooden, open plat.				
EAST TEXAS & GULF RY. CO., Hyatt to Wurtsbaugh, Texas, 3.6 mi. (Abandoned 1934)									
Official guide listed gas car run in 1933									
GULF, TEXAS & WESTERN RY. CO., Seymour to Mineral Wells, Texas, 108 mi. (Merged into SL-SF Ry.)									
600	Brill	1923	21749	Midwest 68hp gas	10 win., bag. 50 pass.	43′	15T	to SL-SF No. 600	
601	Brill	1925	22122	Brill 55 68hp gas	10 win., bag. 50 pass.	43′	15½T	to SL-SF No. 601	
651	Brill	1924	21948	Brill 55 68hp gas	3 win. baggage-express	43′	14T	to SL-SF No. 651	

ROAD NOS.	BUILDER	DATE	BLDR. NO.	ENGINE & DRIVE	BODY TYPE	LGTH.	WT.	DISPOSITION	NOTES & COMMENTS

HASKELL TRACTION CO., Haskell, Texas. (Abandoned)

Had one gas car in 1909.

JEFFERSON & NORTHWESTERN RR CO., Jefferson to Naples, Texas, 48.93 mi. (Abandoned 1942)

ROAD NOS.	BUILDER	DATE	BLDR. NO.	ENGINE & DRIVE	BODY TYPE	LGTH.	WT.	DISPOSITION	NOTES & COMMENTS
(1 car)	Wichita Motor Truck Co.	1922		gas	8 win. bag. 30 pass.	abt. 35'			Pulled 6 win. trailer

HOUSTON & BRAZOS VALLEY RY. CO., Angleton to Bryanmound, Texas, 43 mi. (Merged into Missouri Pacific)

ROAD NOS.	BUILDER	DATE	BLDR. NO.	ENGINE & DRIVE	BODY TYPE	LGTH.	WT.	DISPOSITION	NOTES & COMMENTS
55	Gen. Elect. Wason	1911	3717 9931	GE GM16A1 175hp gas-elec.	17 win. CE bag. 97 pass.	66'	47T	to Mo. Pac. 531	Ex-Akron, Canton & Youngs. 55, ex-ex-Ban. Aroos. 5
56	Gen. Elect. Wason	1912	3722 9931	GE GM16A5 175hp gas-elec.	14 win. CE bag. 91 pass.	68'	48T	to Mo. Pac. 532	Ex-Akron, Canton & Youngs. 56, ex-ex-Ban. Aroos. 6

MOTLEY COUNTY RR, Matador to Roaring Springs, Texas (Merged into Quanah, Acme & Pacific [SL-SF])

ROAD NOS.	BUILDER	DATE	BLDR. NO.	ENGINE & DRIVE	BODY TYPE	LGTH.	WT.	DISPOSITION	NOTES & COMMENTS
M-275	McKeen	1914		McKeen 200hp gas-mech.		55'	30T	gone by 1919	

MINERAL WELLS & LAKEWOOD PARK RY., Mineral Wells to Lake Pinto, Texas, 2 mi. (Abandoned circa 1910)

ROAD NOS.	BUILDER	DATE	BLDR. NO.	ENGINE & DRIVE	BODY TYPE	LGTH.	WT.	DISPOSITION	NOTES & COMMENTS
"Sue" "Es- ther"	Fair. Morse ?			Fair. Morse gas	4 wheel open car, 3 rows of seats				
"Ben Hur"	Stover			Stover 30hp gas	open, 4 rows of seats, 4 wheel long hood				

MOUNT PLEASANT & RED SPRINGS ST. RY., Mt. Pleasant, Texas (Abandoned)

ROAD NOS.	BUILDER	DATE	BLDR. NO.	ENGINE & DRIVE	BODY TYPE	LGTH.	WT.	DISPOSITION	NOTES & COMMENTS
(2 cars)	Fair. Morse Sheffield	1909		Fair. Morse 19 30hp gas	4 wheel, open wood, 25 pass.	20' 4"	4½T		

PARIS & MT. PLEASANT RR CO., Paris to Mt. Pleasant, Texas, 51.43 mi. (Abandoned)

ROAD NOS.	BUILDER	DATE	BLDR. NO.	ENGINE & DRIVE	BODY TYPE	LGTH.	WT.	DISPOSITION	NOTES & COMMENTS
22	Cinn. Car Co.	1922	2610	International gas	7 win. bag. 28 pass. Cin. lt. wt. st.car body	39' 6"		rebuilt to trailer No. 602	Ex-Cotton Belt No. 22, ex-ex-Deering Southwestern No. 82
601	Brill White	1922	21499	White 4 cyl. 40hp gas	8 win. bag. 40 pass. 4 whl. lead trk.	31' 6"	10T		
602	Co. Shops	1939		trailer	10 win. bag. 28 pass.	39' 6"		scrapped	Rebuild of No. 22
603	Brill			Brill 55 68hp gas	10 win. bag. 30 pass.	43' 6"	15½T	scrapped	Secondhand, source not known

PECOS VALLEY SOUTHERN RY. CO., Pecos to Toyahvale, Texas, 40.33 mi. (In operation)

Motor car listed as late as 1941, no other information.

PORT ISABEL & RIO GRANDE VALLEY RR, Brownsville to Port Isabel, Texas, 26.35 mi. (Abandoned)

ROAD NOS.	BUILDER	DATE	BLDR. NO.	ENGINE & DRIVE	BODY TYPE	LGTH.	WT.	DISPOSITION	NOTES & COMMENTS
1	Co. Shops			Pierce gas	4 wheel wooden baggage				Ex-3' 6" gauge car
101-102	Brill	1924	22116	Brill 55 68hp gas	10 win. bag. 29 pass.	43'	14½T		
103				trailer	baggage				
105	Fairmont ?			gas	4 wheel 3 win. CE 8 pass.	abt. 15'		sold to Mo. Pac.	Used as a weed cutter on Missouri Pacific

PORT BOLIVAR IRON ORE RY., Longview to Ero, Texas, 30 mi. (Abandoned)

Open Model "T" Ford sedan pulling home-built 6 window 4 wheel trailer.

QUANAH, ACME & PACIFIC RY. CO., Red River to McBain, Texas, 99.39 mi. (Merged into Burlington Northern)

ROAD NOS.	BUILDER	DATE	BLDR. NO.	ENGINE & DRIVE	BODY TYPE	LGTH.	WT.	DISPOSITION	NOTES & COMMENTS
A-3	Gen. Elect. Wason	8/12	3731	GE GM16C1	15 win. CE bag. 91 pass.	70'	52T		Ex-SL-SF 2113, acq. 1913
2114	Gen. Elect. Wason	8/12	3732	GE GM16C1	15 win. CE bag. 91 pass.	70'	52T		Ex-SL-SF 2114

EITHER OFF THE RAILS or tipsy is this Port Isabel & Rio Grande Valley car, believed to be a Fairmont. No. 105 is at Brownsville in 1940.   *Author's Collection*

ROAD NOS.	BUILDER	DATE	BLDR. NO.	ENGINE & DRIVE	BODY TYPE	LGTH.	WT.	DISPOSITION	NOTES & COMMENTS
RIO GRANDE & EAGLE PASS RY. CO., Laredo to Darwin, Texas, 26.93 mi. (Abandoned)									
One motor car listed in 1945.									
RIO GRANDE CITY RY. CO., Sam Fordyce to Rio Grande City, Texas, 18.03 mi. (Merged into Missouri Pacific)									
102	Brill	1924	22124	Brill 55 68hp gas	10 win. bag 43 pass.	42' 9"	14½T	sold, Imperial Mercantile, 1925	Ex-Sugarland Ry., No. 102
RIVIERA BEACH & WESTERN RY., Robstown to Riviera Beach, Texas (Abandoned 1917)									
1 or 101	McKeen	4/11	102	McKeen 200hp gas-mech.	14 win. CE bag. 38 pass.	70'	40T	sold 1917, scrap. about 1924	Ex-Sand Springs Ry. No. 1, was supposed to have gone to Roby & Northern Ry., but was never delivered.
SABINE & NECHES RIVER RY., Ruliff to Gist, Texas, 13.76 mi. (Abandoned)									
Official Register listed one motor car from 1922 through 1934.									
SAN ANTONIO & ARANSAS PASS RY. CO., Houston to Kerrville, Corpus Christi to Waco, Texas, and branches, 859.98 mi. (Merged into Southern Pacific)									
300	4 Wheel Drive Boston Body	1923		Wisc. 40hp gas	4 win. 4 whl. short hood, bag. 26 pass.	23' 11"	10½T	to Tex. & New Orleans No. 1006	Renumbered 500
301	Unit McKeen	1923	104	Unit 300hp, steam	16 win. CE bag. 77 pass.	70'	48T	to T&NO No. 1007	Ex-Gulf Coast & Santa Fe, M.103, acq. 3/22, renumbered 501
SAN ANTONIO, UVALDE & GULF RR CO., Crystal City to Corpus Christi, Texas, with branches, 318.32 mi. (Merged into Missouri Pacific)									
200	Brill	1924	21983	Brill 55 68hp gas	10 win. bag. 38 pass.	43' 6"	14½T	to Houston Nor. Shore (MP) No. 527	
201	Reo	1924		Reo gas	4 door sedan			converted back to highway use 1928	
SAN BENITO & RIO GRANDE VALLEY RY. CO., Fernando to East Texas, Texas, 83 mi. (Merged into Missouri Pacific)									
100	Fair. Morse	1911		Fair. Morse 24 50hp gas	8 win. 4 whl. 36 pass. bag. wood, clere. roof	34' 2"	12½T	rebuilt to trailer 7/14	
101	Fair. Morse	1911		Fair. Morse 24 50hp gas	8 win. 4 whl. 36 pass. bag. wood, clere. roof	34' 2"	12½T		
102	Fair. Morse	1911		Fair. Morse 24 50hp gas	4 win. 4 whl. bag. wood, clere. roof	34' 2"	12½T		
200-201	American Car	1911		trailer	4 whl., open, 5 bench, wooden	abt. 20'		sold, poss. to Matamores, Mex.	
no #	Co. Shops			trailer	4 whl. wood, bag. mail, express	abt. 10'			

ROAD NOS.	BUILDER	DATE	BLDR. NO.	ENGINE & DRIVE	BODY TYPE	LGTH.	WT.	DISPOSITION	NOTES & COMMENTS
SUGARLAND RY. CO., Cabell to Anchor Jct., Texas, 38.94 mi. (Merged into Missouri Pacific)									
102	Brill	1924	22124	Brill 55 68hp gas	10 win. bag. 38 pass.	43'	14½T	sold Rio Grande City Ry. (No. 102)	
TEXAS MEXICAN RY., Laredo to Corpus Christ, Texas, 160 mi. (In operation)									
508	St. Louis Car Westinghouse	1935	1575 A060	West. Beard-more 950hp dies.-elec.	Mail-bag.	43'		retired 12/50	Ex-Boston & Maine 1141, shortened
TEXAS CITY TERMINAL RY. CO., Texas City to Texas City Junction, 6.39 mi.									
(2 cars)	Fair. Morse	1910		Fair. Morse 50hp gas	8 win. 4 whl. clere. roof, wood, bag. 35 pass.	34' 2"	12T		
22	McKeen	1912		McKeen 200hp gas-mech.	10 win. CE bag. 40 pass.	55'	58T	burned, car shed fire, 1923	
26	GMC Stewart & Stevenson	1923		GMC gas	6 win. hood front, bag. 24 pass.	abt. 20'	abt. 10T		
TEXAS MIDLAND RR, Paris to Ennis, Texas, 125.2 mi. (Merged into Southern Pacific)									
5001	Gen. Elect. Wason	10/12	3752	GE GM16C1 175hp gas-elect.	19 win. C&RE, bag. 101 pass.	70'	52T	to T&NO No. 1008	
5002	Gen. Elect. Wason	10/12	3753	GE GM16C1 175hp gas-elect.	19 win. C&RE, bag. 101 pass.	70'	52T	to T&NO No. 1009	
TRINITY VALLEY & NORTHERN RY. CO., Dayton to Lumm, Texas, 18 mi. (Abandoned 1933)									
1928 "Moody's" lists one motor car.									
TEXAS SOUTH-EASTERN RR CO., Diboll to Vair, Texas, Blix to Lufkin, Texas, total 19.91 mi. (In operation)									
400	(no other information)								
UVALDE & LEONA VALLEY INTERURBAN RY. CO., Uvalde, Texas (Abandoned about 1913)									
(4 cars)	Fair. Morse Sheffield	1910		Fair. Morse 19 30hp gas	5 win. 4 whl. wood	20' 18"	4½T		
UVALDE & NORTHERN RY. CO., Uvalde Jct. to Camp Woods, Texas, 37 mi. (Abandoned)									
1928 "Moody's" lists one passenger (motor) car.									
WACO, BEAUMONT, TRINITY & SABINE RY. CO., Weldon to Colmesneil, Texas, 114.97 mi. (Abandoned)									
	Ford			Ford A gas	2 door sedan				Pulled 2 win. 4 wheel wooden trailer
WEATHERFORD, MINERAL WELLS & NORTHWESTERN RY. CO., Weatherford to Graford, Texas, 43.57 mi. (Merged into Missouri Pacific)									
7 & 11	McKeen	1912		McKeen 200hp gas-mech.	19 win. CE 105 pass.	70'	37½T	said to have gone to the T&P	
WICHITA FALLS & SOUTHERN RR CO., Wichita Falls to Dublin, Texas, 169 mi. (Abandoned)									
(1 car)	Brill	1924	21995	Brill 55 68hp gas	10 win. bag. 40 pass.	43'	15½T		Two other cars, one a Brill Model 250 gas-elect. bag. RPO and a trailer, were canceled.
900	Twin Coach Co. Shops	ca. 1938		Twin gas	9 win. bus				Baggage door built midway down body. This unit may never have been placed in service.

Utah

AREA: 84,916 sq. miles
CAPITAL: Salt Lake City
POPULATION (1927): 522,000

RAIL MOTOR CARS figured prominently in the operation of two of Utah's "big three" electric interurban lines.

The Salt Lake & Utah started passenger service with three Hall-Scott gas cars which were sold when the line was electrified.

The Salt Lake, Garfield & Western purchased a used ACF gas motor car when the road was de-electrified.

The SL&U sold its three cars to three different railroads, while the SLG&W was the third line to own its sole motor car.

Two other Utah railroads operated rail motor cars, and what a contrast they offered: the Tooele Valley had a tiny Fairbanks-Morse car that resembled a single-truck streetcar, while the Southern Utah Railroad at Price operated its enormous McKeen "Mallet," the largest McKeen (and the last) ever built.

All of Utah's rail motor cars had gas-mechanical drives.

NEW AND SHINY, these three motors were lined up outside the Hall-Scott works at Oakland, Calif., one fine day in 1913 and photographed for posterity. Numbers 501-503 were headed for the Salt Lake & Utah. The interior of the 501 also is shown.
Both: Vernon Sappers Collection

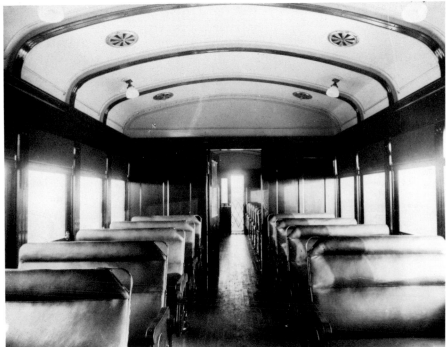

SHOVEL-NOSED ex-Seaboard rail-car MC-3 of the Salt Lake, Garfield & Western served the holiday crowds heading for the Saltair Amusement Park at the edge of Great Salt Lake. This unit later became the M-300 of the California Western of *Skunk* fame.
Al Barker Collection

LAST McKEEN CAR built for passenger service ran on the Southern Utah, shown in a photo published shortly after it was built in 1916.
Author's Collection

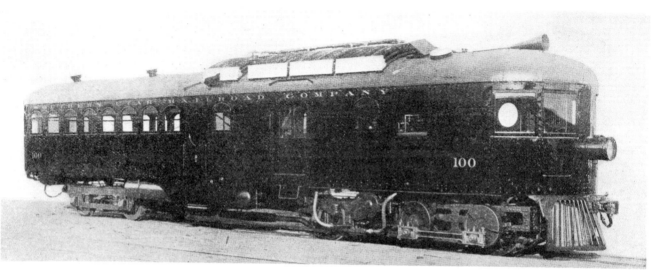

ROAD NOS.	BUILDER	DATE	BLDR. NO.	ENGINE & DRIVE	BODY TYPE	LGTH.	WT.	DISPOSITION	NOTES & COMMENTS
SALT LAKE, GARFIELD & WESTERN RY., Salt Lake City to Saltair Beach, Utah, 10 mi. (In operation)									
MC-3	Amer. Car & Foun.	1935	1432	Hall-Scott 168hp gas-mech.	14 win. CE bag. 57 pass.	64' 1"	26½ T	sold, Cal. West. (M-300) 1963	Ex-Aberdeen & Rockfish No. 106, ex-ex-Seaboard AL No. 2026
SALT LAKE & UTAH RR, Salt Lake City to Payson, Utah, 60 mi. (Abandoned)									
501	Hall-Scott	1913	11	Hall-Scott 150hp gas-mech.	13 win. bag. 52 pass.	60'		sold to Valley & Siletz 1922	
502	Hall-Scott	1913	12	Hall-Scott 150hp gas-mech.	13 win. bag. 52 pass.	60'		sold to Lowville Beaver River	
503	Hall-Scott	1913	13	Hall-Scott 150hp gas-mech.	13 win. bag. 52 pass.	60'		sold to Nev. Copper Belt 1915	
SOUTHERN UTAH RR CO., Price to Hiawatha, Utah, 18 mi. (Abandoned)									
100	McKeen	1916		McKeen 300hp gas-mech.	9 win. CE, bag. 48 pass.	58' 3"	45½ T	retired, body at Helper, Utah	
TOOELE VALLEY RY. CO., International to Warner, Utah, 7 mi. (Abandoned)									
1	Fair. Morse Brill	1910	16790	Fair. Morse 24 50hp gas	8 win. 4 wheel wood, clere. roof, bag. 35 pass.	34' 2"	12½ T		

Vermont

AREA: 9,609 sq. miles
CAPITAL: Montpelier
POPULATION (1927): 352,000

APPARENTLY THE ONLY luck that the West River Railroad had with rail motor cars was bad.

This fits pretty well with the whole history of the line, whose struggles with the river after which it was named and other problems led to author Victor Morse to call his definitive book on the line *36 Miles of Trouble* (Stephen Greene Press, 1959).

It wasn't until late in its history that the railcars arrived on the scene. In 1933, James G. Ashley took over the operations, with high hopes that he could do what no one else ever had—turn a profit.

One of the first things Ashley did was to buy a Four-Wheel-Drive (FWD) motor and trailer set from the nearby Hoosic Tunnel & Wilmington Railroad. These cars were notoriously poor in operation, and I am sure the HT&W was glad to get rid of it. True to form, the unit soon caught fire and was destroyed.

A Brill 55, the Lehigh Valley's first railcar, was borrowed, but it proved inadequate and was returned.

Finally a Boston & Maine gas-electric unit was purchased. This car had started out life as a Sykes gas-mechanical car, a notoriously poor operating unit that the B&M had engaged Brill to modify. It apparently worked fairly well, but by this time economic factors worsened, and Ashley took this car and attempted to start another railroad. Known as the Norfolk Branch Railway down in Connecticut, Ashley's other railroad apparently had no better luck than had the West River.

Two other lines in the state—the White River and the Bristol—each had a tiny Fairbanks-Morse unit, but were abandoned early on.

FROM THE LOOKS OF IT, this Fairbanks-Morse Sheffield car on the Bristol Railroad was set up to carry freight and baggage on both end platforms and maybe on the roof, too.
Harold K. Vollrath Collection

WEST RIVER Sykes railcar originally had a mechanical drive but was rebuilt to a gas-electric by Brill. It certainly sports a rather fierce radiator. *Al Barker Collection*

133

STREETCAR-LIKE No. 4 pauses at Bethel, Vt., in 1916, awaiting, perhaps, the somber-looking gentleman on the platform. This Fairbanks-Morse Sheffield unit was the only railcar of the White River RR Co.
Harold K. Vollrath Collection

ROAD NOS.	BUILDER	DATE	BLDR. NO.	ENGINE & DRIVE	BODY TYPE	LGTH.	WT.	DISPOSITION	NOTES & COMMENTS
BRISTOL RR CO., Bristol to New Haven Jct., Vt. 6.14 mi. (Abandoned)									
5	Fair. Morse Sheffield	1918		Sheffield 33hp gas	7 win. 4 whl. CE, 24 pass.	22' 10"	7½T		Ex-St. Joseph Vy. No. 152 (Ind.) acq. 1918
WEST RIVER RR CO., Brattleboro to South Londonderry, Vt., 38.4 mi. (Abandoned)									
50	Four Wheel Drive	1923		Wisc. 95hp gas	5 win. 4 whl. bag. 12 pass.	25' 6"	9T	burned 1934	Ex-Hoosac Tunnel & Wilmington, No. 50, acq. 1933
60	Four Wheel Drive	1923		trailer	9 win. 4 whl. 40 pass.	29' 9"	8T	burned 1934	Ex-HT&W No. 60, acq. 1933
3	Brill	1925	21877	Brill 55 68hp gas	10 win. 42 pass. bag.	43'	14½T	returned to Lehigh Vy.	Ex-Lehigh Valley No. 3
(1 car)	Sykes St. Louis Brill	1925 1927	1329A 22367	Brill gas-elect.	8 win. bag. 30 pass. hood front	52' 8"		to Norfolk Bran. Ry. after WR aban.	Ex-NY, NH&H No. 1120, orig. mech. drive, rebuilt to gas-elect. by Brill
WHITE RIVER RR CO., Rochester to Bethel, Vt. 19.34 mi. (Abandoned)									
4	Fair. Morse Sheffield			Sheffield gas	5 win. CE, 4 wheel wood, deck roof				

Virginia

AREA: 40,815 sq. miles
CAPITAL: Richmond
POPULATION (1927): 2,546,000

THE TWO LARGEST operators of rail motor cars in this state had their terminals within a couple of blocks of each other, and had been electrified lines operating out of the Washington, D.C., area.

In 1936, the Arlington & Fairfax, a short interurban-type railway, was in bad shape financially. In a bid to cut costs, the A&F acquired a fleet of Evans Auto-Railers. Each was a small bus equipped with guide wheels so that it could run on either rails or paved roads. Eventually, the fleet numbered some 16 units.

I believe the original intention was to run into downtown Washington instead of having to transfer passengers to the local transit system as they had done with electric cars. But the A&F was unable to get the required permission to do this, and as far as I can determine, the rail buses never operated in the street.

Be that as it may, the results were unsatisfactory, and the whole idea was scrapped in favor of regular highway buses. Some of the Evans units were sold to other short lines.

The other line in the area was the more famous Washington & Old Dominion. This line had managed to get rid of its

electric passenger service shortly before World War II.

During the war, a concerted drive by local residents succeeded in forcing the company to restore passenger service. An interesting group of secondhand rail motor cars was assembled, including one of the pioneer Budd stainless steel rail-car sets and a Mack gas-electric demonstrator. This passenger service held on until the early 1950s, when the railroad resumed freight-only operation.

(Top Two Photos) DOODLEBUG TRIO of the Washington & Old Dominion is lined up here at Rosslyn in 1949. Mack, Electro-Motive and Brill built 45, 46 and 52 respectively. Onetime interurban W&OD did not have the luxury of standardization when purchasing these used vehicles.
    Both: George E. Votava Collection

ORIGINAL Brill-Service railbus, built in October of 1921, was sold to Virginia's Winchester & Western. This is its builder's photo.
    Pennsylvania Historical Society

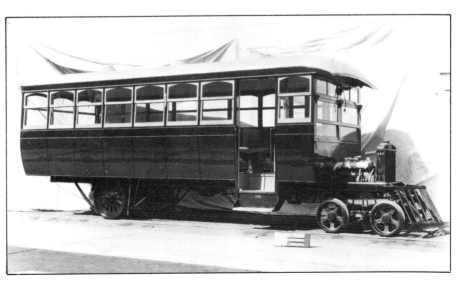

SUBURBAN Washington, D.C., trolley line Arlington & Fairfax took the wires down and acquired several smart-looking Reo railbuses, including the 104 and 108 pictured here at Rosslyn, Va., on January 29, 1939.
George E. Votava Collection

ROAD NOS.	BUILDER	DATE	BLDR. NO.	ENGINE & DRIVE	BODY TYPE	LGTH.	WT.	DISPOSITION	NOTES & COMMENTS
ARLINGTON & FAIRFAX RY., Rosslyn to Falls Church, Va.									
97-99	Evans	1936		Reo Gas	6 win. CE bus body, round front		6T	95-98 sold to W.&OD as work equip.	"Autorailer"
100-111	Evans			Reo Gas (Chevrolet & Ford engines also used)	5 win. CE bus body, flat front, 23 pass.			102, 108, 109 sold Arcade & Attica 107 to Courd. & Port. Allegheny	At least one bus was sold to Narragansett Pier RR, others may have been sold to other lines or converted for highway use.
CHESAPEAKE & WESTERN RY., Elkton to Bridgewater, Va., 27 mi. (Abandoned)									
51	Mack Brill	1920	70000	Mack AB 4 cyl. 30hp gas	8 win. 4 whl. lead trk. 25 pass.	27'	5½T		
75	Edwards			Buda 108hp gas	10 win., bag. 40 pass.	43'	17T		Secondhand, possibly from Gainesville & N.W.
50	Brill Service	1922	21491	Midwest 30hp gas	5 win. 20 pass. rear bag. sect.	31'6"	9½T		There is some question as to whether this unit actually operated on the C&W
FRANKLIN & PITTSYLVANIA RY. CO., Rockey Mount to Angles, Va., 21 mi. (Abandoned)									
50	Edwards	1923		Buda GL-6 108hp gas	8 win. OP bag. 27 pass.	30'	8½T		
MARION & RYE VALLEY RY., Marion to Sugar Grove, Va. 18 mi. (Abandoned)									
(1 car)	Edwards	1925		(2) Buda 108hp gas	11 win. bag. 52 pass.	43'	21½T	sold to Cen. of Georgia 11/34	
VIRGINIA BLUE RIDGE RY., Tye River to Woodson and Massies Mill, Va., 19.28 mi. (Abandoned)									
(1 car)	Brill	1922		Midwest 68hp gas	10 win. bag. 40 pass.	43'	14½T		

ROAD NOS.	BUILDER	DATE	BLDR. NO.	ENGINE & DRIVE	BODY TYPE	LGTH.	WT.	DISPOSITION	NOTES & COMMENTS
VIRGINIA CENTRAL RY., Fredericksburg to Orange Court House, Va., 38.1 mi. (One mile in operation)									
M-1									
M-2, M-3	Edwards	1923		Buda gas	8 win. OP bag. 30 pass.	30'	9½T		
M-100	Brill	1924	21994	Brill 55 68hp	10 win. bag. pass.	43'	14½T		Ex-Clinton & Okla. West (ATSF) 100
T-3				trailer	6 win. OP bag.				
WASHINGTON & OLD DOMINION RR, Rosslyn to Purcellville, Va. 47 mi. (Abandoned)									
45	Mack Osgood Bradly	1928	161001 9115	(2) Mack AP 120hp gas-elect. re-eng. (2) Cummins 200hp diesel engs.	15 win. bag. 65 pass.	76'7"	58T	scrapped 1952	Ex-NYC M-14, ex-ex-Mack demo. M-200 acq. 1943.
46	Electro-Mot. Co., St. Louis Car	1926	155 1403	(2) Winton 200hp gas-elect.	9 win. RPO bag. 40 pass.	70'	47½T	demot. cir. 1945, scrapped 1950	Ex-Gulf, Mobile & Ohio 1801, acq. 11/43
52	Brill	1928	22544	Brill 250hp GE re-eng. Cummins 250hp DE	7 win. RPO bag. 40 pass.	75'6"	62T	scrapped 1951	Ex-NYC M-403, acq. 1944
4688	Budd	1933		Lycoming 190hp gas-elect.	11 win. bag. 30 pass.	50'	12½T	scrapped 1949	Ex-Pennsy 4688, acq. (leased) 1943, purchased 1945
4689	Budd	1933		28hp aux. eng.	12 win. 46 pass.	50'	11T	scrapped 1949	Ex-Pennsy 4689, acq. (leased) 1943, purchased 1945
WINCHESTER & WESTERN RR, Winchester to Wardensville, Va., 42 mi. (Abandoned)									
10	York Wagon Co., Service	5/21		Midwest gas	8 win. hood type bus, 4 whl. 34 pass.	28'	6T		
11	Brill Service	4/22	21365	Midwest gas	8 win. 4 whl. ld. truck, 28 pass.	29'	5½T		
12	Edwards	1923		Buda 108hp gas	8 win. CE bag. 30 pass.	30'	9½T		Ex-Cape Fear Ry., acq. 1928
1	York Wagon Co.	5/21		trailer	8 win. bag. 12 pass.				

Washington

AREA: 68,192 sq. miles
CAPITAL: Olympia
POPULATION (1927): 1,562,000

TWO OF THE MORE interesting short lines of the United States were only about 40 miles apart in the state of Washington—the Hartford & Eastern and the Skagit River Railways.

The Hartford & Eastern was built with Rockefeller money to exploit mines in the Monte Cristo area, and was subsequently taken over by the Northern Pacific Railroad.

Apparently the mines never amounted to much so in 1915 the Northern Pacific rented the line to the Rucker Bros., a sawmill operation in that area.

This firm purchased an open White bus equipped with flanged wheels and a rather large rail motor car built by Hofius Steel & Equipment, a local firm which primarily built logging equipment. Neither of these cars seems to have been particularly successful; the Hofius car was sold to the Valley & Siletz Railroad of Oregon after only two years of use.

About 1917 three very small, lightweight rail buses were built for the line by the New Haven Carriage Co. of Portland, Oregon.

By this time the spectacular beauty of the area was being exploited, and a rather large (for the time) resort hotel was built at the end of the line, where there were also some famous ice caves. This hotel was called the "Big 4 Inn" after nearby Big Four Mountain. Appar-

ently in the last years of operation, the tourist trade was just about the only traffic the road had.

In 1929 a Brill 55 gas car was purchased, but the Great Depression did the line in, and that car was sold to the Skagit River Railway. This line was owned by the city of Seattle, and was built to serve the construction of a series of three dams on the Skagit River to produce power for the Seattle City Light Department.

The first section of the railroad was powered with 2½-ton Signal trucks with flange wheels which pulled trailers, one of which was an old demotorized bus. As construction proceeded up the canyon, and the first dam began to produce electricity, the railroad was electrified and a great variety of electric locomotives and ex-interurban trailers were purchased to accommodate a very active tourist trade that soon developed. The idea was to show the beauty of the area and also let the citizens of Seattle know what they were getting for their money.

Locomotives were obtained from the Puget Sound Electric, Tacoma Municipal Belt, Spokane Coeur D'Alene & Palouse, Portland Railway Light & Power, Seattle Municipal Railway, and the Washington Water Power Co. Passenger cars came from the Puget Sound Electric and the Oregon Electric.

There remained, however, some non-electrified track, so some largely home-built locomotives and railcars were added. Strangely, the demotorized bu[s] was remotorized, and its body is still i[n] existence and on display in the area.

Finally one Brill Model 55 from th[e] Hartford & Eastern was obtained, and [a] brand-new Model 55 was purchased i[n] 1928. Due to the fact that new da[m] construction inundated most of th[e] right-of-way, the railroad was aba[n]doned in 1945.

Most of the other short lines i[n] Washington were owned by lumber con[m]panies, although the Bellingham Bay [&] British Columbia (which owned a 70-foo[t] McKeen car) was bought out by th[e] Milwaukee Road, and the little Water[s]ville Railway was owned by that city.

STYLE SETTERS were Hartford & Eastern railbuses. Unit 22, packed with holiday makers, leaves the Big Four Inn with a four-wheel trailer. The open, four-wheel railbus is H&E No. 2. Both were built by White.
Author's Collection and John A. Taubeneck

(Opposite Page) BARLOW PASS on the ruggedly scenic Hartford & Eastern played host to railcritter 21, a White with a New Haven Carriage body. *John A. Taubeneck Collection*

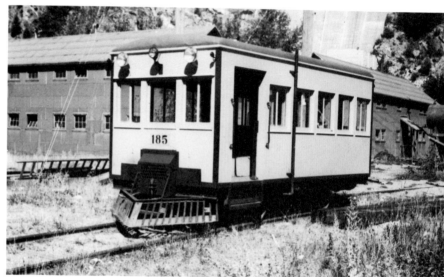

NEATLY PAINTED and ready to roll, these Skagit River units present an appealing sight. Brill Model 55 No. 4 was bought secondhand from the Hartford & Eastern, while boxy No. 185 was built in company shops. *Ralph Shears; Author's Collection*

LONGVIEW PORTLAND & NORTHERN No. 91 poses with proud officials, but author could find no documentation on it. *John T. Labbe, S.M. Morris Collection*

ROAD NOS.	BUILDER	DATE	BLDR. NO.	ENGINE & DRIVE	BODY TYPE	LGTH.	WT.	DISPOSITION	NOTES & COMMENTS
BELLINGHAM BAY & BRITISH COLUMBIA RR CO., Bellingham to Glacier, Wash., 44.54 mi. (Merged into Milwaukee Road 1919)									
1	Fairbanks-Morse			Fair. Morse gas	4 wheel			to CMSP&P 1919	
Kul-shan	McKeen	9/09		McKeen 200hp gas-mech.	14 win. CE, bag. 64 pass.	70'	34T	to CMSP&P 1919 5908	
COWLITZ, CHEHALIS & CASCADE RY., Chehalis to Cowlitz, Wash., 32 mi. (Abandoned)									
(1 car)	Co. Shops White	3/16		White 60hp gas	5 win. open bus, 21 pass. 4 whl. lead trk. hood		6T		
3	Skagit Steel Hickey Motor White Motor	2/23		White gas	7 win. CE, 42 pass. rear bag. sect.	28' 7½"	10½T		
LONGVIEW PORTLAND & NORTHERN RY. CO., Longview Jct. to Ryderwood, 30.26 mi.									
20	Skagit Steel	1927		Buda 150hp gas	13 win. CE, 40 pass.	50'3"	21T	sold, Trona Ry. No. 22, Cal. West. Ry. M-200	
HARTFORD & EASTERN RY. CO., Hartford to Monte Cristo, Wash., 42.12 mi. (Abandoned)									
2	White	1915		White 4 cyl. 40hp gas	4 whl. open bus, 5 rows of seats				
3	Hofius Steel	1916		Wisc. 6 cyl. 125hp gas	7 win. CE, 4 whl. lead trk. 30 pass.	31'	10T	sold, Valley & Siletz, 1918	
21	New Haven Carr., White	1917		White, 40hp, 4 cyl. gas	open bus, 4 whl. lead trk., hood front				
22	New Haven Carr., White	1917		White, 40hp, 4 cyl. gas	7 win. 4 whl. lead truck, bus body				
23	New Haven Carr., White	1917		White, 40hp, 4 cyl. gas	8 win. 4 whl. lead trk. bus body				
100	Brill	1929	22785	Brill 55, 68hp gas	10 win. bag. 36 pass.	43'	14½T	sold, Skagit Riv. Ry., No. 4	

Also had at least two 4 wheel flat cars equipped with "park bench" type seats, about 16 seats.

ROAD NOS.	BUILDER	DATE	BLDR. NO.	ENGINE & DRIVE	BODY TYPE	LGTH.	WT.	DISPOSITION	NOTES & COMMENTS
PUGET SOUND & CASCADE RY. CO., North Burlington to Finney Creek, Wash., 31.9 mi. (Abandoned)									
4	Co. Shops GMC Truck	1925		GMC gas	7 win. 4 whl. lead truck, hood front bag. 35 pass.				Skagit Steel built lead truck
SKAGIT RIVER RY., Rockport to Concrete, Wash. (Abandoned)									
1	Co. Shops Federal	1918		Federal gas.	8 win. 4 whl. lead truck, 28 pass.			on display at Marblemont, Wash.	Built as bus with round windows, made into a trailer
4	Brill	1929	22785	Brill 55 orig. re-eng. GMC 110hp gas	10 win. bag. 36 pass.	43'	14½T		Ex-Hartford & Eastern No. 100
5	Brill	1928	22651	orig. Brill 55, re-eng. Hall-Scott 75hp	10 win. bag. 36 pass.	43'	14½T		
185	Co. Shops			gas	5 win. wood, bag. pass.				
(2 units)	Signal Truck	1922?		Signal gas	open truck, 4 whl. lead truck				Pulled trailers as well as general trucking
WATERVILLE RY. CO., Waterville to Douglas, Wash., 5 mi. (Abandoned)									
(1 car)	White New Haven Carr.	1922		White 4 cyl. 40hp gas	4 win. 4 whl. lead truck, bus body, rear bag. sect.				

West Virginia

AREA: 24,181 sq. miles
CAPITAL: Charleston
POPULATION (1927): 1,696,000

WEST VIRGINIA is the proto-typically Appalachian state. It had many railroad short lines, most of them associated with the coal-mining industry, and most are now gone.

But one rather interesting operation remains. It is the Nicholas, Fayette & Greenbriar Railroad Co., which is jointly owned by the Chessie System and Conrail.

In the middle 1920s, the C&O acquired two linking lines—the Sewell Valley and the Greenbriar and Eastern, which ran from Meadow Creek to Nallen. The New York Central's Charleston branch ran as far as a place called Swiss, which was only 28 miles from Nallen.

A new line was built from Nallen to Swiss, and the NYC added its branch from Swiss to Gauley (back on the C&O's main line) to a new jointly owned line from Gauley to Meadow Creek.

This arrangement is still in force, s you can see C&O and Conrail uni sitting next to each other at Meado Creek. But, alas, the Brill 55s that pr vided passenger service are long gon as are the rather famous and lon lasting pair of cars on the Buffalo Cree & Gauley, which operated rail moto cars and steam locomotives long afte any other West Virginia railroad.

TO SERVE a new branch line jointly owned by the C&O and New York Central, three trim Brill Model 55s were seconded from the C&O to carry the banner of the Nicholas, Fayette & Greenbriar RR. Here's car 121 at Duo.   *G. Gabrill, Jr.*

SHARING a berth with Teakettle No. 8, Mack/Brill railbus No. 9 of the Central West Virginia & Southern is photographed at Hambleton, W. Va., in 1936.
William Montgomery,
Louis Saillard Collection

ROAD NOS.	BUILDER	DATE	BLDR. NO.	ENGINE & DRIVE	BODY TYPE	LGTH.	WT.	DISPOSITION	NOTES & COMMENTS
BUFFALO CREEK & GAULEY RR CO., Dundon to Widen, W. Va., 18.6 mi. (In operation)									
A	Mack Brill	11/21	60005 21369	Mack AC 64hp gas	7 win. 4 whl. ld. truck, bag. 32 pass.	32′ 6″	10T	to Strasburg Ry. Museum	Orig. Lewisburg, Milton & Watsontown No. 20, to Penna. RR No. 4738, to Artemus & Jellico No. 1
B	4 Whl. Drive St. Louis	8/20	1286	Wisc. 62hp gas	5 win. 4 whl. bag. 20 pass.	22′	9T		Ex-Kanawha, Glen Jean & Eastern No. 1
CENTRAL WEST VIRGINIA & SOUTHERN RR CO., Hendricks to Armentrout, W. Va., 29.5 mi. (Abandoned)									
9	Mack Brill	7/21	70008 21346	Mack AB 30hp gas	8 win. hood frt. 4 whl. lead trk. 25 pass.	27′	5½T		
10	Brill	7/21	21347	trailer	4 wheel bag.	12′ 6″			
FAIRMONT & CLARKSBURG RY.									
C1	Brill	1901	11235						Rebuild of a compressed air car
FAIRMONT & NORTHERN TRACTION CO., Fairmont, W.Va. (Abandoned)									
(1 car)	Fairbanks-Morse	1911		Fair. Morse 30hp gas	5 win. CE, 4 whl. wood, deck roof				
GREENBRIAR & EASTERN RR CO., Greenbriar & Eastern Jct. to Greenbriar & Eastern Shops, W. Va., 10.95 mi. (Merged into Nich. Fay. & Greenbriar [C&O-NYC])									
100	Mack Brill	7/21	70009 21371	Mack AB 30hp gas	8 win. 4 whl. ld. trk., hood front, 25 pass.	28′ 8″	6T	scrapped 1/29	
KANAWHA, GLEN JEAN & EASTERN RR CO., Glen Jean to Tamroy, W. Va., 8 mi. (Abandoned)									
1	4 Wheel Dr. St. Louis Car	8/20	1286	Wisc. 62hp gas	5 win. 4 whl. bag. 20 pass.	22′	9T	sold to Buff. Creek & Gauley	
MIDDLE CREEK RY., Hartland, W. Va. (Abandoned)									
101	Brill White			White, 40hp gas	8 win. CE, hood front, 4 whl. ld. truck, bag. 30 pass.	31′ 6″	10T		Prob. secondhand, poss. Mt. Jewett, Kinzua & Ritersville No. 10
NICHOLAS, FAYETTE & GREENBRIAR RR CO., Swiss to Meadow Creek, W. Va., 71 mi. (In operation)									
121	Brill	1924	21933	Cont. H-14 90hp gas	10 win. bag. 22 pass.	43′ 6″	17½T	sold for scrap 10/49	Ex-C&O 9025
122	Brill	1924	21934	Cont. H-14 90hp gas	10 win. bag. 30 pass.	43′ 6″	17½T	sold for scrap 10/45	Ex-C&O 9026
123	Brill	1924	21935	Cont. H-14 90hp gas	3 win. baggage	43′ 6″	18½T	sold for scrap 10/45	Ex-C&O 9000
POND FORK & BALD KNOB RR, West Jct. to Rick Lick, W. Va., 12.99 mi. (Merged into Ches. & Ohio)									
1	Brill	1922	21524	Service 30hp gas	8 win. hood type bus body, 4 whl. lead truck	29′	5½T	prob. to C&O (No. 1000?)	
SEWELL VALLEY RR CO., Meadow Creek to Nalan, W. Va., 39.5 mi., became part of the Nicholas, Fayette & Greenbriar, jointly owned by the C&O and the NYC									
121	Brill	1924	21933	Cont. H-14 90hp gas	10 win. bag. 22 pass.	43′ 6″	17½T	to NF&G 121	
122	Brill	1924	21934	Cont. H-14 90hp gas	10 win. bag. 30 pass.	43′ 6″	17½T	to NF&G 122	
123	Brill	1924	21935	Cont. H-14 90hp gas	3 win. baggage	43′ 6″	18½T	to NF&G 123	
124	Mack Brill	6/21	70005 21292	Mack AB 30hp gas	8 win. hood type bus body, 4 whl. lead truck	28′ 8″	5½T	to East. Ky. Sou. No. 215	

LETTERS, rather than numbers, denoted the two motor cars owned by the Buffalo Creek & Gauley. Car A, a Brill/Bulldog Mack, is seen at Dundon, W. Va., in May of 1958. Car B, of Four Wheel Drive parentage, is also at Dundon.

(Top Photo) Harold K. Vollrath Collection; (Bottom Photo) William G. Young, Tom King Collection

Wisconsin

AREA: 56,154 sq. miles
CAPITAL: Madison
POPULATION (1927): 2,918,000

ONLY THREE short lines in Wisconsin had rail motor cars, but given the fact that the state had only a couple more, this isn't too bad a record.

The most prominent of these, the La Crosse & Southeastern, a subsidiary of the Cargill interests, had a rather strange roster. One of its cars was built by the Meister Car Co. of Sacramento, Calif., for the Ocean Shore Railway, operating out of San Francisco. The second was one of very few cars built by the Eklund Car Co. of Minneapolis, and the third was a Unit Steam car with a body built by the Laconia Car Co. of New Hampshire. The Unit car failed even before it could be put into revenue service.

Another road, the Fairchild & Northeastern, pretty much went from nowhere to nowhere, and had some rather mysterious Sykes cars. Mysterious, that is, in that the bodies apparently were not built by the St. Louis Car Co., which built bodies for the few other Sykes cars.

The last line—the Stanley, Merrill and Phillips Railway—was more a logging road than anything else, and had only one car, a little Fairbanks-Morse type 24, which managed to burn up after only two years of service.

144

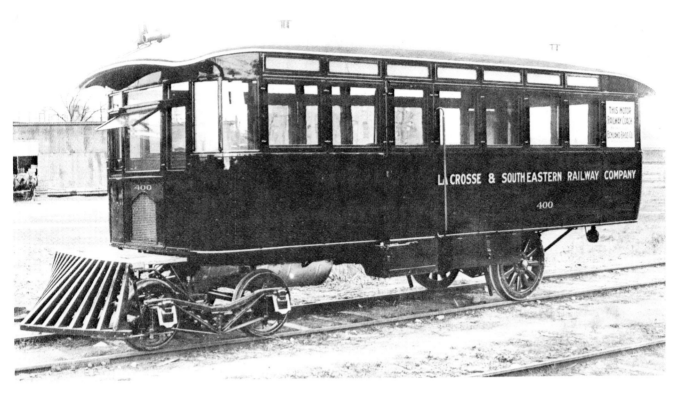

(Above) ECKLAND BROS. of Minneapolis built this railbus for the LaCrosse & Southeastern. With No. 400 came a matching trailer.
Willis Hendrick Collection,
Short & Narrow Rails

MUCH BIGGER was No. 402, a Unit/Laconia car powered by a Stanley steam engine. Really a demonstrator, it didn't work out and was returned to the builder.
R. Miner Collection,
Short & Narrow Rails

ROAD NOS.	BUILDER	DATE	BLDR. NO.	ENGINE & DRIVE	BODY TYPE	LGTH.	WT.	DISPOSITION	NOTES & COMMENTS
FAIRCHILD & NORTHEASTERN RR, Fairchild to Greenwood, Wis., 23.52 mi. (Abandoned)									
(2 cars)	Sykes	1923		Sterling 175hp gas-mech.	30 pass., bag.	52'	15T		
(1 car)		1923		trailer	40 pass.	39' 2"	12T		
LA CROSSE & SOUTHEASTERN RY. CO., La Crosse to Viroqua, Wis., 40.81 mi.									
62	Meister Car.	1917		Buda SSU 60hp gas	10 win. CE bag. 31 pass.	40' 4"	11½ T		Ex-Ocean Shore Ry. (Calif.) No. 62, acq. 1920
400	White Eklund	1919		White 4 cyl. 50hp gas	6 win. CE, 4 whl. lead truck, 32 pass.				
401	Eklund	1919		trailer	4 wheel bag.				
402	Unit Laconia	1920		Stanley steam	12 win. bag. 45 pass.			returned to builder	Unit demo 1202
STANLEY, MERRILL & PHILLIPS RY. CO., Stanley to Jump River, Wis., 33 mi. (Abandoned)									
10	Fairbanks-Morse, Brill	1909	16790	Fair. Morse 24 50hp gas	8 win. OP clere. roof, 4 wheel, bag. 20 pass.	34' 2"	12½ T	burned 9/8/11	

(Above) FAIRBANKS-MORSE gas car No. 10 of the Stanley, Merrill & Phillips meanders through the trees in a scene prior to its fiery end on September 8, 1911.
Bill O'Gara Collection,
Short & Narrow Rails

Wyoming

AREA: 97,914 sq. miles
CAPITAL: Cheyenne
POPULATION (1927): 241,000

BOTH WYOMING short lines that had rail motor cars are still in operation, albeit as part of the Union Pacific System. Perhaps no big thing, but how many other states have this distinction?

Both lines obtained their units on the secondhand market.

The two motor cars that the Laramie, North Park and Western operated were Edwards cars from the Burlington, and the Saratoga and Encampment Valley's lone McKeen was a repossessed unit which had operated on the Peoples Electric Railway of Muskogee, Oklahoma.

RATHER HANDSOME is this Edwards-built car, No. 9508, of the Laramie, North Park & Western. The LNP&W acquired two of these from the Burlington.
William Montgomery, Louis Saillard Collection

ROAD NOS.	BUILDER	DATE	BLDR. NO.	ENGINE & DRIVE	BODY TYPE	LGTH.	WT.	DISPOSITION	NOTES & COMMENTS
LARAMIE, NORTH PARK & WESTERN RR CO., Laramie, Wyo. to Coalmont, Colo., 111.35 mi. (Merged into Union Pacific)									
9506	Edwards	2/26		(2) Buda 60hp gas	9 win. bag. 27 pass.	41'	21½T		Ex-CB&Q 9506, acq. 3/31
9508	Edwards	4/26		(2) Buda 100hp gas	5 win. bag. 22 pass.	43'	21½T		Ex-CB&Q 9508, acq. 3/31
SARATOGA & ENCAMPMENT VALLEY RR, Wolcott to Encampment, Wyo., 44.5 mi. (Merged into Union Pacific)									
M 1	McKeen	1911	121	Samet 150hp gas-mech.	15 win. CE bag. 38 pass.	70'	40T	to Un. Pac. sec. M-9, 1928	Built for Peoples Elect. Ry. (Muskogee, Okla.), reposs. by McKeen

Index

Note: Page numbers with asterisks (*) indicate illustrations or caption references. Listings in the tables are not indexed except for names of the operators.

A

Aberdeen & Rockfish Railroad Co. 98, 102, 102*
Abilene & Southern Railway 127
Akron, Canton & Youngstown Railway Co. 105
Alabama & Florida Railroad 12, 13*
Alabama, Tennessee & Northern Railroad Corp. 11, 11*, 12
Alaska Northern Railroad 14, 15
Alaska Railroad 16
Alaska Road Commission 14
Albany & Northern Railway 39, 40, 72
Alexandria & Western Railway 62
Amarillo Traction Co. 127
American Car & Foundry 18, 21, 26*, 61, 62*
American Potash Co. 21
American Railroad Passenger Car 69
American Traction Co. 75
Angelina & Neches River Railroad Co. 127
Anthony & Western 56
Apalachicola Northern Railroad Co. 36, 36*, 37
Appalachian Railway 100
Arcade & Attica Railroad Corp. 95
Arizona & New Mexico Railway Co. 93, 93*
Arizona Southern 17
Arkansas Northwestern Railroad 19
Arkansas Railroad Co. 19
Arkansas Valley Railway, Inc. 57
Arlington & Fairfax Railway 135, 136, 136*
Arnica Salve Line 52, 52*
Artemus-Jellico Railroad 58, 59
Asherton & Gulf Railway 127
Ashland Railway 12
Ashley, Drew & Northern Railway 36
Ashley, James 35, 133
Atlanta & St. Andrews Bay Railway Co. 36, 36*, 37, 37*
Atlantic & Carolina Railroad Co. 100
Atlantic & Western Railway 98
Atlantic Northern Railway 55
Augusta Northern Railway 122
Aurora, De Kalb & Rockford Traction Co. 49

B

Baby Zephyr 51*
Baltimore & Ohio Railroad 48
Baltimore & Washington Transit Co. of Maryland 67
Baltimore, Chesapeake & Atlantic Railway Co. 67
Bamberg, Ehrhardt & Walterboro Railway Co. 122
Bangor & Aroostook Railroad Co. 105
Bartlett & Western Railway 127
Batesville & Southwestern Railroad 79
Beaver-Penrose & Northern Railway 32
Beebe, Lucius 39
Bellefonte Central Railroad Co. 115
Bellevue & Cascade Railway 54, 55
Bellingham Bay & British Columbia Railroad Co. 139
Big Four Railroad (CCC&StL) 39, 72
Billings Traction Co. 83
Birmingham & Southeastern Railroad Co. 12
Black Mountain Railway Co. 101
Bloomington, Pontiac & Joliet Electric Railway 49
Blue Ridge Railway 122
Blytheville, Leachville & Arkansas Southern Railroad Co. 19
Bonlee & Western Railway Co. 101
Boston & Maine Railroad 35, 89, 89*, 133
Boston & Worcester 69
Boston, Revere Beach & Lynn Railroad Co. 69, 70

Bowden Railway 40
Bowen Motor Railways Co. 72, 114
Boyne City, Gaylord & Alpena Railroad 72
Bridgton & Harrison Railroad Co. 64, 64*, 65
Brill, J.G. 8, 18, 21, 23, 39, 48*, 56, 58, 61, 66*, 72, 72*, 85,
                94*, 99*, 114, 114*, 117*, 125, 135, 135*, 142*
Bristol Railroad Co. 133, 134
Brookville Locomotive Co. 85
Brownsville & Matamoros Bridge Co. 127
Brownsville Street & Interurban Railway 127
Bryan & Central Texas Interurban Railway 127
Bryan & College Interurban Railway Co. 127
Bucklin, H.E. 52
Budd, Edward G. Manufacturing Co. 109
Buffalo Creek & Gauley Railroad Co. 58, 143, 144*
Burlingame Railway 24
Burlington Northern 11
Butler County Railroad Co. 81

C

Cadiz Railroad 59
Caldwell Traction Co. 47
California & Oregon Coast Railroad Co. 110
California Western Railway & Navigation Co. 21, 24, 26
Camas Prairie Railroad 46
Cambria & Indiana Railroad Co. 115
Cape Fear Railways Inc. 98, 99*, 101
Cape Girardeau & Chester 81*
Cape Girardeau & Northern Railway 81
Cape May, Delaware Bay & Sewells Point Railway 92
Cargill 144
Caro Northern Railway Co. 127
Carolina & Northeastern Railroad 101
Carolina & Northwestern Railway Co. 101
Carolina Traction Co. 122
Carrollton Railroad 59
Cassville & Exeter Railway 82
Central of Florida Railway Co. 37
Central New York Southern Railway 94*, 95
Central West Virginia & Southern Railroad Co. 142*, 143
Charlotte Harbor & Northern Railway Co. 37
Charlotte Rapid Transit Co. 101
Chattahoochee Valley Railway Co. 11, 12, 40
Charles City Western Railway 54, 54*, 55
Chesapeake & Western Railway 136
Chesapeake Beach Railway Co. 66, 67
Chessie System 142
Chestnut Ridge Railway Co. 115
Chicago & Eastern Illinois Railway 52, 61
Chicago & Illinois Midland Railway Co. 49
Chicago & North Western Railway 74
Chicago, Attica & Southern Railroad Co. 52, 53
Chicago Motor Vehicle Co. 54
Chicago, Peoria & St. Louis Railroad Co. 49, 107
Chicago, Springfield & St. Louis Railway Co. 48*, 49
Chicago, Terre Haute & Southeastern Railway Co. 52, 53
Chitina Auto Railer 14, 14*
Chowchilla Pacific Railway 22*, 24
Christie & Eastern Railway Co. 62
Cincinnati, Bluffton & Chicago Railway Co. 52, 53
Cincinnati Car Co. 81, 125
Cincinnati, Indianapolis & Western Railroad 48
City of Prineville Railroad 10, 110, 112*
Claremont & Concord Railway Co. 89, 89*
Clarkesville Railroad Co. 40
Clinton & Oklahoma Western Railroad Co. 107
Clinton, Davenport & Muscatine Railway 54
Clinton Street Railway 107

Collins & Glenville Railroad 39, 40, 40*
Colorado, Kansas & Oklahoma Railroad 57
Colorado Railroad 32, 33*
Columbia & Nehalem River Railroad 110, 110*
Columbus & Greenville Railway 78
Condon, Kinzua & Southern Railroad Co. 110, 112*
Conrail 142
Connecticut Company 35
Consolidated Street Railway 56*, 57
Copper River & Northwestern Railway 14
Cornwall & Lebanon Railroad 115
Cotton Belt Route (SSW) 18, 80, 81
Coudersport & Port Allegheny Railroad Co. 115
Cowlitz, Chehalis & Cascade Railway 141
Crystal City & Uvalde Railway 127
Cumberland & Pennsylvania Railroad Co. 67

D

Dan Patch 73
Dan Patch Lines 21, 56, 73, 85, 107
Dansville & Mt. Morris Railroad Co. 94, 94*, 95
Death Valley Railroad Co. 21, 23*, 24
Deering & Southwestern Railroad Co. 81
De Kalb & Western Railroad Co. 79
Delaware Northern 94
Dents Run Railroad 115
Denver, Laramie & Northwestern 30, 32
De Queen & Eastern Railroad Co./Texas, Oklahoma &
    Eastern Railroad Co. 19
Detroit & Mackinac Railway Co. 72, 72*, 73
Detroit, Toledo & Ironton Railroad 74
Diamond & Caldor Railway Co. 24
Doniphan, Kensett & Searcy Railway 19
Drake Railway Automatrice Co. 73
Dunn, Michael J. 98

E

East Broad Top Railroad & Coal Co. 114, 114*, 115
East Carolina Railway 101
East Jordan & Southern Railroad Co. 72, 73
East Texas & Gulf Railway Co. 127
Eastern Kentucky Railway Co. 58*, 59, 60
Edison-Beach car 14*, 52, 89, 96*
Edwards Car Co. ..8*, 10*, 13*, 21, 37*, 39, 98, 99*, 100*, 121*, 147*
Eklund Car Co. 144, 145*
Elberta Zephyr 19*
El Dorado & Wesson Railway 18*, 20
El Dorado Springs Railway Co. 32
Electric Short Line Railway (Luce Lines) ...73, 74*, 75, 77*
Electro-Motive Corporation ..11*, 21, 66, 67*, 83*, 85, 114, 125, 135
Elkin & Alleghany Railroad 99*, 101
Ephrata & Lebanon Street Railway 115
Escanaba & Lake Superior Railroad Co. 73
Eureka Nevada Railway Co. 85*, 87
Evans Automotive Products Co. 121*
Evans Auto-Railer 120, 135, 136

F

Fairbanks-Morse 8*, 9*, 36*, 39*, 52, 61, 72, 85, 86*, 105*,
                              122, 124, 131, 145*, 146*
Fairburn & Atlanta Railway & Electric Co. 40
Fairchild & Northeastern Railroad...............144, 146
Fairmont & Clarksburg Railway 143
Fairmont & Northern Traction Co. 143
Fairmont Railway Motors Co. 23*, 47
Fayetteville Street Railway & Power Co. 101
Federal Storage Battery Car Co. 68*
Ferdinand Railroad Co. 52, 53
Fernwood, Columbia & Gulf Railroad 78, 78*, 79
Flemingsburg & Northern Railroad 58, 59*, 60
Fonda, Johnstown & Gloversville Railroad Co. ..66, 94*, 95
Ford, Henry 74

Fort Smith, Subiaco & Rock Island Railroad Co. 20
Fort Worth & Rio Grande Railway 124
Four Wheel Drive Auto Co. 61, 69, 133, 144*
Fox & Illinois Union Railway 33*, 48*, 50
Frankfort & Cincinnati Railroad Co. 58, 60
Franklin & Pittsylvania Railway Co. 136
Fresno Interurban Railway Co. 24
Frisco (SL-SF Railway) 80, 81, 124

G

Gainesville & Northwestern Railroad 41
Gainesville Midland Railway Co. 41
Galesburg Great Eastern Railroad Co. 50, 51*
Gallipolis & Northern Traction Co. 105
Galloping Geese 30
General Electric 8*, 18, 39, 73, 77, 80, 105, 126*
Georgetown & Gray's Peak 32
Georgia Car and Locomotive Co. 39
Georgia Northern Railway Co. 39*, 41, 42*
Gilmour & Pittsburgh Railroad Co. 46, 47
Grasse Valley Railroad Corp. 89, 94, 96, 97*
Graysonia, Nashville & Ashdown Railroad 20
Great Northern Railway 83*
Great Western Railway 30, 32
Greater Winnipeg Water District 66
Greenbriar & Eastern Railroad Co. 143
Greene County Railroad Co. 42
Greene, Forrest 39
Greenwich & Johnsonville Railway Co. 96
Grice and Long 114
Gulf, Texas & Western Railway Co. 124, 127
Gulf Coast Lines (Missouri Pacific) 124
Hall-Scott Motor Car Co. 21, 21*, 22*, 49*, 52, 85, 109, 131
Hampton & Branchville Railroad Co. 121, 121*, 122
Hanover Railway 50
Hartford & Eastern Railway Co. 138, 138*, 141
Haskell Traction Co. 128
Hawaii Consolidated Railway 44, 44*, 45
Hawkinsville & Florida Southern Railway Co. 42
Hendersonville Traction Co. 101
Hetch-Hetchy Railway 7*, 24, 25*
Hicks Car & Locomotive Works 52
Hocking & Sunday Creek Traction Co. 105
Hofius Steel & Equipment Co. 109, 137
Holton Interurban Railway Co. 21, 22*, 25
Hoosic Tunnel & Wilmington Railroad Co. 69, 70, 133
Houston & Brazos Valley Railway Co. 128
Hoxie-Walnut Ridge Railway 20
Hueneme, Malibu & Port Los Angeles Railway 25
Huntington & Broad Top Mountain Railroad & Coal Co. ...114-116

I

Illinois Central Electric (The) 50
Illinois Central Gulf Railroad 78
Illinois Terminal Railroad System 49*, 50
Independence & Monmouth Railway 110
International Motor Car Co. 10*
Interstate Commerce Commission 7
Iowa Southern Utilities 54

J

Jacksonville & Havana Railroad Co. 50, 51*
Jamestown, Chatauqua & Lake Erie Railroad 96
Jefferson & Northwestern Railroad Co. 128
Jefferson Southwestern Railroad 50
Jonesboro, Lake City & Eastern Railroad Co. 20

K

Kalamazoo Railway Supply Co. 78
Kanauga Traction Co. 106
Kanawha, Glen Jean & Eastern Railroad Co. 143
Kansas City & Memphis Railway Co. 20

Kansas City Southern 18
Kennebago Bus Co. 64, 65*
Kentucky & Tennessee Railway 60
Kentwood & Eastern Railway Co. 62
Kinder & Northwestern Railroad Co. 62
Kosiusko & Southeastern Railroad Co. 79
Kuhlman, G.C., Car Co. 52*

L

Laconia Car Co. 144
La Crosse & Southeastern Railway Co. 103, 144, 145*
Lake Erie, Franklin & Clarion Railroad 114*, 116
Lakeside & Marblehead Railroad 105*, 106, 106*
Lancaster, Franklin & Clarion Railroad 116
Laurinberg & Southern Railroad Co. 101
Laramie, North Park & Western Railroad Co. 147, 147*
Leavenworth & Topeka Railroad Co. 57
Leavenworth, Kansas & Western Railway 57
Lee County Central Electric Railway 50
Lehigh & New England Railroad 58
Lehigh Valley Railroad 36*, 133
Lenox Railroad 60
Lewisburg, Milton & Watsontown Passenger Railway 58, 116
Lewistown Terminal Railroad 47
Liberty-White Railroad 80
Ligonier Valley Railroad Co. 114, 116
Lima & Defiance Railroad Co. 106
Lincoln, Oxford & Southern 89
Little River Railroad Co. 123
Live Oak, Perry & Gulf Railroad Co. 36, 37, 114
Long Beach Railway 95*, 96
Longview, Portland & Northern Railway Co. 140*, 141
Lorain, Ashland & Southern Railroad 106
Louisiana & North Western Railroad Co. 61, 63
Louisiana, Arkansas & Texas Railway Co. 66
Louisiana Southern Railway 61, 63
Los Angeles & San Diego Beach Railway 27
Lowville & Beaver River Railroad Co. 94, 96

M

Mack Trucks, Inc. 8*, 21, 26*, 81, 82*, 84*, 120, 121*, 135
Macomb & Western Illinois Railroad 50
Macon & Birmingham Railway Co. 41*, 42
Magma Arizona Railroad 17
Maine Central Railroad Co. 64
Mammoth Cave Railroad Co. 60
Manahawken & Long Beach Transportation Co. 92, 92*
Manchester & Oneida Railway Co. 55
Manhattan Beach Railroad 96
Manhattan City & Interurban Railway 57
Manistee & Northeastern Railroad .6*
Manistique & Lake Superior Railroad 73
Manitou & Pikes Peak Railroad 30, 31*, 32
Marietta, Columbus & Cleveland Railroad 106
Marine Railway Co. (The) 98
Marion & Rye Valley Railway 136
Maryland & Delaware Coast Railway 66*, 69
Maryland & Pennsylvania Railroad Co. 66, 67*, 69
Mascot & Western Railroad 17
Maxton, Alma & Southbound Railroad 102
McCloud River Railroad 21
McGuire-Cummings Manufacturing Co. 48*
McKeen Motor Car Co. 30, 46*, 54, 73, 81, 85, 94*, 105,
106*, 107, 109, 109*, 122, 131, 138
Meister Car Co. 7*, 21, 23*, 25*, 85, 86*, 144
Memphis & Rugby Railway Co. .123

Mid-Continent Railway Museum .83
Middle Creek Railway 143
Middle Tennessee Railroad Co. 123
Middletown & Unionville Railroad Co. 102, 103
Midland Continental Railroad 102, 103

Midland Terminal Railway 30, 32, 33*
Midland Valley Railroad 18
Midlothian & Blue Island Railroad 50
Milledgeville Railway 41*, 42
Milwaukee Road 52, 54, 138
Mineral Wells & Lakewood Park Railway 128
Minerets & Western Railroad 27
Minneapolis, Anoka & Cuyuna Range 74
Minneapolis, Northfield & Southern Railway 73, 75
Minneapolis, Red Lake & Manitoba Railway Co. 77
Minneapolis, St. Paul, Rochester & Dubuque Electric
   Traction Co. (Dan Patch Line) (Other listings also
   under Dan Patch Line) 73, 75, 76
Minnesota & International Railway Co. 74
Minnesota & Northwestern Electric Railway Co. 77, 77*
Minneapolis & St. Louis Railroad .74
Minnesota, Dakota & Western Railway Co. 77
Minnesota Western Railroad 73
Minnesota Western Railway 73, 74, 76
Mississippi & Skuna Valley Railroad 78, 78*, 80
Mississippi Central Railroad Co. 79*, 80
Mississippi River & Bonne Terre Railway 82
Missouri & Arkansas Railway 19
Missouri & Kansas Interurban Railway 56, 57
Missouri & North Arkansas Railway 18, 18*
Missouri Pacific Railroad 18, 43*
Missouri Southern Railroad Co. 82
Mitchell Street & Interurban Railway 104
Mixed Train Daily 39
Mobile & Pensacola Railway & Navigation Co. 12
Model T Ford 21, 22*, 23*, 36, 98
Modesto & Empire Traction Co. 21, 27
Monongahela Railway 116
Montana Western Railway (The) 83*, 84
Montana, Wyoming & Southern Railway Co. 84
Moody Foundation 109
Moody's Railroads 30
Morehead & North Fork Railroad Co. 60
Morristown & Erie Railroad Co. 91*, 92
Morse, Victor 133
Motley County Railroad 128
Mount Hood Railroad Co. 110, 112*
Mount Jewett, Kinzua & Ritersville Railroad Co. 116
Mount Pleasant & Lakewood Park Railway 128
Mount Tamalpais & Muir Woods Railway 27
Muscatine, Burlington & Southern Railroad Co. 54, 55

N

Nantucket Central Railway 69, 70, 70*
Nantucket Railway 69, 70
Narragansett Pier Railroad Co. 120, 121, 121*
Nashville Interurban Railway 123
Nebraska, Kansas & Gulf 56
Nevada-California-Oregon Railway 86*, 87
Nevada Central Railroad 6*, 88
Nevada Copper Belt Railway 85, 85*, 86*, 88
Nevada County Narrow Gauge 21, 22*, 27
Nevada Northern Railway Co. 85
New Berlin & Winfield Railroad .116
New Bern-Ghent Street Railway .102
New Haven Carriage Co. 137
New Holland, Higginsport & Mt. Vernon Railway 102
New Mexico Central Railway Co. 93, 93*
New Orleans & Lower Coast Railroad 61, 61*, 62*, 63
New York Central System 142
New York, New Haven & Hartford Railroad 35
New York Railway 94
Nezperce Railroad 47
Nicholas, Fayette & Greenbriar Railroad Co. 142, 142*, 143
Northeast Oklahoma Railroad Co. 107
Norfolk Branch Railway 35, 133
Norfolk Southern Railway 98

Norfolk Southern System 39
Northern Pacific Railroad 46, 74, 137
Northwestern Motor Car Co. 21
Northwestern Pacific Railroad 85
Norwalk & Shelby Railroad 72, 105*, 106

O

Oahu Railway 44, 44*, 45, 45*
Ocean Shore Railway 21, 27, 144
Official Guide 7, 30, 98
Official Railway Equipment Register 7
Oil Belt Railway 50
Oil Fields Shortline Railroad 107
Okalona, Houston & Calhoun City Railroad 79*, 80
Oklahoma & Arkansas Railway Co. 108
Oklahoma & Southwestern Railway Co. 108
Oklahoma, New Mexico & Pacific Railway Co. . . 107, 108
Okmulgee Northern Railway 107, 10
Oneida & Western Railroad Co. 124
Oregon Electric Railway 138
Oregon, Pacific & Eastern Railway 109, 109*, 111
Oregon Short Line 46*

P

Pacific & Eastern Railway 111
Pacific & Idaho Northern Railway Co. 46*, 47
Pacific Body Building 46
Pacific Coast Railway Co. 21, 23*, 27
Pacific Southwest Railway Museum 23*
Panama Traction Co. 117*, 120
Paris & Mt. Pleasant Railroad Co. 81, 125*, 128
Patton Motor Car Co. 64
Pecos Valley Southern Railway Co. 128
Pekin & Petersburg Interurban Railway 50
Pennsylvania Railroad 58, 90
Penobscot Central Railway 64, 65
Peoples Railroad Co. 12
Peoples Electric Railway 107, 108
Perry, Otto 66
Pierce-Arrow 30
Pittsburgh & Shawmut Railroad Co. 118
Pittsburgh & Susquehanna Railroad Co. 118
Pittsburgh, Lisbon & Western Railroad Co. 116
Pittsburgh, Shawmut & Northern Railroad Co. 94
Plum Island Street Railway 69
Pond Fork & Bald Knob Railroad 143
Port Bolivar Iron Ore Railway 128
Port Isabel & Rio Grande Valley Railroad . . . 124, 128, 129*
Port Shirley Street Railway 69, 70, 71*
Portland & Oregon City Railway Co. 111
Portland & Southwestern Railroad 113
Portland Railway, Light & Power 138
Potlatcher 47*
Prattsburgh Railway Corp. 98
Prescott & Northwestern RR Co. 19*, 20
Prouty-Pierce 84
Puget Sound & Cascade Railway Co. 141
Puget Sound Electric Railway 138
Public Service Corporation of New Jersey 90, 91*, 92

Q

Quakertown & Delaware River Traction Co. 118
Quanah, Acme & Pacific Railway Co. 128
Quincy Railroad 23*, 27

R

Rapid City, Black Hills & Western Railroad Co. 104, 104*, 122
Remington Arms Co. 69
Reo Speedwagon 64*
Ringling Circus 81
Rio Grande & Eagle Pass Railway Co. 124, 129
Rio Grande City Railway 124, 129

Rio Grande Railway 124
Rio Grande Southern Railroad Co. 30, 30*, 31*, 32
Riviera Beach & Western Railway 129
Rogue River Valley Railway Co. 111*, 113
Rucker Brothers 137
Russell Co. 61*, 66

S

Sabine & Neches River Railway 129
St. Joseph Valley Railway Co. 52, 52*, 53, 72
St. Louis & Hannibal Railroad Co. 81, 81*, 82*, 83
St. Louis Car Co. 21, 39*, 56, 66, 67*, 83*, 84, 85, 144
St. Louis, Kennett & Southeastern Railroad 20
St. Marys Railroad Co. 42, 43*
St. Simons Railway Co. 43
St. Tammany & New Orleans Railway & Ferry Co. . . . 61, 63
Sacramento Valley & Eastern Ry. 28
Sacramento Valley & Eastern Railway 28
Saillard, Louis 78
Salem, Falls City & Western Railway 109*, 113
Salem, Winona & Southern Railroad Co. 82
Salt Lake & Utah Railroad 131, 131*, 132
Salt Lake, Garfield & Western Railway 26*, 132
San Antonio & Aransas Pass Railway Co. 124, 129
San Antonio, Uvalde & Gulf Railroad Co. 124, 129
San Benito & Rio Grande Valley Railway Co. . . 124, 126, 129
San Cristobal Railway 30, 33
San Diego, Cuyamaca & Eastern Railroad 16, 27
San Francisco, City of 7*
San Francisco Municipal Railway 25*
San Joaquin & Eastern Railroad Co. 21, 27, 29*
San Luis Valley Southern Railway Co. 34
Sand Springs Interurban Railway 107, 108
Sandy River & Rangely Lakes Railroad 64, 65, 65*
Sanford Traction Co. 36*, 38
Santa Ana & Orange Motor Co. 28
Santa Fe Railway (AT&SF) 93
Santa Maria Valley Railroad Co. 21, 23*, 28
Saratoga & Encampment Valley Railroad 147
Savage, Col. Marion W. 73
Schuykill & Dauphine Traction Co. 119
Seaboard Air Line 43*
Searcy & Kensett Railway 20
Seattle City Light Department 137
Seattle Municipal Railway 138
Seward Peninsula Railroad 14, 15
Sewell Valley Railroad Co. 143
Sheffield Velocipede Car Co. 134*
Shelby County Railway 82*, 83
Short Line Association 78
Shreveport, Alexandria & Southern Railway System 63
Sibley, Lake Bistineau & Southern Railway System 63
Sierra Railway of California 21, 28
Silver Peak Railway 88
Silverton Northern Railroad Co. 31*, 34
Sioux City, Crystal Lake & Homer Railway 84, 85
Skagit River Railway 21, 26*, 137, 140*, 141
Skunk 26
Smalley Rail Car Co. 36*, 114
Smokey Mountain Railway Co. 102
Sonora-Baja California Railroad 21
Soo Line 73, 74
South Georgia Railway Co. 36, 43, 52, 114
Southern Pacific Railroad 93, 126
Southern Industrial Railroad 55
Southern Railway 36, 39, 122
Southern Utah Railroad Co. 131, 132, 132*
Southwest Missouri Railroad 80*, 81, 83
Sperry Rail Service 72
Spokane, Coeur d'Alene & Palouse Railway 138
Stanley, Merrill & Phillips Railway Co. 144, 146, 146*
Stewartstown Railroad Co. 119

Stockton Terminal & Eastern Railroad 28
Stone Harbor Railroad Co. 92
Strang cars 73
Strang, William B., Jr. 56
Strasburg Railway Museum 58, 89
Studebaker 122
Suffolk Traction Co. 98
Sugarland Railway Co. 130
Sumpter & Choctaw Railway Co. 12, 13
Sumpter Valley Railway Co. 113
Super Skunk 26
Susquehanna & New York Railroad Co. 36*, 114, 119
Sykes Co. 35, 133, 144

T

Tabor & Northern Railway Co. 54, 55
Tacoma Municipal Belt 138
Tallulah Falls Railway Co. 43
Tampa & Jacksonville Railway 38
Tanana Valley Railroad 14, 14*, 16
Tedder, Russell 36
Tele-dector Co. 72
Tennessee & Cumberland River Railroad 124
Tennessee & North Carolina Railway Co. 102, 124
Tennessee, Alabama & Georgia Railway 11, 12
Tennessee, Kentucky & Northern Railroad Co. ... 122, 124
Tennessee Railroad Co. 122*, 124
Texas 39
Texas & New Orleans Railroad Co. (Southern Pacific) 124
Texas City Terminal Railway Co. 125*, 130
Texas Mexican Railway 130
Texas Midland Railway 124, 126*, 130
Texas South-Eastern Railroad Co. 130
Third Avenue Railway 94
36 Miles of Trouble 133
Thomson-Graf-Edler 21, 44, 87*
Tindle, Ralph 56
Tionesta Valley Railway Co. 119
Tonopah & Goldfield Railroad Co. 88
Tonopah & Tidewater Railroad Co. 21, 21*, 28, 85
Tooele Valley Railway Co. 131, 132
Townsville Railroad Co. 102
Towson & Cockeysville Electric Railway Co. 69
Trans-Florida Central Railroad 36, 38, 38*
Tremont & Gulf Railway Co. 63
Trenton Fast Line 90
Trinity Valley & Northern Railway Co. 130
Trona Railway 21, 28
Tucson, Cornelia & Gila Bend Railroad 16, 16*, 17
Tuckaseegee & South Eastern Railway 103
28th & 29th Street Crosstown Railroad 96*
Twin Coach Co. 54, 126*
Twin Falls Railway Co. 46*, 47

U

Uintah Railway Co. 30, 34
Unadilla Valley Railway Co. 94, 98
Union Pacific Railroad 21, 46, 72, 72*, 107, 147
Union Railroad of Oregon 113
Union Transportation Co. 90*, 92
Unit Railway Car Co. 144
Uvalde & Leona Valley Interurban Railway Co. ... 130
Uvalde & Northern Railway Co. 130

V

Valley & Siletz Railroad Co. 109, 113, 13
Ventura County Railway 21*, 2
Verde, Tunnel & Smelter Railroad 16, 17, 17
Virginia & Carolina Southern Railroad Co. .. 99*, 100*, 10
Virginia & Rainy Lake Railway 7
Virginia & Truckee Railway 87*, 8
Virginia Blue Ridge Railway 13
Virginia Central Railway 13
Visalia Electric Railroad 21, 2

W

Waco, Beaumont, Trinity & Sabine Railway Co. 13
Warren & Ouachita Valley Railway 2
Washington & Old Dominion Railway 135, 135*, 13
Washington, Brandywine & Point Lookout Railroad Co. ... 6
Washington & Lincolnton Railroad Co. 4
Washington, Idaho & Montana Railway Co. ... 47, 47
Washington, Spa Springs & Gretta Railroad Co. .. 66*, 68*, 6
Washington Water Power Co. 13
Warner & Webbers Falls Railway 107*, 10
Wason Manufacturing Co. 74*, 85, 126
Waterloo, Cedar Falls & Northern Railway 54, 5
Waterville Railway 138, 14
Watson Car Co. 9
Waukegan, Rockford & Elgin 5
Wayne 3
Waynesburg & Washington Railroad Co. 11
Webber Falls, Shawnee & Western Railway 10
West River Railroad Co. 35, 133, 13
Western Pacific Railroad 2
Westmoreland Interurban 5
Weatherford, Mineral Wells & Northwestern Ry. Co. ... 127*, 13
White, John H., Jr. 6
White Ecklund 10
White Motor Co. 25, 44, 85, 90, 91*, 94*, 110
White Mountain Central Railroad 64
White Pass & Yukon Railway 14, 1
White River Railroad Co. 133, 134
White Sulphur Springs & Yellowstone Park Railroad .. 81, 84, 84*
Wichita & Northwestern Railway Co. 56, 56*, 58
Wichita Falls & Southern Railroad Co. 126*, 130
Wilkes-Barre & Hazelton Railroad 118*, 119
Willamette Pacific 113
Willamette Valley & Coast Railroad Co. 113
Willamina & Grande Ronde Railway 113
Williamsport & North Branch Railway Co. 120
Wilmington, Brunswick & Southern Railroad Co. .. 103
Wilmington, New Castle & Delaware City Traction Co. .. 35
Winchester & Western Railroad 135, 137
Wisconsin & Michigan Railroad Co. 72*, 73
Wolfboro Railway 89
Woodstock & Sycamore Traction Co. 51

XYZ

Yale Short Line 52
Yellow Coach 90
Yosemite Valley Railroad 21
Yreka Western Railroad 29
Yuma Valley Railroad 16, 17
Yakatut & Southern Railroad 14, 15*, 16
Youngsville & Sugar Grove Street Railway 117*, 120

For more details on manufacturers and the larger railroads, see *Interurbans Without Wires* or *Doodlebug Country*, both by the author and both published by Interurban Press.